The Sleepy Dinosaur

by Karen Wallace

Illustrated by Ross Collins

W

Notes on the series

TIDDLERS are structured to provide support for children who are starting to read on their own. The stories may also be used for sharing with children.

Starting to read alone can be daunting. **TIDDLERS** help by listing the words in the book for a check before reading, and by providing visual support and repeating words and phrases. These books will both develop confidence and encourage reading and rereading for pleasure.

If you are reading this book with a child, here are a few suggestions:

1. Make reading fun! Choose a time to read when you and the child are relaxed and have time to share the story.

2. Talk about the story before you start reading. Look at the cover and the blurb. What might the story be about? Why might the child like it?

3. Look also at the list of words below – can the child tackle most of the words? Encourage the child to employ a phonics approach to tackling new words by sounding the words out.

4. Encourage the child to retell the story, using the jumbled picture puzzle.

5. Give praise! Remember that small mistakes need not always be corrected.

Here is a list of the words in this story.

Common words:

a	in	too
does	it's	with
he	me	where
hot	no	

Other words:

cave	muddy	tree
dark	sleep	volcano
dinosaur	sleepy	
leafy	swamp	

Where does a sleepy dinosaur sleep?

Does he sleep
in a cave?

No, it's too dark.

8

Does he sleep
in a swamp?

No, it's too muddy.

Does he sleep
in a tree?

13

No, it's too leafy.

Does he sleep
in a volcano?

No, it's too hot.

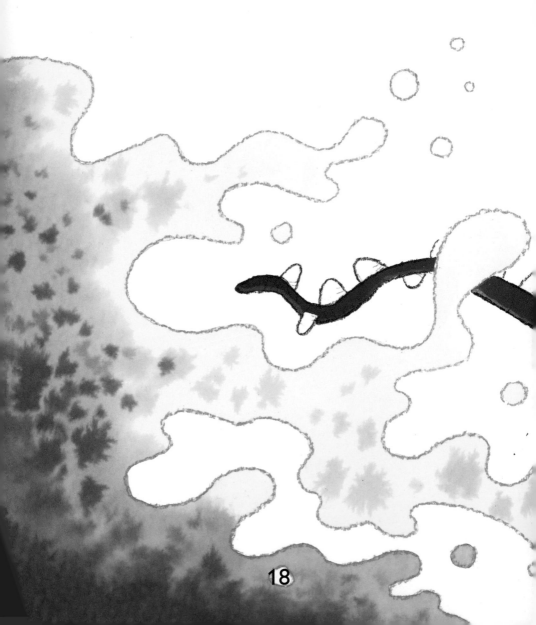

19

Where does a sleepy dinosaur sleep?

He sleeps with me!

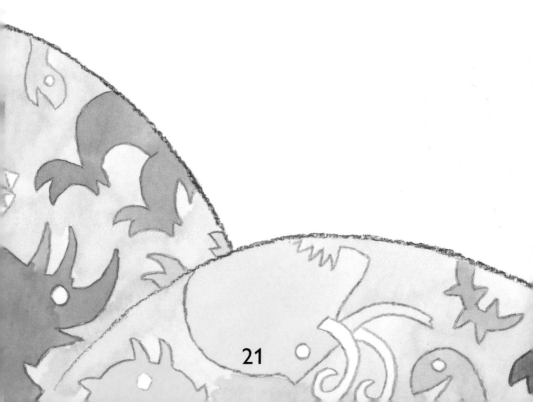

Puzzle Time

Can you find these pictures in the story?

Which pages are the
pictures from?

Turn over for answers!

Answers

The pictures come
from these pages:

a. pages 8–9

b. pages 18–19

c. pages 14–15

d. pages 4–5

Franklin Watts
First published in Great Britain in 2016 by
The Watts Publishing Group

Copyright (text) © Karen Wallace 2016
Copyright (illustration) © Ross Collins 2016

The rights of Karen Wallace to be identified
as the author and Ross Collins to be
identified as the illustrator of this Work have
been asserted in accordance with the
Copyright, Designs and Patents Act, 1988.

Series Editor: Jackie Hamley
Series Advisor: Catherine Glavina
Series Designer: Cathryn Gilbert

A CIP catalogue record for this book is
available from the British Library.

ISBN 978 1 4451 4609 6 (hbk)
ISBN 978 1 4451 4612 6 (pbk)
ISBN 978 1 4451 4610 2 (library ebook)

Printed in China

Franklin Watts
An imprint of
Hachette Children's Group
Part of The Watts Publishing Group
Carmelite House
50 Victoria Embankment
London EC4Y 0DZ

An Hachette UK Company
www.hachette.co.uk

www.franklinwatts.co.uk

FSC
www.fsc.org
MIX
Paper from
responsible sources
FSC® C104740

CAMINO
WINDS

John Grisham

CAMINO WINDS

HODDER &
STOUGHTON

First published in Great Britain in 2020 by Hodder & Stoughton
An Hachette UK company

1

Copyright © Belfry Holdings, Inc. 2020

The right of John Grisham to be identified as the Author of the Work has been
asserted by him in accordance with the Copyright, Designs and Patents Act 1988.

A CIP catalogue record for this title is available from the British Library

Hardback ISBN 978 1 529 34245 1
Trade Paperback ISBN 978 1 529 34246 8

Printed and bound in Great Britain by Clays Ltd, Elcograf S.p.A.

Hodder & Stoughton policy is to use papers that are natural, renewable
and recyclable products and made from wood grown in sustainable
forests. The logging and manufacturing processes are expected to
conform to the environmental regulations of the country of origin.

Hodder & Stoughton Ltd
Carmelite House
50 Victoria Embankment
London EC4Y 0DZ

www.hodder.co.uk

CAMINO
WINDS

CHAPTER ONE
THE LANDING

1.

Leo spun to life in late July in the restless waters of the far eastern Atlantic, about two hundred miles west of Cape Verde. He was soon spotted from space, properly named, and classified as a mere tropical depression. Within hours he had been upgraded to a tropical storm.

For a month, strong dry winds had swept across the Sahara and collided with the moist fronts along the equator, creating swirling masses that moved westward as if searching for land. When Leo began his journey, there were three named storms ahead of him, all in a menacing row that threatened the Caribbean. All three would eventually follow their expected routes and bring heavy rains to the islands but nothing more.

From the beginning, though, it was apparent that Leo would go where no one predicted. He was far more erratic, and deadly. When he finally petered out from exhaustion over the Midwest, he was blamed for five billion in property damages and thirty-five deaths.

But before that he wasted no time with his classifications, advancing swiftly from tropical depression to tropical storm to a full-blown hurricane. At Category 3, with winds of 120 miles per hour, he hit the Turks and Caicos head-on and blew away several hundred homes, killing ten. He skirted low beneath Crooked Island, took a slight left, and aimed for Cuba before stalling south of Andros. His eye weakened as he lost steam and limped across Cuba, once again as a lowly depression with plenty of rain but unimpressive winds. He turned south in time to flood Jamaica and the Caymans, then, in a startling twelve-hour period, he reorganized with a perfect eye and turned north toward the warm and inviting waters of the Gulf of Mexico. His trackers drew a line straight at Biloxi, the usual target, but by then they knew better than to make predictions. Leo seemed to have a mind of his own and no use for their models.

Once again he rapidly grew in size and speed, and in less than two days had his own news special on cable, and Vegas was posting odds on the landing site. Dozens of giddy camera crews raced into harm's way. Warnings were posted from Galveston to Pensacola. Oil companies scurried to extract ten thousand rig workers from the Gulf, and, as always, jacked up their prices just for the hell of it. Evacuation plans in five states were activated. Governors held press conferences. Fleets of boats and airplanes scrambled to reposition inland. As a Category 4, and veering east and west along a steady northbound trek, Leo seemed destined for a historic and ugly landfall.

And then he stalled again. Three hundred miles south of Mobile, he faked to his left, began a slow turn to the east, and weakened considerably. For two days he chugged along with Tampa in his sights, then suddenly came to life again as a Category 1. For a change he maintained a straight course and his eye passed over St. Petersburg with winds at a hundred miles per hour. Flooding was heavy, electricity was knocked out, flimsier buildings were flattened, but there were no fatalities. He then followed Interstate 4 and dumped ten inches of rain on Orlando and eight on Daytona Beach before leaving land as yet another tropical depression.

The weary forecasters said farewell as he limped into the Atlantic. Their models ran him out to sea where he would do little more than frighten some cargo ships.

However, Leo had other plans. Two hundred miles due east of St. Augustine, he turned north and picked up steam as his center spun together tightly for the third time. The models were reshuffled and new warnings were issued. For forty-eight hours he moved steadily along, gaining strength as he eyed the coast as if selecting his next target.

2.

At Bay Books in the town of Santa Rosa on Camino Island, the chatter among the clerks and customers was of nothing but the storm. Indeed, across the island, as well as from Jacksonville to the south and Savannah to the north, everyone was watching Leo and talking about him nonstop. By now most folks were well informed and could say with authority that no Florida beach north of Daytona had taken a direct hit in decades. There had been plenty of glancing blows as the hurricanes hurried north toward the Carolinas. One theory was that the Gulf Stream sixty miles out acted as a barrier to protect the Florida beaches and it would do so again with pesky Leo.

Another theory was that the luck had run out and it was time for the Big One. The models were a hot topic. The hurricane center in Miami was now plotting a trajectory that sent Leo farther out to sea without landfall. But the Europeans had him coming ashore south of Savannah as a Category 4, with massive flooding in the low country. If Leo had proved anything, though, it was that he cared nothing for the models.

Bruce Cable, the owner of Bay Books, kept one eye on the Weather Channel while he hustled customers and chided his staff to get about their business. There wasn't a cloud in the sky, and Bruce bought into the legend that Camino Island was immune to dangerous hurricanes. He'd been there for twenty-four years and had not seen a destructive storm. His store hosted at least four readings a week, and a major appearance was on for tomorrow night. Surely Leo would not disrupt the pleasant homecoming Bruce had planned for one of his favorite authors.

Mercer Mann was ending a two-month summer tour that had been wildly successful. Her second novel, *Tessa,* was the talk of the trade and currently in the top ten on all the bestseller lists. Its reviews were glowing and it was selling faster than anyone had expected. Labeled literary fiction, as opposed to one of the more popular genres, it had seemed destined for the lower rungs of the lists, if it made it at all. Its publisher, along with its author, had dreamed of selling thirty thousand in hardcover and e-book combined, but the novel was already beyond that.

Mercer had deep roots on the island, having summered there as a girl with her grandmother, Tessa, the inspiration for the novel. Three years earlier she had spent a month on the beach in the family cottage and managed to entangle herself in some local mischief. She had also had a quick fling with Bruce, just another in his long line of trysts.

But Bruce wasn't thinking about another fling, or at least he was trying to convince himself he wasn't. He was busy running the store and drumming up a crowd for Mercer's big event. Bay Books was a powerhouse on the national bookstore circuit because Bruce could always pull in a crowd and move the inventory. The New York publishers clamored to get their writers to the island, and many of them were young ladies on the road and looking for a good time. Bruce loved writers and he wined and dined them, promoted their books, and partied with them.

Mercer had been down that road and wasn't going back, primarily because she was being escorted on her summer tour by a new boyfriend. Bruce didn't care. He was just delighted she was on the island and riding high with a superb new novel. He had read the galleys six months earlier and had been promoting it ever since. As usual, when he loved a book, he had sent dozens of handwritten notes to friends and customers touting *Tessa*. He had called booksellers across the country and encouraged them to stock up. He had chatted with Mercer for hours on the phone and advised her on where to tour, what stores to avoid, which reviewers to ignore, and which journalists to spend time with. He had even passed along some unsolicited editorial comments, some of which she appreciated, some she ignored.

Tessa was her breakout novel, her golden moment to establish a career that Bruce had believed in since her first book, which had been largely neglected. She had never stopped adoring him, their little fling aside, along with a rather serious breach of confidence that surrounded it, for which he had forgiven her. Bruce was a lovable though roguish character and an undeniable force in the brutal world of bookselling.

3.

They met for lunch the day before her appearance at a restaurant at the end of Main Street in Santa Rosa, six blocks from the bookstore. Lunch for Bruce was always in a downtown restaurant, with a bottle of wine or two, and usually with a sales rep or a visiting writer or one of the locals he supported. Business lunches, with receipts saved for the accountant. He arrived a few minutes early and went straight to his favorite table on the deck, with a view of the busy harbor. He flirted with the waitress and ordered a bottle of Sancerre. When Mercer swept in he stood and hugged her and offered a firm handshake to Thomas, her companion these days.

They took their seats and Bruce poured the wine. Leo had to be discussed because he was still out there, but Bruce quickly dismissed him as nothing but a distraction. "He's headed to Nags Head," he said confidently.

Mercer was prettier than ever, her long dark hair cut shorter, her hazel eyes glowing with all the success that a bestseller could bring. She was tired of the tour, thrilled to be finished with it, but also savoring the moment. "Thirty-four stops in fifty-one days," she said with a smile.

"You're lucky," Bruce said. "As you well know, publishers don't like to spend money these days. You're killing it, Mercer. I've seen eighteen reviews, all but one positive."

"Did you see Seattle?"

"That jerk doesn't like anything. I know him. I called him when I saw the review and said harsh things."

"Bruce, really?"

"It's my job. I protect my writers. I'll punch him if I ever meet him."

Thomas laughed and said, "Hit him a lick for me."

Bruce raised his glass and said, "Come on, cheers to *Tessa*. Number five on the *Times* list and moving up."

They took a celebratory sip of wine. Mercer said, "It's still hard to believe."

"And a new contract," Thomas said, glancing furtively at her. "Can we break the news?"

"It's already broken," Bruce said. "Let's hear it. I want the details."

Mercer smiled again and said, "My agent called this morning. Viking is offering a nice sum for two more books."

Bruce raised his glass again and said, "Awesome. Those people aren't stupid. Congratulations, Mercer. Great news." Of course, Bruce wanted all the details, especially the amount of the "nice sum," but he had a general idea. Mercer's agent was a tough old pro who knew the business and could now negotiate a new two-book deal for seven figures. After years of struggling, Ms. Mann was entering a new world.

"And foreign rights?" Bruce asked.

"We start selling them next week," she said. Mercer's first books had barely sold stateside. There were no foreign royalties.

Bruce said, "The Brits and Germans will snap it up. The French and Italians will love *Tessa* when it's translated, it's their kind of story, and they'll be easy to deal with. You'll be in twenty languages before you know it, Mercer. This is incredible."

She looked at Thomas and said, "See what I mean? He knows the business." They clinked glasses again as the waitress approached.

"This calls for champagne," Bruce announced, then quickly ordered a bottle before anyone could object. He asked about the tour and wanted the scoop on all the stores she had visited. He knew virtually every serious bookseller in the country and visited as many as possible. For Bruce, a vacation was a week in Napa or Santa Fe for food and wine but also to scout out the best independent bookstores and network with their owners.

He asked about Square Books in Oxford, one of his favorites. Bay Books was modeled after it. These days Mercer was living in Oxford and teaching creative writing at Ole Miss, a two-year gig with one year to go and the hope of a permanent position. The success of *Tessa* would put her on a tenure track, at least in Bruce's opinion, and he was scheming of ways to help.

The waitress poured champagne and took their orders. They toasted the new contract again as the clock seemed to stop.

Thomas, who had done little but listen, said, "Mercer warned me that you take your lunches seriously."

Bruce smiled and replied, "Indeed. I work from early to late, and at noon I have to get out of the store. That's my excuse. I usually nap off the lunch midafternoon."

Mercer had been coy about her new friend. She had made it clear that she was seeing someone and that he would have all of her attention. Bruce respected that and was truly pleased she had found a steady, and not a bad-looking one. Thomas appeared to be in his late twenties, a few years younger than Mercer.

Bruce began chipping away. He said, "She tells me you're a writer too."

Thomas smiled and said, "Yes, and quite unpublished. I'm one of her MFA students."

Bruce chuckled at this and said, "Ah, I see. Sleeping with the professor. That'll get you high marks."

"Come on, Bruce," Mercer said, but she was smiling.

"What's your background?" Bruce asked.

Thomas said, "Degree in American lit from Grinnell. Three years as a staff writer for *The Atlantic*. Freelance stuff for a couple of online magazines. About three dozen short stories and two dreadful novels, all fittingly unpublished. I'm hanging around Ole Miss doing the MFA thing and trying to figure out the future. For the past two months I've been carrying her luggage and having a grand time."

Mercer added, "Bodyguard, chauffeur, publicist, personal assistant. And he's a beautiful writer."

"I'd like to see some of your stuff," Bruce said.

Mercer looked at Thomas and said, "I told you. Bruce is always eager to help."

Thomas said, "Deal. When I have something worth reading I'll let you know."

Mercer knew that before dinner Bruce would dig online and find every story Thomas had written for *The Atlantic* and every other publication and would have a fairly firm opinion about his talents.

The crab salads arrived and Bruce poured more champagne. He noticed that his two guests were, so far, light drinkers. It was a habit he couldn't shake. At every lunch and dinner table, and at every bar, Bruce noticed. Most of the female writers he entertained hit the booze lightly. Most of the males were hard drinkers. A few were in recovery, and for those Bruce stuck strictly to iced tea.

He looked at Mercer and said, "And your next novel?"

"Come on, Bruce. I'm living the moment and writing nothing these days. We have two more weeks here before classes start and I'm determined not to write a single word."

"Smart, but don't wait too long. That two-book contract will get heavier as the days go by. And you can't wait three years before the next novel."

"Okay, okay," she said. "But can I have just a few days off?"

"One week, that's all. Look, dinner will be a blast tonight. Are you up for it?"

"Of course. All the gang?"

"They wouldn't miss it. Noelle is in Europe and she sends her regards, but everybody else is quite eager to see you. They've all read the book and love it."

"And how's Andy?" she asked.

"Still sober, so he won't be there. His last book was pretty good and sold well. He's writing a lot. You'll see him around."

"I've thought about him a lot. Such a sweet guy."

"He's doing well, Mercer. The gang is still together and looking forward to a long dinner."

4.

Thomas excused himself to find the restroom, and as soon as he was gone Bruce leaned in and asked, "Does he know about us?"

"What about us?"

"You've forgotten already? Our little weekend together. It was delightful, as I recall."

"Don't know what you're talking about, Bruce. It never happened."

"Okay. Fine with me. And nothing about the manuscripts?"

"What manuscripts? That's a part of my past I'm trying to forget."

"Wonderful. No one knows but you, me, Noelle, and of course the folks who paid the ransom."

"Nothing from me." She took a sip of wine, then leaned in low herself. "But where's all that money, Bruce?"

"Buried offshore and drawing interest. I have no plans to touch it."

"But it's a fortune. Why are you still working so hard?"

A big smile, a big sip. "This is not work, Mercer. This is who I am. I love this business and would be lost without it."

"Does the business still include dabbling in the black market?"

"Of course not. There are too many people watching right now, and, obviously, I don't need that anymore."

"So you've gone straight?"

"Clean as a whistle. I love the world of rare books and I'm buying even more these days, all legit. From time to time I get approached with something suspicious. There's still a lot of thievery out there, and I confess that I'm tempted. But it's too dicey."

"At the moment."

"At the moment."

She shook her head and smiled. "You're hopeless, Bruce. A hopeless flirt, philanderer, and book thief."

"True, and I'll also sell more copies of your book than anyone else. You gotta love me, Mercer."

"I wouldn't call it love."

"Okay. How about adoration?"

"I'll try that. Changing the subject, is there anything I should know about tonight?"

"I don't think so. Everyone is excited to see you again. There were some questions when you disappeared three years ago, but I covered for you, said you had some family drama back home, wherever home might be. Then you got a couple of gigs teaching and just haven't had the time to get back to the island."

"Same characters?"

"Yes, minus Noelle, as I said. Andy will probably stop by for a glass of water and a hello. He asks about you. And there's a new writer you might find interesting. Name's Nelson Kerr, a former lawyer with a big firm in San Francisco. He ratted out a client, a defense contractor who was illegally selling high-tech military stuff to the Iranians and North Koreans, nice guys like that. It was a big stink about ten years ago, now it's long since forgotten."

"Why would I follow that?"

"Right, anyway, his career flamed out but he collected a ton for blowing the whistle. Now he's sort of hiding out. Early forties, divorced, no kids, keeps to himself."

"This place attracts the misfits, doesn't it?"

"Always has. He's a nice guy but doesn't say much. Bought a nice condo down by the Hilton. Travels a lot."

"What about his books?"

"He writes what he knows, international arms smuggling, money laundering. Good thrillers."

"Sounds awful. Does he sell?"

"So-so, but he has potential. You wouldn't like his stuff but you'll probably like him."

Thomas returned and the conversation switched to the latest publishing scandal.

5.

Bruce lived in a Victorian home ten minutes by foot from Bay Books. After the obligatory post-lunch siesta in his office at the store, he left midafternoon and walked home to prepare for dinner. Even in the depths of summer, he preferred to have his fancy meals on the veranda, under a couple of creaky old fans and next to a gurgling fountain. His favorite cuisine came from south Louisiana, and for the evening he had hired Chef Claude, a bona-fide Cajun who'd been on the island for thirty years. He was already in the kitchen, whistling as he hovered over a large copper pot on the stove. They bantered for a moment but Bruce knew better than to hang around. The chef was a big talker and when fully engaged often forgot about his food.

The temperature was in the low nineties and Bruce went upstairs to change. He peeled out of his daily seersucker and bow tie and put on grungy shorts and a T-shirt, no shoes. Back in the kitchen, he opened two cold bottles of beer, gave one to the chef, and took the other one to the veranda to set the table.

At these moments he really missed Noelle. She imported antiques from the South of France and was a master at decorating. Her favorite chore was preparing a table for a dinner party. Her collection of vintage china, glasses, and flatware was astonishing and still growing. Some she bought to stock her store, but the rarest stuff, and the most beautiful, she kept for their private use. In Noelle's book, a gorgeous table was a gift to their guests, and no one could do it like her. She often photographed them both before and during the dinners, and framed the best ones to hang for her customers to admire.

The table was twelve feet long and for centuries had been used in a winery in Languedoc. They had found it together a year earlier when they spent a month on a shopping spree. Flush with ill-gotten cash, they had virtually raided Provence and bought so much stuff that they rented space in a warehouse in Avignon.

On a sideboard in the dining room, Noelle had carefully laid out the perfect dishes. Twelve vintage porcelain plates that had been hand-painted for a minor count in the 1700s. Lots of silverware, six pieces for each setting. And dozens of glasses for water and wine and digestifs.

The wineglasses were often problematic. Evidently Noelle's French ancestors didn't drink as much as Bruce's American writers, and the old glasses held barely three ounces when fully loaded. At a rowdy dinner party years earlier, Bruce and his guests had become frustrated with the need to refill the dainty glasses every ten minutes or so. Since then, he insisted on more modern versions that held eight ounces of red, six for white.

Noelle, who drank little, had acquiesced and found a collection of goblets from Burgundy that would impress an Irish rugby team.

Next to the dishes was a detailed diagram of the proper setting that she had prepared three days earlier when she left town. Bruce went about the business of arranging the linen placemats, the silk table runners, the candelabras, and then the dishes and glasses. The florist arrived and fussed over the table as she rearranged things and bickered with Bruce. When the table was perfect, according to her, Bruce took a photo and sent it to Noelle, who was somewhere in the Alps with her other companion. It was of magazine quality and ready for a dozen guests, though with their dinners the exact number was never certain until the food was served. Strays often materialized at the last moment and added to the fun.

Bruce went to the fridge for another beer.

6.

Cocktails were scheduled for 6:00 p.m. However, the guests were a bunch of writers and none would dare arrive before seven. Myra Beckwith and Leigh Trane showed up first and entered without knocking. Bruce met them on the veranda and mixed a rum and soda for Leigh and poured a stout ale for Myra.

The ladies had been a couple for over thirty years. As writers, they had struggled to pay the bills until they discovered the genre of soft porn romance novels. They cranked out a hundred of them under a dozen pseudonyms and made enough money to retire to the island and live in a quaint old house just around the corner from Bruce. Now, in their mid-seventies, they wrote little. Leigh fancied herself a tortured literary artist but her writing was impenetrable and her novels, the few she got published, sold next to nothing. She was always working on a novel but never finishing one. She claimed to be embarrassed by the junk they'd published but enjoyed the money. Myra, on the other hand, was proud of their work and longed for the glory days creating steamy sex scenes with pirates and young virgins and such.

Myra was a large woman with a crew cut dyed lavender. In a lame effort to hide some of her bulk, she wore loud flowing robes that would work nicely as bedsheets for a queen-size. Leigh, on the other hand, was tiny with dark features and long black hair piled neatly into a bun. Both ladies adored Bruce and Noelle, and the four dined together often.

Myra gulped her brew and asked him, "Have you seen Mercer?"

"Yes, we had lunch today, along with Thomas, her bodyguard these days."

"Is he cute?" Leigh asked.

"He's a nice-looking guy, a few years younger. One of her students."

"Go, girl," Myra said. "Did you ever learn the real reason she left here so abruptly three years ago?"

"Not really. Some sort of family business."

"Well, we'll get to the bottom of it tonight, I can assure you of that."

"Now Myra," Leigh said softly. "We'll not be prying."

"Hell if we won't. Prying is what I do best. I want the gossip. Is Andy coming by?"

"Maybe."

"I'd like to see him. He was so much more fun when he was in the sauce."

"Now Myra. That's a touchy subject."

"If you ask me, there's nothing more boring than a sober writer."

"He needs sobriety, Myra," Bruce said. "We've had this conversation."

"And what about this Nelson Kerr fellow? I find him boring even when he's not sober."

"Now Myra."

"Nelson will be here," Bruce said. "I was thinking he might be a good match for Mercer, but she's occupied at the moment."

"Who made you a matchmaker?" Myra quipped as they noticed J. Andrew Cobb, or Bob Cobb as they called him, walking through the door. As usual, he was wearing pink shorts, sandals, and a gaudy floral print shirt. Without missing a beat Myra said, "Hello Bob. You shouldn't have dressed up for the occasion." She gave him a quick hug as Bruce stepped to the bar and mixed vodka and soda.

Cobb was an ex-con who'd served time in a federal pen for sins that were still vague. He wrote crime novels that sold well but had far too much prison violence, at least in Bruce's opinion. He hugged Leigh, said, "Hello ladies. Always a pleasure."

"A good day on the beach?" Myra asked, looking for trouble.

Cobb's skin was a dark, leathery brown, a perpetual tan that he maintained with hours in the sun. His reputation was that of an aging beach bum who admired bikinis and was always on the prowl. He smiled at Myra and said, "Every day on the beach is a good one, my dear."

"How old was she?" Myra asked.

"Now Myra," Leigh cooed as Bruce handed him a drink.

"Old enough, barely," Cobb said and laughed.

Amy Slater was the youngest of the group and was making more money than the others combined. She had struck gold with a series about young vampires, and there was even a movie in the works. She and her husband, Dan, arrived on the veranda along with Andy Adam. Jay Arklerood was right behind them and managed a rare smile as greetings were made. He was a brooding poet who often dodged the dinners. Myra, the Queen Bee, had no use for him. Bruce fetched drinks, an ice water for Andy, and listened to the banter. Amy went on about her movie, though there were problems with the script. Dan stood quietly by her side. He had retired from employment and took care of the kids so she could write full-time.

The party was buzzing when Mercer and Thomas made their entrance. She swapped hugs as she introduced her new fella. The gang was delighted to see her and gushed about her new book, which most had read. As they talked, Nelson Kerr eased onto the scene and fixed a drink at the bar. He joined the circle around Mercer, and Bruce made the introductions.

After a few minutes, the conversations spun off in different directions. Andy and Bruce discussed the storm. Myra cornered Thomas and began drilling into his past. Bob Cobb and Nelson had gone fishing the day before and needed to relive their catches. Leigh was going through Mercer's novel chapter by chapter and couldn't get enough of the story. Drinks were refilled and no one was in a hurry to sit down to dinner.

The last guest to join them was Nick Sutton, a college boy who spent his summers on the island tending to a fine home owned by his grandparents. As was their annual ritual, they

had fled the Florida heat and were roaming the country in a
camper. Nick worked at the bookstore, and when he wasn't on
duty he surfed and sailed and looked for girls. He read at least
one crime novel a day and dreamed of writing bestsellers. Bruce
had read his short stories and thought the kid had talent. Nick
had lobbied hard for the invitation to dinner and was almost
overwhelmed to be included.

At 7:30, Chef Claude informed Bruce that it was time to eat.
Andy whispered to his host and eased away without another
word. Sobriety was difficult enough during dry evenings. He
wasn't tempted to drink, but the last thing he wanted was a
three-hour dinner with wine flowing.

Bruce pointed to chairs and got them seated properly. He
sat at one end and Mercer, the guest of honor, had the other,
with Thomas to her right. There were eleven in all, the literary
mafia of Camino Island plus Nick Sutton. Bruce passed along
best wishes from Noelle, who hated to miss the fun but was
with them in spirit. Everyone knew she was off in Europe with
her steady French boyfriend and no one was surprised. They
had long ago accepted the open marriage and no one cared. If
Bruce and Noelle were happy, their friends were not about to
question the arrangement.

Bruce had never liked by-the-hour servers buzzing around
his table and eavesdropping on the conversations, so he didn't
use them. He and Claude poured the wine and water and served
the first appetizer course, a small bowl of spicy gumbo.

"It's too hot for gumbo," Myra growled mid-table. "I'll be
soaked."

"Cold wine always helps," Bruce shot back.

"What's the main course?" she asked.

"Everything's spicy."

Bob Cobb said, "So, Mercer, last stop on the tour, right? And I loved the book, by the way."

"Thanks," she said. "Yes, the last stop."

"Coast to coast?"

"Yes, thirty-three stops. Tomorrow is thirty-four."

"You'll have a huge crowd tomorrow, Mercer," Amy said. "A lot of the locals remember your grandmother and they're very proud of you."

"I knew Tessa," Bruce said. "But, as I look around the table, I believe that no one here was living on the island when she died. What was it, Mercer, twelve years ago?"

"Fourteen."

Myra said, "We moved here thirteen years ago to get away from a bunch of writers. Look what's happened. Everyone followed us here."

Bob said, "And I believe I was next, about ten years ago, right after I got paroled."

"Please, Bob," Myra snapped. "No more prison stories. After your last book I felt like I'd been gang-raped."

"Now Myra."

"So you liked it?" Bob asked.

"Loved it."

"Anyway," Bruce said loudly. "I'd like to propose a toast to, first of all, Mr. Leo. May he remain at sea and just go away. And, more importantly, to our dear friend Mercer and her wonderful new book, number five on the big list and rising. Cheers!"

They clinked glasses and took a drink.

"I have a question, Mercer," Leigh said. "Did your grandmother, the real Tessa, really have a steamy romance with a younger man, here on the island?"

"That was the best part," Myra interjected quickly. "That first seduction scene made my teeth sweat. Really well done, girl."

"Thanks, Myra," Mercer said. "Coming from you, that's quite a compliment."

"Don't mention it. Of course I would've gone way overboard."

"Now Myra."

"But yes, once I was old enough to realize what was going on, I suspected Tessa spent a lot of time with the younger man when I wasn't around."

"And that was Porter, in real life?" Leigh asked.

"Yes. Porter lived here for many years. Fourteen years ago they died together in a storm."

"I remember Porter, and the storm," Bruce said. "It was one of the worst we've seen on the island, short of a hurricane."

"Who's talking about hurricanes?" Amy asked.

"Sorry. We've had our share of glancing blows but nothing terrible. The storm that got Tessa and Porter was an old-fashioned summer heat cell that came from the north with no warning."

"And where was Tessa?" Amy asked. "I'm sorry, Mercer, if you don't want to talk about this."

"No, it's fine. Tessa and Porter were not far out, just a lazy summer's day in his sailboat. Porter and the boat were never seen again. Tessa was found in the surf near the North Pier two days later."

Myra said, "Well, thank God you didn't kill her off in your novel. I certainly would have."

"You killed everyone, Myra," Leigh said. "After you ran them through the sex grinder."

"Murder sells, Leigh, almost as much as sex. Remember that when those royalty checks arrive."

"So what's next, Mercer?" Bob Cobb asked.

She smiled at Thomas and said, "Rest for a couple of weeks, though I'm already being hounded by Thomas and Bruce to start another novel."

"I need something to sell," Bruce said.

"So do I," added Leigh, for a laugh.

Jay, the brooding poet, said, "My last book sold twenty copies. No one reads poetry." As always, it was an awkward effort at humor and got a sympathetic laugh or two.

Myra almost blurted something like: And no one *can* read the crap you write. But instead she said, "I've told you before, Jay, you should write some really raunchy fiction under a pen name, make some money, like Bob, and do your little poetry thing as the real you. Still won't sell, though."

Bruce had seen this conversation go off the rails before, and he quickly intervened with "Can we toast the new deal, Mercer?"

She smiled and said, "Oh why not? Secrets are hard to keep around here."

Bruce said, "A new two-book deal with Viking, as of this morning."

They cheered and took turns congratulating Mercer as Claude removed the bowls. He poured more wine, a cold Chablis, and began serving the next course, a small platter of smoked oysters. A breeze materialized from the east and gently ruffled the thick air.

On his trips to and from the kitchen, Claude kept one eye on the small television near the stove. Leo was still out there, drifting, churning, puzzling the experts, with no apparent destination.

7.

Bruce preferred long dinners with gaps between courses for wine and conversation. After he and Claude cleared the oyster shells, they refilled the wineglasses and announced that the main dish would be blackened redfish, a delicacy that might take some time.

Claude went to the stove, where his cast-iron skillet was already warm. From the fridge he removed a tray of marinated fillets and carefully placed two in the skillet. He covered them with his own recipe of Cajun seasoning—garlic, paprika, onion, salt, and spices. The aroma was pungent, delicious.

He hummed as he cooked, happy as always to be at the stove, and he sipped wine and enjoyed the waves of laughter from the veranda. Dinner parties at Bruce's were always an event. Great wines and food, interesting guests, no hurries, no worries.

The evening broke up at midnight when Mercer and Thomas finally said good night. Bruce and Claude cleared the table and stacked the dishes on the counter. Someone else would clean up tomorrow. Regardless of how late he went to bed, Bruce was an early riser and walked to the bookstore each morning at seven.

As soon as Claude was gone, he locked the house, climbed the stairs, stripped, and fell across his bed. Within minutes he was in a coma.

Around 1:00 a.m., Leo finally made his move.

8.

Nick Sutton was a light sleeper, and once awake in the pre-dawn hours he often read for an hour or two before returning to bed. Out of curiosity, he turned on the television to catch the news and presumed things were quiet. Things were not. The forecasters were alarmed because Leo had suddenly turned due west and its projected path was now aimed directly at Camino Island. It was a Category 3, gaining strength, two hundred miles out there and moving at them at ten miles an hour. Nick flipped channels and the panic was growing by the minute. He began calling and waking friends, some of whom were already glued to the Weather Channel.

At 5:00 a.m., he called Bruce and broke the news. Bruce watched the weather for ten minutes and called Nick back with instructions to round up the troops and meet at the store as soon as possible.

By daybreak, the island was in a frenzy. As a barrier, it was designed to take the brunt of any storm and protect the mainland. It was surrounded by water, flat with a high altitude of only twenty-four feet, and susceptible to a major storm surge, though no one on the island had ever witnessed that kind of water.

At 7:03, the sun peeked above the quiet ocean as if the day would be just another sunny one in paradise. Leo was by then a

Category 4 and for the first time seemed determined to trek in one direction without veering left or right. At 7:15, the governor activated full evacuation for the coastal areas north of Jacksonville. "Get out now" was his message, and he hinted strongly that a mandatory evacuation order was forthcoming. "There is no time to prepare," he said grimly. "Just get out now."

Forty thousand people lived year-round on the island, with about half in Santa Rosa proper. There were no other towns to speak of. The city limits were not well defined and blurred with the rest of the island. Because it was early August, the tourist season was slower than June and July, but it was estimated that fifty thousand visitors were staying in oceanside hotels and condos. Early in the morning they were asked to leave, and quickly. Some fled immediately but most lingered and watched cable news with their coffee and breakfast. Only one four-lane bridge linked Camino Island to the mainland and by 8:00 a.m. its traffic was heavy. Each day a thousand employees crossed the bridge to work in the island's hotels, but they were now being turned away. No one was allowed to cross. Everyone was encouraged to head west. Where? It didn't matter. Just get off the island.

As the minutes passed, the forecasters remained unanimous with their projected paths. Leo's eye was headed for downtown Santa Rosa.

At 8:15, the governor ordered the mandatory evacuation and activated two National Guard units. The police began going door-to-door. By law, a resident could not be forced to leave. However, for those who chose to remain, the police took phone numbers of their next of kin and informed them that first responders would not try to save them. The two hospitals were evacuated and the critical patients were taken to Jacksonville. The six grocery stores on the island opened early and were flooded with panicked shoppers desperate for bottled water and nonperishables.

Those who planned to stay were warned that there would be little food and water and no electricity for days after the storm. And there would be almost no medical care.

The warnings were blunt and everywhere: Get off the island!

9.

Bay Books had seven employees—three full-time and four by the hour. All hands were on deck as Bruce barked orders and helped them haul books upstairs to the second floor, where they were stacked on the floor. The tables and chairs in the small café were shoved to the side to make room. Two part-timers, both young men, were sent down to Noelle's store to move her beloved antiques.

A fire marshal stopped by at 8:30 and said to Bruce, "You're only four feet above sea level so you can expect some flooding." The harbor was six blocks to the west, the beach a mile to the east.

"You know there's a mandatory evacuation order," he said.

"I'm not leaving," Bruce said.

The fire marshal took his name, phone number, and Noelle's contact information, then hurried to the store next door. At 9:00, Bruce gathered his employees and told them to grab their valuables and leave the island. Everyone vanished, except for Nick Sutton, who seemed to relish the idea of riding out a major hurricane. He was adamant in his refusal to evacuate.

The shelves of Bruce's office on the first floor were lined

with valuable first editions. Bruce told Nick to continue to box them and deliver them to his home four blocks away. Bruce left and drove to the home of Myra and Leigh, who were frantically throwing clothes and dogs into their old station wagon.

"Where should we go, Bruce?" Myra asked, soaked with sweat and visibly frightened.

"Get on Interstate 10 and head toward Pensacola. I'll check on the house after the storm."

"You're not leaving?" Leigh asked.

"No, I can't. I'm going to watch the store and check on things. I'll be fine."

"Then we're staying too," Myra said without conviction.

"No, you're not. It could be ugly—lots of trees down, some flooding, no power for days. Y'all get out of here and find a hotel room somewhere. I'll call as soon as the phones start working again."

"You're not worried?" Leigh asked.

"Of course I'm worried. But I'll be okay." He helped them load all the bottled water in the house, a box of liquor, three sacks of food, and ten pounds of dog food. He practically shoved them into the car and waved them goodbye. Both were in tears as they began their escape.

He called Amy, who was already on the road and over the bridge. Her husband had an aunt in Macon, Georgia, and that would be their first stop. Bruce promised to check on their home after the storm and call. He tried to drive to the beach but the police were blocking all eastbound traffic. Mercer was not answering her phone.

10.

Tessa had built the beach cottage thirty years earlier. As a child, Mercer had spent her summers there, far away from her warring parents. Larry had always been around to tend to the cottage, and bicker with Tessa about the gardening, and bring fruits and vegetables from his garden. He was a native of the island and would never leave, not even for a threat like Leo.

He arrived early that morning with eight sheets of used plywood, drills, and hammers, and he and Thomas boarded the windows and doors as Mercer hurriedly packed the car. Larry was adamant that they leave as soon as possible. The ground floor of the cottage was eighteen feet above sea level and there were two hundred feet of dunes for protection. He was confident the surge wouldn't reach the cottage but was worried about the wind.

Tessa had died in a storm, and Mercer wasn't about to stay behind. At 11:00, she hugged Larry goodbye and left with Thomas at the wheel, his yellow Labrador perched between them on the console. It took an hour to get to the bridge, and as they inched across it and looked down at the choppy and forbidding waters of the Camino River, the sky darkened and the rains began.

11.

With his rare books secured in a new walk-in vault next to his bedroom, Bruce tried to relax. If that could be possible. The storm hysteria on cable was impossible to ignore and it was frightening to watch Leo tighten his eye in real time and keep it locked on the island. Bruce and Nick Sutton ate sandwiches on the veranda and watched it rain. The housekeeper had been frightened away and had already called from Tallahassee.

Bruce's collection was worth far more than the inventory at his store, or the art on his walls, or the pricey antiques Noelle peddled to her high-end clientele. With his prized editions secured, a chunk of his net worth was safe from any catastrophe—fire, flood, wind, theft. The biggest chunk was buried offshore and no one but Noelle knew about it.

Bay Books was closed and locked tight, as were all downtown stores, restaurants, and coffee shops. No one was interested in shopping or dining out. Main Street was deserted except for the police in yellow rain gear. There was little crime on the island during a normal day. Potential looters lived elsewhere. The biggest fears were rising waters and glass breakage.

Four blocks away, where the stately Victorians had been on display for a century, the fear was falling trees. Some of the oaks had been around for three hundred years, and every house was shaded by thick limbs draped with Spanish moss. The trees were stately, historic, a source of great pride, but in a few hours they would become dangerous.

As Nick returned to the table with a Heineken, Bruce poured another glass of white wine and looked at his checklist. He said, "It might be a good idea if you stay here for the fun. I have no experience with hurricanes but it seems as though the buddy system will be safer. Wind, water, falling limbs, no power—it'll be better to have two of us."

Nick nodded but wasn't convinced. "How much food do you have?"

"For two people, enough for a week. I have a small generator

that will run the basics for a few days. I'll fill the cans with gas.
Are you on your bike?"

"Always."

"Okay. Take my Tahoe to your grandparents' home and load
up all the food and water you can find. Fill the tank with gas.
And hurry."

"You got some beer?" Nick asked. The college boy.

"The wine cellar is stocked with plenty of beer, booze, and
wine. We need to round up some water. Does your grandfather
have a chain saw?"

"Yes. I'll bring it back."

"A plan. Let's hustle."

Nick left and Bruce finished the bottle of wine. He tried to
nap in a hammock but the wind picked up and made too much
noise. There were three bathtubs in the house and he ran them
full. He moved the patio furniture inside and locked all windows and doors. His checklist included the names of thirty-one
people—employees, friends, and, of course, his writers. Of the
whole group, five were staying behind, including Bob Cobb and
Nelson Kerr. Myra and Leigh were puttering along in heavy traffic on I-10, sipping rum, soothing their dogs, and listening to
one of their raunchy romance novels on tape. They giggled like
a couple of drunks. Amy and her family were already in Macon.
Jay Arklerood, the poet, was headed to Miami. Andy Adam had
fled early, partly out of fear that his fragile sobriety could not
survive the chaos of a deadly hurricane. Bob Cobb was tucked
into his condo with a woman. Nelson Kerr was sitting on a pier
in a rain suit watching the waves churn and enjoying the excitement, for the moment. His condo was not far from Bob's and
they planned to keep in touch when Leo rolled in.

His winds were 155 miles an hour, on the verge of rising to a Category 5, with projections of catastrophic damage and loss of life. He was also moving faster, almost fifteen miles an hour due west, with landfall now predicted at 10:30 p.m. at the heart of the island. By 4:00 p.m., the rains were torrential as the outer bands settled in with gusts strong enough to snap branches. Debris flew and scattered across the streets. At 5:30, a policeman knocked on Bruce's door and asked what the hell he was doing at home. Bruce explained that he had already checked with the authorities and was staying put. He asked about his neighbors and was told that everyone had left.

When Nick returned around 6:00, the island suddenly got very dark. The sky turned black as thick clouds swirled violently not far above them.

Bruce hooked up his small generator and switched off all circuits except for the outlets in the den and kitchen. No other electricity was in use. They had plenty of flashlights and batteries. Dinner was steaks on the grill and frozen French fries with a bottle of pinot noir.

At 7:00 p.m., with the winds howling at eighty miles an hour, Bruce called the gang for the last time. Myra and Leigh were in a motel in Pensacola with their five dogs, who were causing trouble because they were nervous and barking. Amy was high and dry in Macon. Jay was staying with a friend in Miami. Andy Adam was at his mother's in Charlotte. All were worried about their homes and about Bruce's safety. They were glued to their televisions, and the predictions grew more ominous by the hour. Bruce assured everyone that he and Nick were safe and well prepared. He promised to check on their property as soon as possible and call when cell service was restored. Good night and God bless.

According to the state disaster chief, the most vulnerable section of the island was a half-mile stretch of beach known as Pauley's Sound. It was on the far north end, near the Hilton, and, like most of the oceanfront, had been heavily developed with clusters of condos, old and new cottages, mom-and-pop motels, beachside bars and cafés, and tall modern hotels. The Sound was only a few feet above sea level and there were no dunes to protect it from a surge. Both Bob Cobb and Nelson Kerr lived there in a gated development known as Marsh Grove. Bruce called them last. Bob and his lady were hunkered down for the night. He seemed nonchalant and had obviously been drinking. Nelson Kerr was sitting in the dark and wishing he had fled too. Bruce invited him to hustle over to his house where things would certainly be safer, but Nelson said the police had closed all the streets. Trees and power lines were already down and the rain was falling in sheets.

By 8:00 p.m., the sustained winds were over a hundred miles an hour and howled with a roar so loud and constant that Bruce and Nick had trouble sitting still. With flashlights, they roamed the downstairs, looking cautiously through windows to gauge the damage, to see if limbs had fallen, to see if rainwater was flooding the street. They would sit for a moment in the den and try to enjoy a taste of bourbon, then a gust would blow through and rattle the house. Or they'd hear a *crack* in the distance.

The cracking sounds were the worst. With the first two, neither Bruce nor Nick was certain what was happening. Then they realized that wind was snapping off thick limbs, which sounded like nearby shotgun blasts. With each one they flinched and eased carefully toward a window.

For the past fifteen years Bruce had owned the Marchbanks House, an 1890 Victorian built the old way and designed to withstand hurricanes. At the moment he wasn't worried about losing a roof or a porch, but there were two ancient oaks on the property with limbs large enough to do serious damage.

In the midst of the storm, as if the howling, rattling, and cracking were not enough, an odd cadence emerged. The roar was constant and slowly rising, and every minute or so a band of even stronger gusts swept through, as if to warn that heavier action was still out there over the water and not far behind. The gusts passed, the storm returned to its steady noise and strength, and Bruce and Nick took a sip of bourbon and hoped there would be no more gusts. Then a limb cracked and they peeked out the windows.

Just after 9:00, the power lines gave way and began to snap. The island was pitch black as the storm grew louder.

After two hours of getting battered by winds over a hundred miles per hour, the boys had had enough. Bruce thought about an attempt at humor with something like "Well, I guess we should've left," but why bother? The eye was still two hours away and the winds had not reached their peak. The street was solid water from the rain and the surge had yet to arrive. Bruce was certain the ground floor of Bay Books was taking water.

But for the moment he and Nick were dry and safe. There was little they could do until morning. At 10:30 p.m., the projected time for the arrival of the eye, Bruce was certain that the house was about to shear off its foundation and crash into Dr. Bagwell's across the street. Its floors and ceilings vibrated and the walls were literally shaking. The great fear was that a limb might crash through the den and open up the house to torrents of rain and more wind. They would be forced to flee and seek shelter, but where? There was no place to go.

It was almost 11:00 when the winds stopped and the night became perfectly still. Bruce and Nick stepped outside and waded to the street, where they looked at the sky and saw stars. A TV expert said that Leo's eye would pass in about twenty minutes, and Bruce was tempted to take a look at downtown and check on his store. But again, why bother? He couldn't stop the flooding. The cleanup would begin in the morning. He had plenty of insurance coverage.

They walked down the street, wading in ankle-deep water, and did not see another person, not another light. Evidently the policeman had been right—all of his neighbors had the good sense to leave. In the darkness it was impossible to see where all those limbs had landed, but there was debris everywhere.

The tranquility, along with the bourbon, settled their nerves, if only for a moment. As the minutes passed, a gentle wind arrived from the west and reminded them that the storm was only half over.

12.

Leo's two-week reign of terror climaxed officially at 10:57 p.m. Eastern Standard Time when the center of his eye came ashore along the northern tip of Camino Island. True to form, he wiggled a bit at the end, moved to the north, and stalled just long enough to maintain a Category 4 ranking, with top winds at 145 miles per hour, almost reaching the rare status as a Cat 5 at 156 miles an hour. Not that it really mattered. Eleven miles per hour mean little in such a powerful storm, and long before and long after the eye came and went its winds battered the island. Old cottages built decades earlier were blown off their stilts. Newer ones hung on but lost windows, doors, roofs, decks. The top storm surge around the eye was fifteen feet in some areas, enough to flood hundreds of cottages, homes, motels, and stores. Main Street was under four feet of water, and some of the older homes in the historic section took in water for the first time in history.

Along the ocean, all boardwalks and piers were gone. Inland, limbs and entire trees blocked streets and driveways. Parking lots were covered with roof shingles, garbage, more jagged tree limbs. In the docks and harbors, boats of all sizes were strewn about like scattered firewood.

Though virtually everyone had fled, some of the few who stayed behind did not survive. At sunrise, the first siren could be heard wailing across the island.

13.

Bruce slept for two hours on a sofa in the den and awoke with cobwebs and a stiff back. The wind was gone, the house was quiet and dark, the storm was over. He walked to a window and saw the first hint of sunlight. He put on rubber boots and walked outside where he waded through six inches of water and looked at his house from across the street. A few squares of slate were missing from the roof and a third-floor gutter had been ripped off, but the house was in remarkable shape. All of the heavy oak limbs that he had worried about were still where they should have been. Four doors down to the west, the floodwaters had made it all the way to the Keegan home but had stopped at the front steps.

He reached into a pocket and removed a cigar. Why not have a smoke? He clipped and lit it, and for a long time stood in muddy water in the middle of Sixth Street as the sky lightened and morning arrived. The clouds were thinning, the sun was rising, the day would be hot and humid, and there was no electricity to cool things. There were no sounds and not another human in sight. He walked south along Sixth to Ash and the water disappeared. The asphalt on Ash was visible. A door opened and Mr. Chester Finley walked onto his porch and said good morning.

"Had a little wind, didn't we?" he said with a smile. He was holding a bottle of water.

"Just a little. You guys okay?" Bruce asked.

"We're fine. The Dodsons took a hit but they're not here."

"Smart folks. I'm around if you need some help." Bruce walked around the corner and gawked at the Dodsons' pretty Victorian. A huge limb had sheared off from an oak in their backyard and literally cut the house in half. He walked on and stopped in front of the Vicker House, 1867, purchased by Myra and Leigh thirteen years earlier. They had painted it pink with royal blue trim, and it had survived well enough. A limb had crashed through a front window and Bruce suspected there was substantial water damage. He and Nick could handle the cleanup with the chain saw. That might be their first project.

As he was returning to Sixth Street, he heard the unmistakable thumping of a helicopter. He stopped and listened as it grew closer, and soon enough a Navy Seahawk came into view, flying low to survey the aftermath. Rescuers in uniforms had arrived, and that was a welcome thought. The chopper flew away and minutes later another one buzzed downtown. It was smaller, with the gaudy paint job of a news station.

14.

Mercer and Thomas sipped coffee in bed and waited for the first reports. They were in a motel near Dothan, Alabama, one that had waived the No Pets rule and allowed them and the dog to check in after dark. The traffic had been brutal and they had been forced to keep driving west to find a room. The cable stations had blacked out shortly after 10:00 p.m. when the winds became too strong, but by 6:00 a.m. they were up and running. Not long after sunrise a helicopter ran a live shot along the beach as an excited reporter on board tried to describe the damage. A large condo building was gutted. Another had partially collapsed. Roofs were missing. Some of the smaller beach houses were almost flattened. The empty parking lots were littered with debris. Naval vessels were unloading near Main Beach, the busiest place on normal days. Mercer could not catch a glimpse of Tessa's cottage, but there was little doubt it had been damaged. Inland, thousands of trees were down, with streets blocked by limbs and entire trees. A church steeple had been toppled.

Near the center of Santa Rosa, the streets were under water that appeared to be about knee deep. Rescue crews in boats were moving slowly about. One man waved at the helicopter. The screen cut to a reporter on the ground who quickly recapped his heroic efforts to remain outdoors all night as his crew grappled with their camera. He said that emergency management expected the island to be without electricity for at least a week.

The National Guard had already arrived. The island was virtually deserted but they had just received the first report of a fatality up at Pauley's Sound; more later. The bridge was closed and would be examined for damage.

It was obvious the island was a mess and would remain so for weeks or months. Mercer and Thomas had no desire to rush back into the rubble and they couldn't get to the cottage anyway. Larry was there, she hoped, and he would do the best he could. Nor did they wish to hang around a motel when Mercer's apartment in Oxford was only six hours away.

Thomas left to find breakfast and something for the dog. Mercer got in the shower, worried about Larry but happy not to be on the island, happy that the book tour was over, though the ending was not exactly what she had wanted, and happy most of all to be going home. She and Thomas had been living out of their luggage for two months.

CHAPTER TWO
THE CRIME SCENE

1.

Bruce, who had absolutely no experience with a chain saw, quickly yielded the tool to Nick, who had at least held one before. It took them ten minutes to figure out how to start the damned thing, but Nick was soon rampaging around the backyard, slicing up even the thinnest of limbs and branches. Bruce followed at a safe distance and gathered the debris. He was tossing some limbs into a pile when a Santa Rosa policeman appeared from nowhere. Bruce signaled and Nick reluctantly shut down the chain saw. Another one could be heard in the distance.

The officer introduced himself, and after a few minutes of storm talk said, "There are some fatalities, sorry to say. Looks like most were on the north end."

Bruce nodded and wanted to know what this had to do with him.

The officer went on, "Your friend Nelson Kerr took a head wound and didn't make it."

"Nelson!" Bruce said in disbelief. "Nelson's dead?"

"Afraid so. And he left your name and number as his local contact."

"But what happened to him?"

"Don't know. I was not at the scene. I was told to find you. My captain asks that you come to the scene and identify the body."

Bruce shot a bewildered look at Nick, who was too stunned to speak, and said, "Well, sure. Let's go."

The officer looked at Nick and said, "Better bring that chain saw. We might need it."

Parked in front of the house was a green and yellow John Deere all-terrain vehicle, a Gator, a two-seater with four-wheel drive. Bruce sat in the front, shoulder to shoulder with the officer, and Nick crawled into the back. They took off, turned west, and began dodging limbs and debris in the street. They moved away from downtown, zigzagging slowly through the devastation.

The damage was overwhelming. Every street was blocked with trees, limbs, downed wires, lawn furniture, boards, shingles, garbage, and standing water. Dozens of homes had been hit with limbs and branches. Only a few of the residents were outdoors, and those who were cleaning up appeared dazed. On Atlantic Avenue, a main thoroughfare to the beach, National Guardsmen were everywhere with chain saws, picks, and axes. The street was barely passable but the officer slowly worked the Gator through the cleanup chaos.

He said, "Looks like Pauley's Sound got hit the worst. The Hilton really got hammered. Already found two bodies in the parking lot."

"How many fatalities?" Bruce asked.

"Three so far. Your friend and those two but I'm afraid there'll be more." He turned off Atlantic and onto a narrow street that ran north and south. They weaved around thick limbs and debris, turned again and headed east and before long stopped at Fernando Street, the main drag along the beach-front. More Guardsmen were working to clear it. The officer stopped and they helped shove an overturned car out of the way. A hundred yards to the east, the ocean was calm, the sun was up and already hot.

Nelson Kerr lived in a three-story row house that lined a dead-end street not far from the Hilton. The units were heavily damaged, with blown-out windows and roofs torn off. They stopped in the street and walked to a driveway where Bob Cobb was waiting. Bruce shook his hand and Bob hugged him. His eyes were bloodshot, his long gray hair disheveled. "Rough night, partner," he said. "Should've left with the smart folks."

"Where's Nelson?" Bruce asked.

"Around back."

Nelson was lying crumpled over a short brick wall that ringed his patio. Definitely dead. He was wearing jeans, a T-shirt, old sneakers. Another policeman, a sergeant, was standing guard, obviously uncertain about what to do next. He offered a hand and said, "This your friend?"

Bruce felt weak in the knees but gamely stepped forward for a closer look. Nelson's head was hanging off the side of the brick wall. There was a bloody gash above his left ear. Below the body was a limb from one of several Japanese crepe myrtles. Other limbs and leaves littered the scene.

Bruce stepped back and said, "Yes, that's him."

Nick leaned closer for a look and said, "That's Nelson."

The sergeant said, "Okay. Do you guys mind staying here with the body while we get some help?"

"What kind of help are you talking about?" Bruce asked.

"Well, I'm not sure. I guess we need the medical examiner to pronounce him dead. Just stay with him, okay?"

"Sure, whatever," Bruce replied.

"He left your name, address, and phone number, and he also wrote down the name of some folks in California. Mr. and Mrs. Howard Kerr. I assume they're his parents."

"Probably. I've never met them."

"I guess we need to call them." The sergeant looked at Bruce as if he could use some help.

Bruce wanted no part of that call and said, "That's your job. But the phones are down, right?"

"We have a satellite phone back at the staging area at Main Beach. I guess I'll get back there and make the call. I don't suppose you could do that, could you?"

"No sir. I don't know those people and it's not my job."

"Okay. Y'all just stay here with the body."

"Will do."

Bob asked, "Can we look around his house?"

"I guess. We'll be back as soon as we can." The two policemen got in the Gator and drove away.

Bob said, "These folks were a bit luckier. The surge stopped here at the front steps. I live two streets over and got five feet of water on the ground floor. I sat on the stairs and watched it rise. Not a good feeling."

"I'm sorry, Bob," Bruce said.

"I wouldn't call Nelson lucky," Nick said.

"Good point."

They returned to the rear patio and stared at the body. Bob said, "I can't imagine what he was doing outside in the middle of the storm. A really stupid move."

"Didn't he have a dog?" Bruce asked. "Maybe his dog got out."

"He did have a dog," Bob remembered. "A little black mutt, knee high, called him Boomer. Let's find him," Bob said as he opened the rear door. "I suppose it's prudent not to touch anything."

They stepped inside onto a wet floor in the unlit kitchen, looking for any sign of a dog. Nick observed, "If the dog was here wouldn't we know it by now?"

"Probably," Bruce said. "I'll check the upstairs. You guys poke around down here."

Five minutes later every room had been checked and there was no dog. They regrouped in the kitchen, where the heat and humidity were rising by the minute. They went out to the patio and stared at Nelson.

Bruce said, "We should at least cover the body."

"Good idea," Bob said, as if still in a daze. Nick found two large towels in a bathroom and gently placed them over the body. Bruce was suddenly nauseous and said, "I need to sit down, fellas." Nelson had shoved four metal deck chairs under a table wedged in a corner of the patio, and they had not been scattered by the wind. They pulled them out, dusted off the debris, and sat in the shade twenty feet from the body. Nick found three bottles of warm beer in the fridge and they toasted their dead comrade.

Bruce said, "You got to know him pretty well, right?"

Bob replied, "I guess. He moved here, what, two years ago?"

"Something like that. His third novel had just been published and was selling well. He'd been divorced for a few years, no kids, and wanted to get away from California."

They sipped their beers and studied the white towels. Nick said, "This really doesn't make any sense. How could the dog get out in the middle of a major hurricane?"

"Maybe the damned thing had to pee," Bob said. "Nelson let him out for a quick one, the dog got freaked out in the storm, got away, and Nelson panicked and tried to get him. That branch snapped and hit him in the head. I'll bet he's not the only fool who got hit by a falling limb last night. Bad timing. Bad luck."

Bruce said, "He had just finished a novel. I wonder where the manuscript is."

"Wow. That's valuable stuff. Did you read it?" Nick asked.

"No, but I had promised to. He was just finishing the second draft. As far as I know, he had not sent it to New York."

"It's probably in his computer, don't you think?"

"More than likely."

Nick asked, "What happens to it?"

There was a long pause as they considered this. "Wasn't he a lawyer?" Nick asked.

"He was, a big firm in San Francisco," Bruce said. "I'm sure he has a will, and the will appoints an executor who'll take charge of his affairs. It'll be a mess."

Bob said, "If he's been here for two years then he's likely to be a resident of Florida. Of course he is. He has Florida tags on his car. So wouldn't the lawyer be here?"

"Hell if I know. He probably has, had, lawyer friends everywhere."

Nick stepped into the condo and closed the door behind him.

Bob said, "We could wait here for hours, you know? These poor cops are chasing their tails right now."

"We passed a bunch of National Guardsmen on the way over, so help has arrived."

"What about your place?"

"Got lucky. Lots of downed limbs, no real damage. Nothing like around here."

Bob said, "I should've left. Now I have to rip out carpets and drywall and shovel out mud and crap. A week with no electricity. Temps in the nineties. You have plenty of food?"

"I'm okay. I have a small generator so the beer is still cold. Come stay with me and Nick. There's food, and when it's gone we'll go looting, have some fun."

"Thanks."

Nick cracked the door and said, "Hey, fellas, come take a look."

They walked into the den where Nick lit a wall with a flashlight. Bob asked, "Where'd you get that?"

"Found it on the sofa. Look at those specks next to the bookshelves. Could be dried blood. There's more on those books just to the right there."

Bruce took the flashlight and examined the wall. There were eight to ten dark specks of something, perhaps blood. Perhaps not. But whatever the substance there was no way that Nelson or his housekeeper, if he had one, would have allowed the stains to remain where they were. Bob examined them and shook his head.

"Follow me," Nick said, and they walked down a narrow hall to the bathroom. He lit the vanity and said, "See those pinkish stains beside the faucet? Could've been left behind by someone trying to wash away bloodstains."

"You read a lot of crime novels?" Bob asked.

"Hundreds. They're my favorite."

"So where's the bloody hand towel or rag or whatever?" Bruce asked.

"Gone. There was no electricity, but the hot water pressure would've worked until the tank ran dry. Our suspect couldn't toss the hand towel in the washing machine because it wasn't working. And it's empty now. He couldn't leave behind the evidence, so he simply left with it."

"Our suspect?" Bruce asked.

"Indulge me here. This could be serious."

"It's already serious," Bob said.

"Got that."

Bruce said, "You're thinking somebody came over here in the middle of a Category 4 hurricane, caught Nelson in the den, whacked him in the head, dragged his body outside, tried to clean up the blood, and then ran off. Seriously?"

"Stranger things have happened," Nick said. "Actually, it was the perfect time to kill somebody and make it look accidental."

"I like it," Bob said. "But where's the blood on the floor?"

They looked at their feet. All six were on a wet and stained rug. Nick said, "It's too dark in here to see anything, but what if, and, again, just indulge me, but what if we're standing in the middle of a crime scene?"

Bob said, "I didn't do it, I swear."

Bruce said, "Let's take a closer look at his head."

They studied each other's eyes for a second, then tiptoed back to the patio. Nick took the lead and inched closer to the corpse. He lifted a towel and leaned down. The bloody gash above Nelson's left ear was sickening and, to their untrained eyes, certainly looked ghastly enough to cause death. Using the towel and being careful not to touch him with his fingers, Nick tried to lift Nelson's head, but his neck was already stiff.

Nick stood and said, "Okay, here's what I think we should do. Let's roll the body off and let it land on the deck. We need to see his face and the other side of his head."

Bruce said, "Not so sure about that. The cops have seen him and they'll know we messed with the corpse."

Bob said, "I agree. I ain't touching him."

Nick said, "Okay, then we can put him back to where he is right now. But we need to see everything."

"Why?" Bruce asked. "What's your theory?"

"The killer hit him once inside and knocked him out, then dragged him out here and whacked him again, probably more than once, to finish him off."

"In the middle of the storm?" Bruce asked. "With rain coming down in sheets?"

"Exactly. The killer wasn't worried about getting wet. Don't you see? It was the perfect time to kill him."

"With what?" Bob asked.

"Exactly! With something the killer found in the apartment. He didn't show up at the door with a gun or a knife. He got inside, maybe it was someone Nelson knew but sure as hell didn't know what he wanted, and he let him in because he was roaming around in a Cat 4. The guy grabbed a fire poker or a baseball bat or something he probably knew was in the apartment, and used it."

"You've read too many crime novels," Bob said.

"You've already used that line," Nick replied.

They stood still and gawked at poor Nelson. Bruce retreated to the shade and returned to his chair. Nick and Bob slowly did the same. The sun was bearing down, the temperature getting hotter. Around them the rescue was coming to life as more choppers buzzed about and more chain saws were heard in the distance.

It had been an hour since the cops left.

2.

Nick stood and without a word walked to the corpse, pulled off the towels, grabbed Nelson by his legs, and rolled him off the brick wall. He landed on the patio, faceup. Bruce and Bob hurried over for a look.

His right eye was swollen shut and there was another gash above it. "Just what I suspected," Nick mumbled to himself. "Would you please get me the flashlight?"

Bruce found it on the kitchen table and brought it outside. Nick took it and knelt low over the head, as if searching for lice. He found a knot on the crown of the skull, hidden by thick hair, and continued his search. When he finished he reclined against the brick wall and said, "Looks like the limb hit him at least three times. Want to explain that?" He was looking at Bruce, who was speechless.

Bob said, "Okay, okay. Now let's put him back up there before the cops get here."

"No! The cops need to see this," Nick said. "We're talking about murder, guys, and the cops do the investigating. Or at least they're supposed to."

Bruce said, "Okay, but cover him up. I can't stand to see his face like that."

Nick gently placed the two towels over Nelson.

Bob, who in another life had spent time in a federal prison, was nervous. "Look, we probably left some fingerprints in there. Shouldn't we try to rub things down?"

"Hell no," Nick said. "The cops said we could go inside. If our prints are there it's because we were there. Doesn't mean we're involved in the crime. And if we start rubbing things we might destroy prints left by the killer."

"Good point," Bruce said. "Do you think he left the murder weapon behind?"

Nick, now the head sleuth by default, thought for a second and said, "I doubt it. He probably fled in the storm and it would've been easy to discard anything in this mess. But we should look around."

"I'm not going back in there," Bob said. "In fact, I'm thinking about leaving now. I need to start ripping out carpet."

"We'll help you," Bruce said.

"You can't leave," Nick said. "You found the body and the cops will want to talk to you. They asked us to stay here."

"Right," Bruce said. "Let's stay put until they tell us to leave."

Nick said, "I'll be inside. You guys want another hot beer?"

Both nodded and Nick brought out two more bottles. He left them on the patio and walked around the kitchen, careful not to touch anything. He found a dish towel and used it to open cabinets and cupboards. In the den, he noticed that the set of four fireplace tools was intact in the wrought iron holder. Using the flashlight and not touching the tools, he carefully examined the poker, tongs, shovel, and brush. Only the poker was a possibility. The tongs would be too unwieldy. The shovel and brush could not deliver a lethal blow, at least in his amateur opinion. With his cell phone, he took photos of the stains on the wall in the den.

On the patio, Bruce asked, "Who in the world would want to kill Nelson Kerr?"

"I can't begin to imagine," Bob said. After a long pause he asked, "Do you really believe this, Bruce?"

"I don't know. Maybe we're getting ahead of ourselves. I say we take a deep breath, wait for the cops, and let them deal with it."

"I agree. But right now they're running in circles. Hell, we're all stunned. I'm not sure we're thinking that clearly right now. I was up all night, not a wink of sleep, and scared to death. I'll be honest."

Upstairs, Nick entered the master suite, which was even darker. He opened the shades and eased around the room, touching nothing. The bed was unmade. There were clothes on the floor. Nelson kept the downstairs neat but not his bedroom. Nick walked through the other bedroom and found nothing of interest—no more blood, no possible murder weapon. He looked in the two bathrooms; nothing.

On the patio, Bob said, "You know, it's possible that he got hit by more than one limb. Look, they're all over the place. I'm not sure I'm buying this murder story."

"And the blood on the wall?"

"Are you sure it's blood?"

"No. I'm not sure of anything, except our pal Nelson there is quite dead."

"Should we move him out of the sun? Hell, he's just roasting."

"It's not bothering him. No, we're not touching him again."

They sipped their hot beer and studied Nelson. The shadows were shifting and they would soon lose their shade.

In the garage, Nick found Nelson's shiny BMW sitting unscathed. An impressive rack of fishing rods covered one wall. A bag of golf clubs was in the corner. On a small workbench, Nelson had neatly arranged the usual assortment of household tools, gadgets, and supplies. Extra lightbulbs. Cans of insect and wasp repellent. Nothing was out of place. Indeed, his garage was tidier than his bedroom. A designer tool kit sat unopened and Nick toyed with the idea of having a look inside. He was particularly interested in the hammer, if it hadn't been removed, but he resisted the temptation to touch it. Let the cops do that.

Bob said, "There are some bad guys in his past, right? I mean, he wrote about some pretty nasty boys."

"Have you read his books?"

"Most of them. Good stuff. He got booted from his law firm, right?"

"That's always been his version. He was a partner in a big firm in San Francisco, doing well but wanting to get out, or so he says. Said. He found out one of his clients was selling military software to Iran and North Korea and he blew the whistle. The Feds paid him well but his legal career was over. He took the money, lost a lot of it in a divorce, and came here to start over again. Apparently, somebody was after him."

"So you're still into the murder scenario?"

"I think so. It looks pretty suspicious." Bruce sipped his

beer. "You know, Bob, this is too weird. Nelson's lying there baking and his family has no clue. You know they're worried sick."

"I'm sure the police will notify them. Now that you've identified the body."

"You would hope so, but these local boys are overwhelmed right now. I mean, what if that was your brother lying there? Wouldn't you want to know?"

"You ever met my brother?"

"Come on, Bob."

They took a sip, stared at Nelson, listened as another helicopter approached. Bob said, "I wonder what Sherlock Holmes is doing in there."

Nick was studying the seven iron with the flashlight. The clubs were high-end Pings, a set that Nick, a serious golfer, recognized, and they were arranged in the bag in perfect order. Wedges on the bottom row. Irons, four through nine, in the middle. Then the fairway woods and driver, all with matching Ping head covers. Nick remembered a Scott Turow novel, *Personal Injuries,* in which the head of a two iron had been filed down to make a bladelike weapon. It landed perfectly at the base of the antihero's skull and killed him instantly.

The seven iron had not been filed or modified, but there was something on it. A liquid that had dried and perhaps a few sprigs of turf. With the flashlight in one hand, Nick took close-up shots of the clubs. He was suddenly aware that he was drenched with sweat and breathing heavily. He left the garage and returned to the patio where Bruce and Bob were still sitting, still watching Nelson.

Nick removed both towels and said, "I'm taking photos of everything."

"Why?" Bob asked.

"Just to have them. Who knows?"

3.

At noon, almost two and a half hours after the cops had left, they heard something in the street. An ambulance had arrived and two first responders were unloading a gurney. A downtown-beat policeman who Bruce knew well met them in the driveway.

"Hello, Nat," Bruce said with a smile and a handshake. He was delighted to see a familiar face, and a man in a uniform.

"Hello, Bruce. What the hell are you doing here?"

"Guarding the body. Guy's name is Nelson Kerr, a friend of mine. He gave me as his contact."

"I know Nelson," Nat said, stunned. "He's dead?"

"Afraid so."

"Let's have a look."

Bruce introduced Bob and Nick and they walked to the patio, the medics behind them. Nat leaned over the corpse, pulled back one of the towels, and gawked at Nelson's face. Bruce was saying, "For some reason he came out during the storm and got hit by a limb, or something like that. Bob here found him lying up there on the brick wall."

"Who moved him?" Nat asked.

"We rolled him off. Not sure the limb did the damage, Nat. It looks like he took at least three blows to the head. This might be more complicated than we think."

Nat stood and removed his cap and looked at Bruce. "What are you talking about?"

"We found some spots on a wall in the den. Might be dried blood. And some stains in a sink that could also be blood."

Nick said, "It's a homicide, Officer. Someone hit Nelson over the head inside, dragged him out, finished him off, and tried to make it look like storm damage."

"In the middle of a hurricane?"

"Yes, sir. The perfect time to kill someone."

"And who are you?"

"Nick Sutton. I work at the bookstore."

Bob said, "He thinks he's Sherlock Holmes, but he might be on to something."

Nat was not equipped to deal with situations like this. He paced around for a moment, scratching his head, and finally said, "Okay, show me the blood."

Nick took him inside. Bruce asked one of the medics, "So what's happening on the island?"

"Chaos. The National Guard is clearing roads. They just found three dead folks under a beach cottage, just up the road here. The body count is seven so far. Thankfully, most folks left the island."

The second medic said, "Most of the floodwater has receded but there's still two feet downtown."

"I own Bay Books on Main. I suppose it was flooded."

"About five feet, sir."

Bruce shook his head, mumbled, and said, "Well, it could've been worse."

Nat followed Nick out of the condo and pulled out his radio. He disappeared around the side and talked to someone privately.

Bruce asked the first medic, "Any phone service?"

He shook his head. "All the cell towers were knocked out. It could be days. Y'all really think he was murdered?"

Nick said, "Either that, or that same limb hit him three times in the head."

"Which limb?"

Bruce pointed and the medic strained to look.

Nat returned with purpose and said, "Okay, I talked to my lieutenant and he said don't touch the body. He's trying to find our homicide guy."

"I didn't know we had a homicide guy," Bruce said. "I can't remember the last murder on Camino Island."

Nat said, "It's Hoppy Durden. He also does bank robberies."

"I can't remember the last bank robbery."

"He's not very busy."

Bruce said, "Look, Nat, might I suggest you guys contact the state police and get an investigator in here?"

"Sir, you're confused. Right now no one is coming onto the island. The bridge is closed and all roads are blocked. We're trying to get injured folks off the island."

"I get that, but at some point real soon the bridge will open so the cleanup crews can get in, then the homeowners."

"Just stay in your lane, sir. Somebody else is in charge of that." His radio squawked and he stepped away again. The medics were called to another emergency, and so Bruce, Bob, and Nick were again sitting in the sun on the patio watching Nelson roast. Thankfully, Nat had covered him again with the towels.

The officer returned to the patio, said he had been called

away, and instructed the three to remain with the body, and don't touch anything, and he would try and find Hoppy but he was probably busy somewhere else. It was all hands on deck and the right hand had no idea what the left hand was doing.

Luckily, Hoppy Durden arrived fifteen minutes later. Bruce knew who he was but had never met him. As far as he knew, Hoppy spent no time in his bookstore. He was a large man with an ample belly and his sweaty uniform stuck to his skin. Introductions were made and Bruce outlined their murder theory. Hoppy looked at Nelson's wounds, as if he'd seen dozens of murder victims, then followed Nick into the condo, which was as hot as a sauna. When they emerged, Hoppy flung sweat from his forehead and said, "Looks like this might be a crime scene." He was noticeably excited. With a real murder in the works, he had the perfect excuse to avoid more chain saw duty down along the beach.

He got his camera and began taking photos of Nelson. He strung yellow crime scene tape around the back patio, down the drive, across the front yard, and along the flower beds. Bruce wanted to ask why so much yellow tape was needed when there was no one around. He had several questions and even more suggestions but decided to keep them to himself. Hoppy kept calling for backup but no one else arrived. Using his phone, he videorecorded brief statements from Bruce, Bob, and Nick. He asked them to please stay out of the condo. As Hoppy went about his business, he offered them bottles of cold water from his cooler. They drained them.

Bob was finally excused and left to deal with his flood damage. Bruce and Nick promised to come help as soon as possible.

The same medics returned with their gurney and loaded

up Nelson. Hoppy explained that he would be taken to the city hospital where there was a small morgue in the basement.

Bruce said, "I thought the hospital was evacuated."

"It is. But it has a generator."

"Who does the autopsy?" Bruce asked. After spending half an hour with Hoppy he was not feeling good about the investigation.

"Well, assuming we do one, I guess it'll be the state medical examiner."

"Come on, Officer Durden. There has to be an autopsy. If this is a murder, you have to know the cause of death, right?"

Hoppy rubbed his chin and eventually nodded. Yes.

Bruce pushed but not too aggressively. "Why not just load him up and take him to the crime lab in Jacksonville? That's where they do autopsies, right?"

"Yes. I know the examiner there. You may be right. We can probably pull some strings and get off the island without much trouble and drive down to Jacksonville."

"And we need to make sure his family in California is notified," Bruce said.

"Can you do that for me? I need to get back to the staging area."

"Sorry. That's your job."

"Right."

Hoppy followed the gurney down the driveway to the ambulance. Bruce and Nick watched as they loaded it and drove away.

CHAPTER THREE
THE LOOTERS

1.

Larry lived in a brick house a mile inland and three miles south of Mercer's cottage. He spent the morning with his chain saw clearing limbs and debris from his front yard, then left in his pickup to explore. But it was hopeless. Trees were down everywhere and all streets were blocked. He returned home, loaded a backpack with food and water, and set out on foot to check on his properties. He looked after five of them, all vacation homes on the beach owned by old clients. The devastation was unlike any he'd seen in his fifty-plus years on the island. Trees were strewn across roofs, lawns, cars, and trucks. Trees that would take days to cut up and remove stretched across streets and roads. Entire subdivisions were isolated. It took two hours to get to Fernando Street, the main drag along the beach. There he found less damage, primarily because there were fewer trees. The dunes had served their purpose and held back the storm surge, but the homes and cottages had been battered by the wind.

He saw few people moving about, a good sign that most folks had fled. Helicopters and small planes buzzed about like menacing insects, so help was on the way. He passed a crew of Guardsmen clearing the road and stopped to chat with a sergeant. According to him, the northern end took the brunt of the storm. The Hilton was gutted. The body count was at eight and rising. The injured were being taken to Jacksonville. The bridge was now open to first responders, but the residents would be kept away for days.

At Mercer's cottage, Larry found the front lawn covered with leaves, small branches, broken boards, and roofing shingles. He went inside and found no water damage, no leaks. The roof had held the place together nicely. On the deck facing the ocean he surveyed the cottage and was proud that his plywood sheets had protected all doors and windows. He would leave it boarded up for a few days. The boardwalk over the dunes was intact until the end, where the final platform and steps had been washed away by the surge. He looked up and down the beach and saw that both piers were gone. He sat on the boardwalk, hung his feet over the dunes, sipped a bottle of water, and watched the action. A mile away at a public beach a staging operation was getting organized. A Navy Seahawk chopper circled as another attempted to land on the beach. An amphibious landing craft approached from the sea. There were advantages to living close to the naval base in Jacksonville.

When he finished the bottle, he returned to the cottage, studying the roof as he walked. A few shingles were missing, but nothing major. Three houses down, the deck had been blown away and all windows were shattered.

He locked the cottage and returned to Fernando Street to

head home. With no phone service there was nothing to report. He lived alone and had enough food and water for two weeks. He was relieved that he had been lucky. His home was not damaged. However, with no electricity conditions would not improve. He suspected that in a day or so he would be wishing he was in a nice, cool motel two hundred miles away.

Next time, he would probably evacuate with the sensible folks.

2.

The cleanup effort at Bob's lasted less than an hour. After ripping out the first-floor carpets and hauling out the ruined rugs, the three were soaked with sweat and exhausted.

During a break, Bob said, "You know, I really should wait until the insurance adjuster takes a look. Don't you think?"

Bruce quickly replied, "Great idea. He'll hire a crew to clean up, right?"

"It's in the policy," Bob said. "I pay six thousand a year for supplemental flood insurance, so I'm covered."

Nick said, "Here's a better idea. Let's load up the food, water, and booze and get out of here. Take it all back to Bruce's and set up camp."

Bob said, "But my car took five feet of water. It won't start. I've already tried."

Nick said, "Okay, but Nelson's BMW is high and dry. He won't be using it. I've got the keys in my pocket."

"You took his keys?"

"Sure. They were on the kitchen counter. House keys too."

"What if the cops come back to investigate?" Bruce asked.

"I doubt if they'll be back this week, and they can get in if they want."

"You want to steal his car?" Bob asked.

"No, I want to borrow it. Downtown is at least three miles away, and through a minefield. It's a disaster, Bob, every dog for himself. Different rules apply. I say we raid Nelson's fridge and pantry and take the good stuff. It's just going to rot anyway."

Bruce said, "I like it. We take the food, borrow the car, bring it back when the roads are clear. The cops are far too busy elsewhere."

"What if they stop us?"

"For doing what? They won't know we're driving a dead man's car."

"All right, all right."

In his upstairs guest room, Bob emptied two large plastic containers filled with old clothes. They loaded them with four thawing steaks and a chicken from his freezer, some cold cuts and cheese, eight bottles of beer, three bottles of bourbon, and two bottles of vodka. Bob locked his condo and they set off, lugging their loot.

Bob said, "If the cops see us they'll start shooting."

"Do you see any cops?"

"I don't see anyone."

Minutes later, they arrived back at Nelson's, all three panting and even more exhausted. They entered through the rear patio so they would not be seen, though there was no one to see them. Bruce went to the garage and tried to open the overhead door. It wouldn't budge until he found the manual bypass switch next to the motor. He and Nick grunted and pulled until the door was open. They quickly filled the trunk with canned goods and boxes of pasta from the pantry, bacon, eggs, and cheese from the fridge. The freezer was empty except for two steaks and two frozen pizzas. Gluten free. They took them, then made a generous haul from Nelson's bar. He liked good Scotch and they helped themselves to it, along with every other bottle they could grab. Luckily, they found an entire case of imported sparkling water.

Since Bruce knew more cops than Bob or Nick, he was chosen as the driver. Nick lifted the yellow crime scene tape and Bruce eased the car under it. They were in the street, their borrowed car packed with loot, and headed toward downtown, certain they would be stopped and arrested. The fifteen-minute drive took two hours as they weaved around fallen trees, got blocked at almost every turn, negotiated through police barriers, and waited at unnecessary checkpoints. They passed a few residents cleaning up, all dazed and tired. They passed a few other cars. The police and Guardsmen were busy, stressed, suspicious, and of little help. They were in rescue mode and had no time for curious sightseers. One helpful policeman saved them with directions that led to a gravel road along a marsh.

They parked in Bruce's driveway and immediately ran to the kitchen for a bottle of water. The generator was rattling away on the terrace and Bruce turned it off. He had less than five gallons of gasoline. All breakers were off except for the refrigerator, freezer, and a circuit that cooled and lit the kitchen and den. The rest of the house was hot and muggy.

They unloaded the car, stashed away the food and drinks, opened three bottles of cold beer, and sat in the den for a long rest. Bob, who had slept not a wink before, during, and after the storm, soon nodded off in his chair. Nick followed him on the sofa. Bruce needed a nap too but his mind was racing. He restarted the generator and set the thermostat on 80. Tomorrow's priority would be gasoline.

He left his men to their slumbers and began walking. His bookstore was only four blocks away, and as tired as he was, he needed the exercise. The floodwaters had receded to a point about a block from the harbor. Two police cars were parked in the center of Main Street. Barricades kept away traffic that did not exist.

Bruce knew one of the officers and shook hands with both of them. They passed along the latest rumors: The phone company was hard at work on a temporary cell tower. Might have service as early as tomorrow. Ten dead now, with about a dozen missing but there was no way to know if they were really missing or in a motel somewhere. A tornado did some damage ten miles to the west, but no one was hurt. The bridge was open to rescue personnel, volunteers, and supplies, but not to residents. Not sure when the islanders would be allowed to return. Electricity was a priority but would take days. Crews were arriving from as far away as Orlando. Generators were pouring in. All stores were ordered closed until further notice. Except for Kroger, which had a large generator and was open for business. More Guard units were on the way.

Bruce walked to his store and unlocked the front door with great trepidation. One day before, he and his crew had managed to move ten thousand books to the second floor, where they were now safe and dry. As were the rugs and most of the shelving. On the first floor the heart pine floors were wet and muddy and probably ruined. Judging from the stains on the wall behind the cash register, the floodwaters reached a height of exactly four and a half feet before they receded.

Oh well. He had plenty of insurance and plenty of money. Everything could be repaired, and before long he would be back in business. It could've been far worse. He climbed the stairs and walked onto the balcony where he had shared many cappuccinos and lots of good wine with friends and touring writers. He had met Nelson there, not that many years ago.

The madness of the past twenty-four hours had muddled his brain and made clear thinking impossible. During the storm, his frightened thoughts had been on physical survival. Once it passed, he went into a panic phase as he desperately worried about damage to his home and store. And now, after seeing Nelson, he was on the verge of bewilderment. The murder theory was giving him headaches.

He breathed deeply and tried to imagine the phone call to Nelson's parents. Surely the police had made contact by now, and surely his family was frantically trying to reach someone on the island who knew more. He felt an obligation to at least attempt to contact them. Not for the first time he contemplated loading up Bob and Nick and making a run for it. In his car, not Nelson's. They could drive two hours, probably south, and find cell service and a motel. Bruce could call the Kerr family and also check in with Mercer, Myra and Leigh, and other friends. But once off the island it might be impossible to return.

And where was Nelson's dog? And how many pets were lost in the storm?

The breathing helped little and his nerves were still frayed. He walked up a narrow stairway to his old apartment on the third floor and found a bottle of single malt. The air was thick and musty so he returned to the balcony and poured a strong one. After a few sips he felt himself relax, and soon he was able to hold on to one thought at a time.

He assumed the state crime lab would conduct a proper autopsy. The storm had caused other fatalities and the lab might get stressed somewhat, but for a murder it would certainly take its time. If the autopsy confirmed Nick's theory, then what was the next step? Trusting Hoppy Durden to get to the bottom of things seemed like a joke. He seemed to have little interest in a possible homicide. Who would inform Nelson's parents that he was not only dead but had been murdered? It was entirely plausible that Hoppy and his bosses would show little sympathy for some clown venturing outdoors in a Cat 4 and getting hit by falling limbs. Faced with what appeared to be an unsolvable crime, they could easily decide to embrace the theory that there was no crime at all, just an accident. Nelson was new to the island, kept to himself and had few friends, and he was a writer anyway and those folks are known to be odd. Blame it on flying debris and close the file.

Bruce finished his drink, returned the bottle to the apartment, and left Bay Books. He walked to Noelle's shop to assess the damage.

3.

There was enough charcoal to fill the grill, and Bruce built a raging fire. He cooked Nelson's steaks first, for their dinner, then grilled sausages, hot dogs, pork chops, and everything else in the freezer, which was running at one-quarter speed. When the coals were perfect, he put on two whole chickens.

They ate on the veranda, in fading sunlight, and washed

down the steaks with a bottle of Syrah. When they finished, Bruce cleared the table and poured more wine.

Bob suddenly stood, cracked his knuckles, and said, "Okay, boys, I have to get this off my chest. I'm not sure I'll tell the cops. I don't know what to do so I want your advice." He was suddenly fidgety and nervous, and began pacing back and forth. "I had a woman with me last night, said her name was Ingrid. Met her on Friday at the bar in the Hilton. A real looker, probably forty years old, with a body like you've never seen. Said she had a black belt and lived in the gym. Said she was staying at the hotel for a few days of beach time. I took her home, she spent the night, and man she was something. A real handful, all muscle and tone. She hung around. We had lunch with Nelson on Saturday and he couldn't take his eyes off her. She stayed over that night too, couldn't get enough. She almost killed me. I'm fifty-four, you know, and my stamina ain't bad, a lot of practice, but I couldn't keep up. I thought about bringing her to dinner Sunday at your place to meet Mercer, and of course to show off, but thought better of it. When the storm turned our way, she was planning to leave, at first. Then she decided to stay, which was okay with me. If I could ride out the storm, then so could she. When it hit, though, she panicked, I mean really freaked out and wanted to go back to the hotel. I was worried about the flood surge because my street is lower than the others, and when I said I thought we might get some water she went nuts on me. We had a fight, nothing physical, I figured she could snap my neck if she wanted to, but there was a lot of yelling and cussing. She bolted, just after dark. I mean she ran out of my condo into the storm with me yelling at her the whole time. She went crazy, slap-ass crazy. And I let her go. I mean, hell, she was just a hookup, you know. Nothing serious. I figured if she wanted to disappear into wind strong enough to roll over a car, then so be it. My last image was her disappearing down the street, leaning sideways into the wind, struggling to keep her feet."

Bob sat down and gulped his wine. They waited, and finally Bruce asked, "Is that the end of it?"

"No. A few minutes later, Nelson called. The last call before we lost service. He told me she was at his place and acting really bizarre. What was going on? I said I didn't know. He said he would try to take care of her."

Another pause, and Bruce asked, "Okay, anything else?"

"No. That's all."

For a long time nothing was said. Bob had settled down but was breathing heavily, his eyes drooping, defeated. "I don't know how to handle this," he mumbled.

Bruce said, "Well, you have to tell the police, that's for certain."

"I suppose, but I really don't want to get involved. After meeting Officer Hoppy I don't have much faith in these cops. Hell, he'll probably suspect me and I don't need that."

"How can he suspect you?"

"I have a record."

"Come on. That's history. You can't be a suspect."

"Stranger things have happened."

"Did you get her last name?" Nick asked.

"Murphy. Ingrid Murphy, from Atlanta. But I doubt if any of that is true."

"The hotel will have records," Bruce said.

"Maybe. Right now the hotel is about to tilt over. You saw it today. They'll probably condemn it."

Nick said, "I doubt if she was staying there."

Both looked at him, confused. "What are you talking about?" Bruce asked.

"If she is the last person known to be with Nelson before he was bludgeoned to death, then let's assume she is the killer. Indulge me here, okay? I honestly doubt the same tree hit him four times. Someone took a blunt weapon and cracked his skull, right? Given her physical attributes that Bob has so nicely described, she has the capability."

"So, what's the motive?" Bruce asked.

"There is none. How did she meet Nelson?" Nick asked Bob.

Bob replied, "Like I said, we had lunch."

"Was it her idea?"

Bob scratched his chin, thought for a moment, and said, "Well, sort of. She claimed to be a big reader, liked my books and all, and we talked about other writers on the island. When I said Nelson was a friend, she got excited. Clicked off all his titles, seemed to know them inside and out."

"Odd," Nick said. "Not exactly girl stuff."

"I thought the same thing."

Nick said, "Ingrid just met Nelson and then she killed him, but it wasn't random. She came here for that purpose. The motive was money, because she was paid to do the job. Where did you have lunch?"

"At the Shack, down under the bridge."

"Where I'll bet they don't have cameras," Nick said.

"Herman probably doesn't lock the door at night," Bruce said.

"Who suggested the Shack?" Nick asked.

"So you're still the detective, huh?"

"I'll bet it was her idea."

Bob scratched his chin more, tried to remember. "Matter of fact, it was her idea. She said she had read about the place and wanted to try it. This sounded true because it gets its share of reviews. Travel magazines and stuff. Keep going, Sherlock. I want to hear your theory."

"She set you up. She managed to catch your eye around the hotel bar, where you're known to prowl. She got you in the sack, surprise surprise, and you led her to Nelson, the target. She got lucky when the storm took aim at us and provided the perfect setting. A murder in the middle of a hurricane. She's a pro, fearless, tough, and waited until the storm had passed and daylight was coming and made her getaway. She'll probably never be found. I'll bet you a hundred dollars, which I don't have, that she was not registered at the Hilton."

Bruce appeared dumbfounded. "Anything else?"

"Just speculating, of course. But I'll bet she had a team with her. Probably rented a condo for a week or two. Had plenty of backup and they knew how to get off the island about the time that Leo was leaving. Don't ask me how."

"So what was the murder weapon?" Bob asked.

"We may never know, but it could've been Nelson's seven iron. I looked at his clubs this morning when you two were sitting on the patio. There's a stain and some matter on the seven iron. Could be blood, I don't know. I didn't touch anything. When swung properly, a seven iron, or any iron for that matter, can do some real damage to a skull."

Bruce asked Bob, "And she was strong enough to move his body?"

"Oh sure. I weigh two hundred pounds and she really

bounced me around. Of course I wasn't resisting, mind you. Nelson weighs, weighed, a buck-seventy at most."

Bruce said, "But there was no electricity. How could she find his golf clubs with no lights?"

"He had at least two flashlights. We used one this morning. Maybe she had been there before. Maybe someone else scoped the place when Nelson wasn't home."

"A lot of maybes," Bob said. "You got quite an imagination."

"I do. Let's hear your theory."

"I don't have one and I'm not thinking too clearly right now. Hell, we don't even know if it's a murder. I say we wait till the autopsy."

They sat in the darkness and listened to the distant sounds of their battered island. A gas-engine generator was rattling a street or two over. A helicopter was making a night run in the direction of the beach. A siren wailed far away. But none of the usual languid nighttime sounds—neighbors laughing on their porches, music emanating from stereos, dogs barking, cars easing down the street, the distant horn of a shrimp boat entering the harbor.

Bruce slapped a mosquito on his neck and said, "That's it. Let's go inside." He started his generator, closed the terrace door, and they regrouped in the den where the air was a bit cooler. All lights were off but for a small table lamp by the television. Bruce set it on a card table and said, "How about some poker?"

He poured a round of single malt from Nelson's collection and they toasted their late friend. The alcohol mixed with the fatigue and the poker was cut short. Bob slept on one sofa; Nick on another. Bruce stretched out in his recliner and soon fell asleep to the rickety hum of his generator.

4.

Breakfast was coffee and a cheese sandwich. The gasoline supply was becoming critical and they discussed it as they ate. Nelson's car had half a tank, and Bob suggested they drain most of it with a section of garden hose. Bruce and Nick confessed to having no siphoning experience, so Bob took charge and managed to withdraw about ten gallons without poisoning himself.

With that project complete, they decided that the next priority was returning Nelson's car. Bruce checked the doors and locked the house, set the alarm with his remote, and left in his Chevy Tahoe. Bob and Nick followed in Nelson's BMW, and it took an hour to wind their way around the devastation. Not surprisingly, there was no one at the condo—no homicide team sifting for clues, no neighbors picking up debris. No one had touched the yellow crime scene tape. Bruce lifted it and Bob returned the BMW to its spot. The three met in the garage and stared at the golf clubs, but said nothing. They closed the overhead door, walked into the kitchen, and discussed Nelson's keys. If they left them behind, there was the chance that someone might break in, find them, and steal the car, but they agreed that this was a long shot. If they took them, the police wouldn't know the difference and would have no trouble entering. Nick kept them in his pocket.

As they settled into the Tahoe, Bruce said, "I have an idea. We could sit around here today and tomorrow and get nothing done. I'm kinda bored with this hurricane crap. Let's pack a bag, head to the bridge, and see what the situation is there. If we can escape, we can drive to Jacksonville, visit the crime lab, snoop around and maybe learn something, then we can drive a few hours and find a nice hotel with hot water and phones that work. Who's in?"

"Me," Bob said.

"Let's go," Nick said.

They drove to Bob's cul-de-sac and waited for him to gather some clean underwear and a shaving kit. They weaved through heavy debris and made it to Fernando Street, where the two lanes were now passable. The shoulders, curbs, and bike lanes were piled high with debris, and small bulldozers were pushing more of it around. Dozens of utility crews worked frantically. It took another hour to get to the home of Nick's grandparents, and to his relief it was not heavily damaged. It was half a mile from the beach and the falling limbs had missed the roof. Nick found a trash bag and filled it with perishables from the freezer and refrigerator. The meats and cheeses were already spoiling. Thankfully, his grandparents had been away for two months and there wasn't much food in the house. He couldn't cook and lived on cold cuts and carryout pizza. He threw some clean clothes in a backpack, locked the front door, took a photo to send to his grandparents, tossed the trash bag onto the neighbor's porch, and jumped into the rear seat.

"Where are your grandparents?" Bob asked as they drove away.

"Idaho, last I heard. I really need to call them. I'm sure they're worried sick."

"As are a lot of folks," Bruce said.

Half an hour later they parked in his driveway and hustled about. Bob turned off the generator as Nick again stuffed perishables into two large coolers. Bruce ran upstairs to pack some clothes. He was already thinking about a hot shower. They fixed a box full of sandwiches and loaded up as much food, water, beer, and wine as they could stuff into the Tahoe. They were not sure where they were headed but wanted to be prepared.

At the bridge a thousand emergency lights were flashing and uniformed officers milled around with National Guardsmen. Traffic was being waved on and there was a line of cars and trucks leaving the island. In the other lanes supply trucks, utility crews, and emergency vehicles were arriving. Bruce parked the Tahoe and walked to the crowd at the bridge. He saw a policeman he knew and pulled him aside.

He said, "We're thinking about leaving for a day or so, but don't want to get stranded. How can we get back on the island?"

The officer lit a cigarette and said, "Word is the bridge will open both ways at noon tomorrow, but they are discouraging folks from returning. It could be a week with no electricity."

"Great. What's the body count?"

"Still at eleven, as of midday."

Bruce frowned and shook his head. "We're headed to Jacksonville. Do they have electricity?"

"It was blacked out yesterday. Supposedly getting some power back today."

"Are things better north or south?"

"South. Leo turned to the north and is now drenching Atlanta. I'd go south, probably as far as Orlando, if you're looking for a room."

They crossed the bridge without incident but were soon bumper-to-bumper on the mainland. Thousands of pine trees had been scattered like straw, and crews were working to clear the roads. The traffic lights had been blown away and state police directed traffic. They inched along, listening to the news on the radio and munching on snacks. The thirty-minute drive to Interstate 95 took two hours and the interchange was grid-locked.

According to the news, most of southern Georgia was without power as Leo stalled again near Atlanta. Record flooding was being reported from Savannah to Columbus.

They were clipping along at forty miles per hour on the Jacksonville bypass when their phones came to life. Service at last! Bruce called Noelle in Switzerland and brought her up to date. Nick called his parents in Knoxville and left a voice mail with his grandparents, wherever they were. Bob called a daughter in Texas and reported that he was fine, uninjured, and happily off the island. Bruce called Mercer, who was tucked in her apartment in Oxford and watching cable nonstop. He did not mention Nelson because he did not want a longer conversation. He would have more time later. He called Myra and Leigh, who were still in Pensacola. He called three of his employees to see where they were staying, and asked when they might return.

Nick called the crime lab to see if it was open. Bob had suggested that it had to be because the morgue had to be chilled, right? Nick was told that the lab was operating on a limited basis and expecting full electricity in a matter of hours. He pressed the receptionist for information about their buddy, Nelson Kerr, but got nowhere.

Bob's app said the traffic south was much heavier than that to the west, so they turned onto Interstate 10. Indeed, it thinned considerably twenty miles out of Jacksonville. Nick called motel after motel in the Tallahassee area but everything was booked. So he stretched his search westward and was soon being rejected in Pensacola. Bob called his daughter again and asked her to go online and find some rooms somewhere along the interstate.

Meanwhile, Bruce poked around the crime lab with no luck. Working with a directory, he called several numbers of some officials who appeared to be important, but no one was in.

Bob's daughter called with the good news. She had just booked three rooms at a small resort near Destin. On the beach. By the time they arrived they had been in the Tahoe for eleven hours. At the registration desk, Bruce paid for all three rooms and was informed that they could stay only two nights. They hustled to their rooms and showered.

Alone for the first time in what seemed like a week, Bruce went online and began digging for information about Mr. and Mrs. Howard Kerr in the Bay Area. A website listed four of them. Nelson was forty-three, so Bruce guessed that his parents were in their late sixties or early seventies. The first Howard Kerr he called had never heard of Nelson. But the second one knew him well. Nelson's father sounded like a broken man who had just lost his only son and was bewildered by the things he didn't know. Bruce filled in as many gaps as he could without mentioning the possibility of foul play. If that were established, he would call later. After a few minutes, Mr. Kerr went on the speakerphone so Mrs. Kerr could join them. Bruce carefully explained that there were some mysterious elements about the death and the authorities wanted an autopsy.

The parents were not sure they approved, but Bruce said that, as far as he knew, the police could order an autopsy whenever they wanted.

Why an autopsy? Why were the police involved?

Bruce bobbed and weaved and said that he didn't know

all the facts and details but was trying to gather information. He would know more tomorrow, hopefully, and would update them immediately. Mrs. Kerr broke down, sobbing, and left the conversation.

After an excruciating fifteen minutes, Bruce managed to end the call with a promise to talk tomorrow. He collected his thoughts, tried to shake off the emotion of talking to grieving parents, put on clean shorts and a T-shirt, and walked to the lobby to join his pals for dinner.

5.

Mercer called late that night. The number of fatalities stood at eleven and the news stories looked and sounded awful. She had not spoken to Larry and was worried about the cottage. Bruce told her they had driven by earlier that morning but had not been able to stop. As far as he could tell it appeared to be relatively undamaged, though he'd seen only the west side. The wind and water came from the ocean. Bruce told her about Nelson, a man she had met only once, but she was shocked nonetheless. He hinted that there were strange circumstances around his death and the police were investigating.

In his opinion, the cleanup would take weeks and months. There was no real rush to reopen the bookstore. The customers were gone. The tourists wouldn't return for a year. He suggested that she wait at least a week before returning to the island. He would check on the cottage as soon as possible and meet with Larry. There was really nothing she could do until electricity was restored.

6.

Day Three. The Grand Surf Hotel was on a point at the southern tip of Camino Island, as far away from the destruction as possible. When it opened thirty years earlier it had been the largest and fanciest hotel on the beach, and had become instantly popular with tourists. Locals used it for weddings and parties and fancy dinners. It survived Leo with little damage. Early on the third morning its lights came on and it was open for business. The owners comped all rooms for rescue workers and utility crews, and the relief teams moved their operations to the hotel parking lot. Crates of food were hauled into the kitchen and cooks began preparing meals.

With dozens of crews working around the clock, electricity spread slowly from the Grand Surf north toward Santa Rosa. A large temporary cell tower was powered up and some phone service was restored. The first hint of normalcy returned to the devastated island.

The Santa Rosa chief of police was a veteran named Carl Logan. He and Hoppy Durden, along with the department's only technician, a part-timer, arrived at Nelson's condo and found it locked. They jammed the patio door, put on rubber gloves and plastic shoe coverings, and entered the kitchen. Hoppy walked Logan through the crime scenario as laid out by that kid who worked at the bookstore, and showed him the spatter stains on the wall in the den and the stains on the downstairs vanity. They photographed everything again, with better cameras, and shot a video. At Logan's suggestion, they withdrew to the patio and decided to call in the state police.

There was no word from the crime lab about the autopsy.

7.

After a long morning by the pool, Bruce, Bob, and Nick were bored and worried about home. It was impossible to relax with their thoughts occupied by the destruction and chaos on the island. They called friends, grandparents, insurance adjusters, employees. Bruce tried repeatedly to get Hoppy on the phone but service was not good. They were buoyed by the report that some electricity had been restored. The names of the dead had not been released. At noon, it was announced that the bridge was open to residents but they were strongly encouraged to stay away for a few more days. The temperature was in the mid-nineties and water was scarce. There was little they could do until the cleanup gained momentum.

After lunch, the three packed their small bags, filled the tank with gas, and headed east. Their phones provided comfort and they talked nonstop. Bruce badgered people at the crime lab but got nothing. Nick searched for motel rooms and found two in Lake City, an hour west of Jacksonville. The traffic grew heavier and slowed their progress considerably. Late in the day, Bruce managed to get Carl Logan on the phone, and was relieved to learn that the police were conducting an investigation, at some level. Carl said he was waiting on the state boys to send in a team. At least Hoppy wouldn't be in charge.

They ate pizza for dinner at a roadside joint, returned to the crowded interstate, and finally made it to Lake City.

By 6:00 the following morning, Day Four, they were on the road in an attempt to beat the traffic. They drove an hour into Jacksonville and parked in the lot beside the state crime lab, and waited. At 8:30 they walked into the lobby and Bruce informed the receptionist that he had an appointment with one Dorothy Grimes, assistant to the field director. He did not, but he had spoken to her on the phone yesterday afternoon and was desperate enough to start lying. Of course, Ms. Grimes was busy at the moment. They took seats in the lobby, found coffee, opened newspapers, and gave every impression that they were there for the duration. An hour passed and Bruce spoke again to the receptionist. His tone was not quite as friendly.

The receptionist said, "Ms. Grimes does not have you on her daily calendar."

"We spoke yesterday and agreed that I would stop by this morning. Look, this involves the death of a friend who died in the hurricane. His body is somewhere in this building awaiting an autopsy and I have some valuable information. Can we just treat this as an emergency?"

"I'll see."

"Thank you." Bruce returned to his seat and she returned to her phone. Half an hour later, a robust woman of about sixty stepped off the elevator and glared at Bruce. "I'm Dorothy Grimes, assistant to the field director. What's going on here?"

Bruce was immediately in her face with a sappy smile and a limp handshake. "Bruce Cable, from Camino Island. We survived the storm but our friend did not. Can I please have five minutes of your time? Call it a humanitarian gesture."

She looked him over, then quickly scanned his pals. Shorts, T-shirts, sandals and sneakers. All three were unshaven, red-eyed, rather unkempt, but the poor guys had just been through a major hurricane. "Follow me."

Nick and Bob stayed behind as Bruce disappeared into the elevator. Two floors up, he stepped off and followed Dorothy to her office. She closed the door and said, "You have five minutes."

"Thank you. I need to see the field director, Dr. Landrum. It's rather urgent."

"Well, you gotta talk to me before you talk to him."

"Okay. My friend Nelson Kerr died in the storm. He has no family here and left my name and number as his contact. His body was brought here for an autopsy. At first the police thought he had been killed by flying debris. We think otherwise, and I need to know the results of his autopsy. Please. Just a few minutes with the boss."

"He can't discuss an autopsy with you. Completely against protocol."

"I get that. Nelson's parents are in Fremont, near San Jose. They're desperate for information and don't have a clue about what to do next. I'm their contact here. I have to tell them something."

She pondered this as she stared at him. "Are you suggesting foul play or something like that?"

"Yes. But the autopsy should reveal a lot. Please."

She took a deep breath, then nodded at a chair. "Have a seat." Bruce did as he was told and she left the office. Fifteen minutes later she returned and said, "Follow me."

Dr. Landrum's office was twice as large and consumed one corner of the floor. He was waiting at the door with a generous smile and a handshake. Undergrad at Florida State. PhD in forensic science from Miami. About seventy and on the fading end of a long career in public service. He waved at chairs and they gathered around his desk. Dorothy remained in the room, now armed with a notepad like a legal secretary.

"So you rode out the storm?" Landrum asked pleasantly.

"I did. Not sure how smart it was and wouldn't recommend it. Do you know the island?"

"Oh yes. We enjoy the beaches there. It's an easy day trip for us."

"Ever hung out in downtown Santa Rosa?"

"Sure. Some nice restaurants."

"And the bookstore?"

"Yes. Several times."

"I own it. I opened Bay Books twenty-three years ago. You've probably seen me there."

"You don't say. Was it damaged?"

"It took some water but it's okay. Nelson Kerr was a friend of mine, one of my writers, and I need to tell his parents something. He moved to the island two years ago and has no family there."

"I see. The police chief called and we're sending a crime scene unit to the island today, as soon as we can get across the bridge. I hear it's rather chaotic there. I assume you think it was not an accident."

"Depends on the autopsy, sir. Has it been performed?"

"It has. It was done yesterday. I'm not allowed to discuss it with you until I meet with our investigators."

"I get that. I'm asking for a favor, a little breach in protocol that no one will ever know about. You see, Dr. Landrum, I have some information about the crime, if indeed it was a crime, that I cannot share with you until there is a meeting with the investigators. There is a possible witness, a possible suspect. And a possible motive."

Landrum looked at Dorothy, who was busy scribbling on her pad. She was of no help.

"Are you sworn to secrecy?" he asked Bruce.

"Whatever you want. I need to tell his family something."

Landrum sighed, adjusted his reading glasses, and picked up some papers. "In layman's terms, the deceased died of multiple blows to the head, four to be exact, two of which would have been fatal. His cranium was shattered, massive bleeding around the brain. He was struck at the base of his skull with a sharp object that ruptured his spinal cord, and that alone could have been fatal."

Bruce closed his eyes and tried to absorb it. He managed to mumble, "So he *was* murdered."

"Sure looks like it but it's too early to be certain. I suppose it's possible that a man moving around outdoors in a catastrophic hurricane could get hit by debris more than once."

"But unlikely."

"I agree. I'm sorry for your loss, Mr. Cable."

"Thank you. And I won't breathe a word of this."

"Please don't. And you say you have additional information."

"I do. A friend of mine, and also a friend of Nelson's, knows something. We need to chat with your investigator as soon as possible."

"Are you headed back to the island?"

"Yes, but we're in no hurry. My friend is downstairs in the lobby."

"Does he have time to talk?"

"We have plenty of time these days."

8.

Things thawed considerably over the next hour as Bruce, Bob, and Nick were escorted to a conference room and served coffee and doughnuts. As they waited, Bob griped at Bruce for being so gung ho.

"You could've at least asked me if I wanted to chat with the cops," he growled.

"Oh, you're talking to the cops, Bob, now knock it off. You're a key witness whether you like it or not."

Nick snorted and chimed in, "You knew the killer and had been sleeping with her for days before the murder. You'll be the first witness called at trial."

"What do you know about trials?"

"Tons. They're in all the crime novels."

"Well, I've sat through one, okay, and I've heard the jury say 'guilty as charged,' so I'm not afraid of the courtroom."

"You did nothing wrong, Bob, relax," Bruce said. "Don't you want to find the killer?"

"I don't know, maybe not. If she's a professional, then some very nasty people paid her. Maybe we should leave them alone."

"Not going to happen," Bruce said. "You're in up to your ears."

"Thanks for nothing."

The door eventually opened and an officer in a suit strutted in. He introduced himself as Captain Butler, and passed around business cards. WESLEY BUTLER, FLORIDA STATE POLICE. He found the coffee and joined them at the table. Without removing a pen he asked, "Now who's who? Who have we got here?"

"I'm Bruce Cable, friend of Nelson Kerr. Same for Bob Cobb, who's a writer on the island."

"And I'm Nick Sutton, senior at Wake Forest, summer flunky at the bookstore. Also a friend of Nelson's."

"Okay. I just saw the autopsy report. Looks like your friend got banged up pretty good. I've talked to the police chief on the island and he's described the evidence at the crime scene. We'll get there as soon as we can, hopefully in the morning. I understand it's pretty crazy down there."

All three nodded.

"But the crime scene is intact, as far as you know?"

"As far as we know," Bruce said. "There is no one around. In the spirit of full disclosure, the three of us have been in the apartment more than once. Nick here noticed the stains on the wall and in the downstairs bathroom. I walked around upstairs."

"Why?"

"Well, at first we were looking for Nelson's dog. Didn't find him. We were not suspicious until Nick saw the stains."

Bob said, "Then Nick noticed more than one head wound and we became suspicious."

Bruce said, "And just so you'll know, we borrowed his car two days ago to return to my home, and we cleaned out his refrigerator and liquor cabinet. Didn't think he would mind."

"A bunch of looters," Butler said with a grin.

"Book us. We're guilty. But rules change after a storm when you're worried about survival."

"Okay. You think your prints are in the house?"

"I'm sure they are."

Nick said, "We thought about wiping things down but didn't want to wipe off too much."

"Good move. Not sure I've ever investigated a murder in the middle of a hurricane."

"It's my first and last," Bruce said.

Butler sipped some coffee and said, "Now, the Director says there's more to the story."

"It's likely," Bruce said.

"Okay, let's just have a chat without recording anything. We can do that later. I'm fresh on the case and know nothing. Tell me what happened."

Bruce and Nick looked at Bob, who cleared his throat and began, "Well, there was this woman, said her name was Ingrid."

9.

Halfway through Bob's narrative, Butler began taking notes. The story was too rich not to. He never interrupted, but was obviously intrigued by the details. When Bob finished, Butler asked, "And what day did you meet her?"

"What's today?"

"Friday, August ninth."

Bruce said, "The storm hit late Monday night, August fifth."

Bob stared at his phone and said, "I met her a week ago today, Friday the second."

"In the bar at the Hilton?"

"The outdoor bar. There's a big pool scene with a couple of bars."

"And you hang out there?"

"I do indeed. Plenty of action."

"Any discernible accent?"

"Not really. Nothing that I noticed, and, being a writer, we usually notice accents."

"No accent at all?"

"No sir. Flat, Middle America. Could've been Kansas or California, not the Bronx or East Texas. Definitely nothing foreign."

"How much time did you spend with her?"

"Too much, I suppose. We met Friday afternoon, had drinks, then retired to my condo, it's a five-minute walk, and had leftover lobster salad. Went to bed, did our thing, and she slept over. We were having coffee Saturday morning, and that's when Nelson's name came up. She saw one of his books on the shelf and claimed to be a big fan. I had her pegged as a nonreader or a chick-lit fan at best, and I thought it odd that she would enjoy his books, but I said nothing. The conversation went on and she said she would like to meet him. She suggested the Shack, a dive out by the bridge with really good food."

"Been there too."

"So, I called Nelson and we met him there for a late lunch on Saturday. They hit it off okay and we had a nice visit. Later that afternoon, she and I hung around the beach, then had dinner again. Back to my place. She wanted to have a go Sunday morning but I needed a break. She left and said she was going back to the hotel."

"Any chance she slept with Nelson?"

"Oh, sure, always the chance. Hell, I didn't care. I wasn't thinking about marriage. Tried that twice."

"Did you see her Sunday?"

Bob sipped coffee, scratched his chin, thought hard for a moment. "Yep, we set up on the beach near the hotel and enjoyed the sun. That night I had dinner at Bruce's but didn't take the woman. Nelson was there. Then the hurricane changed its course and all hell broke loose."

"What about a physical description."

"Five-ten, one-thirty, helluva body. She's about forty years old, likes string bikinis, and on the beach got more looks than eighteen-year-olds. Said she lives in the gym and has a black belt. I believe her. Not an ounce of fat anywhere. Brown eyes, long fake blond hair, no tattoos, scars, birthmarks, and I saw it all."

"I don't suppose you took a photo of her. Maybe a selfie?"

"No, I don't do selfies and I don't run around snapping photos. Nor did she."

"Can you think of a spot where she may have been captured on surveillance?"

"I've thought about that a lot. I'm sure the Hilton has cameras all over the place, including the outdoor bars and pool area. There's probably some footage, if it still exists. Right now the Hilton is a mess. It took at least eight feet of storm surge and the ground floor is gutted. The decks, restaurants, patios, terraces were all blown away. Most of its windows are gone. If there were outdoor cameras they were probably ripped off by the wind. The place is barely standing."

"What about the Shack?"

"That's a possibility. I don't know if it survived but it's on the water, the back bay."

Butler reviewed his notes and sipped coffee. He looked at Bruce, then Bob, and asked, "And you think this gal did a number on Mr. Kerr?"

Bob grunted and said, "That's your job, sir."

Bruce nodded at Nick and said, "He has an interesting theory."

"And you're Mr. Sutton?" Butler asked.

"Nick Sutton, rising senior at Wake, summer intern here on the island where I house-sit for my grandparents. I hang around the bookstore, where Bruce pays me minimum wage to haul stock."

"You're overpaid," Bruce said.

"Anyway, I live in the underbelly because I read five or six crime novels a week. As an employee I get a twenty-percent discount, even on paperbacks. At Barnes and Noble I'd get forty off. My entire paycheck, meager as it is, goes for my library."

"Okay, and your theory?"

"She's a professional, hired by big money to knock off Nelson because of something he has written or is writing or planning to write. He has a 'checkered past,' to use a badly overworked cliché. She arrived on the island with a pal, probably a man, who rented a condo near the scene, and they waited. She knew about Bob and Nelson. Easy research. She bumped into Bob, a pushover, and through him met Nelson, her prey. The hurricane presented a unique moment to strike, which she did, and then she and her pal got off the island. Or maybe they're still around, though I doubt it."

"Not bad," Butler said with a smile, but it was blatantly obvious he was just humoring the kid. They can say the darnedest things. "Nice imagination."

"Thanks. I read a lot."

"Any ideas about a murder weapon?"

"Nelson's golf clubs are in the garage. I'd start there."

"Golf clubs?"

"She had to use something from the house. I doubt she showed up with a baseball bat."

"Interesting," Butler said, playing along. "I guess you watch a lot of movies too."

"Not really. I'm too busy reading."

Bruce cleared his throat and said, "Mr. Butler, I have to call Nelson Kerr's parents and tell them something. Should I mention murder?"

"They know he's dead, right?"

"Right, and they know about the autopsy and the involvement by the police."

"I can't tell you what to say, but I would tell them that he died from blunt force trauma to the head, looks suspicious, and the state police have opened an investigation."

"Okay. And how do they get the body to California? I've never dealt with this before."

"Most folks haven't. Hire a local funeral home. They do it all the time."

10.

Butler walked them out of the building and to the parking lot where he lit a cigarette and seemed in no hurry. As they said goodbye and shook hands, Bruce remembered something. "Nelson had just finished his latest novel, or at least an early draft. I was about to read it. The book is not under contract, so no one in New York has seen it. I'm almost certain that it's still in his computer, and that file is pretty valuable to his estate."

Butler nodded confidently. "We'll secure it."

Driving away, Nick said, "I don't trust him. He's cocky, smug, and not very bright. He and Hoppy will make quite a team."

"He didn't care for your postulating, did he?" Bob said with a laugh.

"No, he thinks I'm a nut. You see his type all the time, at least in good crime novels. These guys who've been around think they can look at a crime scene and name the killer. It's called tunnel vision. They embrace their own theory, then march off in the wrong direction. They ignore facts to the contrary and embrace anything that supports their ideas. Happens all the time, especially in real-life wrongful conviction cases where they nail some poor dude while the real killer keeps on killing."

Bruce said, "I didn't think he was that bad."

"He's not too bright, Bruce," Bob said. "Nick's right, for a change."

"It's almost noon," Nick said. "Is anybody else hungry around here?"

"Always," Bruce said. "And thirsty. How many cold beers are left?"

"Plenty," Nick said from the back. "Where are we going?"

"I'm tired of driving and tired of both of you," Bruce said. "I say we go home and end this little road trip."

"Amen," Bob said.

Nick opened one of the coolers, passed out sandwiches and beers, and they enjoyed lunch as they sped around the Jacksonville bypass. Half an hour later they exited Interstate 95 onto the four-lane that ran twenty miles to the bridge and the island. They immediately noticed a caravan of dump trucks loaded with debris headed farther west to the county landfill. They passed a field where hundreds of FEMA trailers were parked. Eastbound traffic was heavy but moving well, at first. But after five miles it slowed, then practically stopped. Most were cars but there were dozens of trailers with backhoes, bulldozers, and loaders headed for the cleanup.

They inched along, sipping beer, listening to 1980s golden hits because they could agree on nothing else. Nick said, "Okay, you want my latest theory?"

Bruce slowly reached over and turned down the volume. He was intrigued by the deft workings of Nick's criminal mind. Bob nodded and asked, "Are you going to tell us regardless of whether we want to hear it?"

"Yes. The real killer is the guy with the cash. Nelson published three novels about arms dealers, drug dealers, money launderers, gun runners, corporate crooks, shady defense contractors, and so on. Right, Bruce?"

"For the most part."

"He seemed to really know his subject matter. Let's assume he pissed off some folks along the way. If so, why would they rub him out now? The books have been published. Most have sold well. It's all fiction, all make-believe anyway, so why get upset?"

"Your point?" Bob asked.

"My point is that what's been said has been said, and Nelson is certainly not the first novelist to write about arms dealers. My point is that the next book, the unfinished novel, is what got him killed. Somebody out there didn't want it published."

Bruce and Bob nodded along.

Nick went on, "Maybe they knew his subject matter. It wouldn't be that hard to figure out, since he always did quite a bit of research. Word got out that Nelson Kerr was writing about their business or their crimes. Or maybe they hacked him, read it, and felt threatened."

Bruce said, "Nelson was afraid of getting hacked and worked offline. His desktop was secure. Other writers have had their stuff stolen. He was a fanatic about keeping his material protected."

Bob asked, "How did he back up his work? The cloud?"

"Don't know, but I doubt if he used the cloud."

"How did he communicate?" Nick asked.

"He used a laptop for emails, but even then he never said much. He was almost paranoid. No social media at all. He changed his phone number every few months."

"So. He was still an amateur and he could get hacked. There's always somebody smarter. If the Russians and Chinese can hack the CIA, then our late buddy Nelson could be hacked. Wouldn't he have sent his manuscript to his agent, maybe his editor?"

"His agent died last year and he was in the process of finding a new one. He and I talked about it at length. A month ago he told me the book was almost finished and no one had read it. He wanted me to have a look and make notes. I'll bet the manuscript is still in his computer. Where else would it be?"

Bob said, "So after she killed him, she took his hard drive?"

"Don't know, yet," Nick said. "But if his hard drive is missing, then one part of the mystery is solved."

"Why didn't you think of this sooner?" Bruce asked. "We could've checked his computer."

"We weren't touching anything," Nick said. "I got the impression that Butler back there sort of suspects us of something anyway."

"I'm glad you said that," Bob replied. "I had the same impression. What will he do when they find our fingerprints?"

"We have solid alibis," Bruce said.

They inched along in silence, at times approaching ten miles per hour, at times sitting still. Bruce's phone buzzed and he answered it. He listened, mumbled something about dogs searching, and shook his head in disbelief. He ended the call and said, "You're not going to believe this. The cops have the road blocked this side of the bridge and they're searching each car with dogs. Can you please tell me why?"

Bob, the ex-felon, had little use for the police. He shook his head and said, "Because they can."

Bruce was exasperated. "I mean, these people just had their homes and businesses blown away, so why would they want to sneak explosives onto the island? These cops are out of control."

Bob said, "For the same reason they send SWAT teams to arrest people for bad checks. Because they can and it's far more dramatic. These guys think they're as tough as Navy Seals and they have to prove it. Look at all that military garb they wear. Why does every Podunk police department have a tank these days? Because the Pentagon has too much of the stuff and sells it cheap. Why do they send canine units to sniff around the county fair? Because they have the damned dogs and need to use them. Don't get me started."

"I think you've already started," Nick observed from the backseat.

"Why does every fender bender need three cop cars and four fire trucks? Because these guys are bored, sitting around the station, and they get their jollies racing up and down the streets with sirens screaming. Tough boys in action. They like to block traffic in all directions, makes 'em feel powerful. They control the situation. Sniffing dogs. Unbelievable. It'll be midnight before we get there."

Bruce paused a few seconds and asked, "Do you feel better now?"

"Not really. I got chewed up by the cops, okay, so I carry a grudge. I'd feel better if this traffic was moving. Whose idea was this road trip after all?"

"Nick's."

"Blame me for everything," Nick said. "I'm just the intern."

Bruce picked up his phone and said, "Look, I've been putting this off, but I need to call Nelson's father and tell him that his son is not only dead but was probably murdered. You guys want to help?"

"Sorry," Nick said.

"He named you as his contact," Bob said. "It's all yours."

The Tahoe stopped in a long curve. For miles ahead nothing was moving. Bruce found the number and punched redial.

11.

Mr. Kerr could barely talk and handed the phone to his daughter, Polly. She introduced herself with "I'm Nelson's sister, his only sibling. Thank you for what you're doing."

She sounded calm, in control. Bruce said, "I really haven't done anything. I'm very sorry for your loss. Nelson was a friend."

"Where is he now?"

"As far as I know, he's in the morgue at the state crime lab. We just left there and are trying to get back onto the island. Things are a mess."

"What happened? What can you tell me?"

Bruce hesitated and did not want to talk about the cause of death. "We met with an investigator for the state police. They have opened a case file and will send a team of technicians to Nelson's condo tomorrow."

"For what purpose?"

"To gather evidence to determine if a crime was committed."

"Was my brother murdered?"

"No one knows the answer to that."

She paused, and Bruce could almost see her gritting her teeth and trying to maintain composure. He tried to imagine their nightmare, stumbling through the dark two thousand miles away and watching the chaos on television. She said, "Okay. I'm leaving in an hour and I'll land in Jacksonville at eight in the morning. That's the plan, though the airline said there could be delays because of everything. I think I have a rental car. Will it be possible for me to get on the island?"

"Probably. The bridge is open and we're trying to get there now."

"I assume there are no hotel rooms."

"Correct. It appears as if most of the hotels are damaged. I have a big house with plenty of room. A couple of friends are staying over and we're sort of camping out. No electricity now but we might get hooked up tomorrow. We have food and water and we're getting by. You're welcome to join us."

"That's awfully generous, Mr. Cable."

"It's Bruce, and I'm not being generous. It's called survival."

"Thank you. This is very hard." Her voice cracked slightly.

"I cannot imagine. I'm sorry."

"Is there something we should be doing?"

"Have you talked to a funeral home?"

"No, not yet."

"Okay, we have. Text me your cell number and I'll text you the number of a reputable funeral home in Jacksonville. I chatted with the director an hour ago. Once he is hired, they will transfer the body to the funeral home and prepare it for shipment."

He realized he sounded like they were discussing a FedEx package.

She said, "Thank you. I'll do that right now. Will you be around in the morning?"

"Oh yes. Waiting for you. We'll go to Nelson's condo and have a look."

CHAPTER FOUR
THE EXECUTRIX

1.

After a hearty breakfast of cold chicken, granola bars, and peanut butter on crackers, Nick stuffed his backpack and set off on his bike for the two-mile ride to his grandparents' home. When he arrived, he called Bruce and reported that their part of the island had electricity. Some of the neighbors had returned, and work groups were getting organized to clean up the debris and tack FEMA tarps across damaged roofs. The busy streets were passable and traffic was moving about, but many of the side streets were still blocked. According to a policeman, the southern half of the island had full power and downtown could expect it later in the day. For the northern half it could be another week.

Bob was antsy and tired of camping out. He wanted to go home, but with no car and no electricity he would be hot and stranded. He hung around and helped Bruce pick up litter in the backyard. They helped a neighbor cut up branches and remove hanging gutters. It was August 10 and a high of ninety-eight was predicted.

At 9:20, Bruce got a text from Polly McCann. She had landed in Jacksonville and was searching for a rental car. "It'll take hours," he said to Bob. "Poor girl."

Bored with hard labor, they headed toward Nelson's place to see if the state police had arrived. For almost an hour, they drove the island to observe the destruction and the cleanup. They stopped at Mercer's cottage and walked around it. Bruce shot a video and sent it to her. Amy lived in a high-end gated community a mile inland. The gate was missing and they drove the streets. Fallen trees were everywhere, but Amy's home had been spared serious damage. He shot another video and sent it to her. The hospital had reopened and its parking lot was full.

Two large vans were parked at Nelson's, one in the drive and the other in the street. To make sure everyone knew serious matters were at hand, both vans were marked in bold letters: FLORIDA STATE POLICE—CRIME SCENE UNIT. Two unmarked cars were parked in the street. A few neighbors gawked from their porches.

Bruce and Bob stood at the police tape and finally caught a glimpse of Captain Wesley Butler. He walked over with a friendly hello, shook their hands, and lit a cigarette. After a round of meaningless chitchat, Bruce asked, "So how's it going in there?"

"Can't discuss it," Butler said, officially.

"Of course not," Bob mumbled sarcastically.

Bruce wanted to ask, "What about the damned hard drive?" But he knew he would get nothing.

Butler asked, "Where's your third amigo, that kid who knew everything?"

"We fired him," Bruce said. "He's off the case. Say, look, Mr. Kerr's sister will be here later today, flying in from California. She'll want to see his place, maybe gather some personal items. What are the rules here?"

Butler was already shaking his head. "Sorry. No one goes in until we're finished and we'll be here all day. Good way to kill a Saturday, huh?"

Well, he's been dead for five days, Bruce thought. About time you got here. But that was unfair. The storm had upset all schedules and routines. Butler excused himself and returned to his work. Two technicians in white mummy suits hauled out a rolled-up rug and placed it in a van.

What about the damned hard drive? Bruce realized that neither he nor the family would know anything about the investigation for days or perhaps weeks. Standing at the police tape, he was as close as he would get to the evidence.

As they were leaving, a neighbor walked over and asked, "What's going on here?"

"It's a crime scene," Bruce said, nodding at the two vans with billboards painted on all sides. "Nelson was killed during the storm."

"Nelson's dead?" the neighbor gasped.

"Afraid so. Head wounds."

"Why are the police here?"

"You'll have to ask them."

They drove to Bob's condo and spent an hour hauling trash and debris to the curb. It was depressing work made even worse by the heat. An insurance adjuster had promised to stop by later in the day. There was a rumor that Curly's Oyster Bar was open down south, near the Grand Surf Hotel, and they decided to explore.

2.

Polly McCann arrived at Bruce's shortly after two and knocked on the door. The doorbell wasn't working because the electricity had not yet reached downtown. She was about fifty, California slim and trendy with a smart boy's haircut and designer eyewear. After a long night on the plane she looked remarkably fresh. Bruce offered her a bottle of cold water and they sat in the den and began covering the preliminaries.

She taught physics at a community college in Redwood City. Her husband chaired the math department. They had two sons, both in college at UC–Santa Barbara. Her parents were in their early eighties and battling more health issues than most of their friends. They were devastated by Nelson's death and unable to make decisions. Polly was his only sibling and had been handling their parents' affairs for years. Nelson's ex-wife had already remarried and divorced again, and would not be a factor. Their parting ten years earlier had left scars, and they truly loathed each other. Mercifully, there were no children.

"He didn't talk about the divorce and I knew better than to ask," Bruce said.

"The marriage was a bad idea from day one," she said. "Nelson finished Stanford Law at the top of his class and took a big job with a high-powered firm in San Francisco. It was a grind, ninety hours a week, lots of pressure. For some reason he decided to further complicate his life by marrying Sally, a real flake who drank too much, worked too little, and was looking for money. I tried to talk him out of it because I couldn't stand the woman, but he wouldn't listen to me. They quarreled constantly, so he put in even more hours at the office. He made partner at thirty-one and was knocking down close to a million a year. Then he realized that one of his clients was illegally selling military software to some authoritarian governments, and he wanted to blow the whistle. He did talk to me about that. He knew his legal career would be over, you can't rat out a client and expect to survive as a lawyer, but he thought the government would make it worth the trouble. Plus, he was really sick of the big-firm racket. So he did the right thing, got a check for five million in return, and happily fled the office. But his timing was bad. He should have pursued the divorce before he blew the whistle. His wife lawyered up and they found evidence of an affair with a coworker. He lost big, cracked up, and we had to put him away for six months. Then he started writing. Does this sound like whatever he's told you?"

"Pretty close. He never told me how much he received from the government. He did say that she had better lawyers and clearly won the divorce. I got the impression it was a brutal ordeal."

"How well did you know him?"

"Have you had lunch?" Bruce was happy to share his peanut butter and crackers, but was suddenly nervous about offering food to a fairly hip Californian. No doubt she survived on nothing but raw vegetables and protein shakes.

She smiled and hesitated and said, "Actually, I'm starving."

"Then step into my kitchen where the air is slightly cooler than out on the street." She followed him to the snack bar and watched as he rummaged through the pantry and found a can of tomato soup. "Perfect," she said.

"And for appetizers we can offer chunky peanut butter and saltines."

"My favorite," she said, much to his surprise.

He put the soup on and opened the peanut butter. "How well did I know Nelson Kerr? Well, I considered him a friend. We're about the same age, with similar interests. He's been here for several dinner parties. I've been to his place. We've had dinners out. My wife fixed him up with one of her friends but the romance lasted less than a month. He was not that aggressive with women. We spent time at the bookstore drinking coffee and talking about books and writers. I thought his pace was a bit slow for a genre author and encouraged him to write more, but I do that with most of my writers."

"Your writers?"

"Yes. There's a clan of them on the island and I'm the den mother. I encourage all of them to write more so I'll have more to sell."

"How well did Nelson sell?"

"His last book did about a hundred thousand copies in print and digital combined, and his numbers were steadily increasing. I pushed him to do a book a year. He was on the right trajectory with his career, but Nelson had a lazy streak. I said that to him once and he gave some lame excuse about still being tired from big law. I said that was nonsense."

"Did you ever read his stuff before he sent it to New York?"

"No. With some writers I do, but I'm known to have a lot of opinions so most shy away from my editing. Nelson asked me to read his latest, said he had finished the first draft and was polishing up the second." Bruce decided he would discuss the hard drive later. There was so much ground to cover.

He poured the soup in a bowl and presented it to her. She smiled and said, "Thanks."

"What color wine do you think goes best with tomato soup?" he asked.

"Let's postpone the wine." She stirred the soup, blew on a spoonful, and tasted it. "Compliments to the chef."

"Don't mention it."

"So, Bruce, was my brother murdered?"

He took a deep breath, walked to the fridge, opened it to fetch a beer, realized he'd had two already, removed nothing, closed the door and leaned against it with his arms folded across his chest. "I'm not sure, but a few things are certain. Number one, Nelson is dead." He described Nelson's body when they found him. He summarized Dr. Landrum's summary of the autopsy and cause of death.

She listened without blinking, without emotion, and without eating her soup.

"And number two. There was a woman involved. Ingrid." He took a deep breath and told Bob's story from start to finish, slowly and with every detail he knew. Polly stared at the table and never picked up her spoon.

"And number three. The police are investigating now, at this moment, and you can't enter Nelson's condo until they're through."

"Sounds like murder to me," she said softly, but again with no emotion.

"It's murder, Polly. Any suspects come to mind? Something from his past that he never shared with anyone here on the island?"

"Well, Ingrid is certainly a suspect."

"Indeed. But why? They had just met. If she had no motive, then she did it for money."

She shook her head and shoved the bowl away. The soup was cold, and it was probably the last can of Campbell's Tomato. Bruce hated to see it wasted, but the stores were reopening and it was time for a grocery run. It takes a disaster to make you appreciate the basics.

"I don't know," she said. "I can't think of anyone. As far as I know, his only enemy is his ex-wife, but she got the money and lost interest. You have a theory?"

"Yes, and mind you I've spent the last five days with Andrew Cobb, 'Bob' as we call him for some reason, who's a convicted felon who now writes some pretty graphic crime novels. He's out there in a hammock snoring off his lunch of oysters and beer. You'll meet him soon enough. And there's a visiting student here named Nick Sutton who works in the store and reads virtually every crime novel published. We've had more than enough time to kick around various theories."

"And your best one is?"

"It's a long shot but we have to start somewhere. Ingrid was a pro who came and went and will likely never be found. The man who paid her is someone who doesn't want Nelson's next book to be published."

"That's pretty farfetched."

"Agreed. But right now we have nothing else."

She squinted her eyes and mulled it over. After a moment she asked, "And do you know what the book is about?"

"Not a clue. Do you?"

She shook her head. "I found his books difficult to read and we never talked about them. In fact, we haven't talked much at all since he moved here. Nelson was a loner, especially after his troubles."

"He was paranoid about getting hacked. It's happened to some writers and musicians. Stuff was stolen. So he wrote offline. Somehow the bad guys knew what he was writing."

"Oh, Nelson was definitely paranoid. He rarely used email. He even thought his phones were tapped. We corresponded by old-fashioned snail mail."

"How quaint. I got the impression that he was always look-ing over his shoulder."

"No doubt," she said. "And he wasn't like that until the whistleblowing episode."

"And you say he cracked up?"

"After the divorce, which, as I said, happened after his departure from the law firm. Severe depression or a nervous breakdown or whatever they called it. We locked him away in a fancy joint for six months and he made a nice recovery. Still in therapy, though."

For the first time, her eyes were moist. She removed her glasses and blinked a few times. "About a month ago, I received an overnight package from Nelson. In a letter he said he was enclosing his latest novel on a thumb drive, wanted me to hold it for safekeeping. He asked me not to read it until further notice. He gave me his new phone number. I wrote him back and asked why he was changing his phone number again, but he never answered, never explained."

"Where's the thumb drive?"

"In my pocket."

"Let's keep it there. And you haven't read the novel?"

"Not a word. And you don't want to?"

Bruce looked at her untouched tomato soup and asked, "Are you finished?" She'd had two sips and two crackers.

"Yes, I'm sorry. My appetite vanished."

"Let's go back to the den where it's cooler."

They moved to the den and he closed the door to the kitchen. Out on the veranda, Bob's bare feet were visible dangling from the hammock.

Bruce said, "I'd rather not read the novel, not now anyway, because I want to answer no if I'm ever asked by the police."

"Will the police find it?"

"I don't know. I'm sure they'll confiscate his computers and get search warrants to look at everything. But if I were a gambler, I'd bet the desktop hard drive was snatched about the same time Nelson was murdered."

"Should I hand over the thumb drive?"

"For now, let's say no. You can always do it later, or not."

"I'm confused. Under your theory, Nelson was likely murdered because of this novel I'm holding in my pocket, right?"

"It's just a theory, and a shaky one at best."

"But it's all you have, right?"

"Right. He was killed by a professional for a reason."

"Got that. So someone has to read the novel to begin unraveling the crime. Who? You? Me? The police?"

Bob's feet slowly dropped to the tiled floor of the veranda. The rest of him followed, and he stood for a long minute stretching and rubbing his eyes like a bear leaving hibernation. As things slowly came into focus, he got his bearings and lumbered toward the door.

Bruce said, "Bob's done with his nap. He's a member of the team so we'll need to brief him."

"And the thumb drive?"

"Sure. He'll have an opinion or two. Plus he's a convicted

felon with a brilliant criminal mind, who doesn't trust cops and prosecutors."

Bob stepped into the den and introduced himself to Polly.

3.

The lights flickered, came on, went off, came on again, and Bruce and Bob held their breath. When it was apparent that the electricity was back for good, they exchanged high fives and couldn't stop grinning. Bruce quickly adjusted thermostats and left to turn off the generator, whose constant rattling had gotten under his skin. Civilization was back, with hot showers, cold water, clean clothes, television, the works. The camping trip was over. However, they managed to temper their excitement in the presence of a grieving sister.

Bob agreed that they should sit on the thumb drive until they heard from Wesley Butler, if indeed he bothered to call. He had promised to do so when his crime scene unit finished its business.

Polly asked, "Do the investigators meet with the victim's family for updates? I'm sorry, but I have no idea what to expect."

Bruce said, "I don't have a clue. Luckily I've not been through this before."

Bob said, "I had a buddy in prison one time. His family went through a murder. It was awful and all that, but to make matters worse the cops wouldn't tell them anything. They finally hired a lawyer to get some information."

"I'd prefer not to hire a lawyer," she said. "I just hired a mortician."

"You won't have to do that," Bruce said, as sympathetically

as possible. "Our police chief is a good guy and I can talk to him."

"Thank you."

"Would you like to rest? Your bedroom is upstairs and is now much cooler."

"That would be lovely, Bruce. Thank you."

She went to her rental car and fetched an overnight bag. Bruce showed her to a guest room and closed the door. He returned to the den and sat across from Bob, who said, "I like her."

"She's far too old for you, Bob. She's almost your age."

"Well, Ingrid was forty or so, so I can be flexible."

"You'll never outgrow the young divorcées in string bikinis."

"I hope not. Why did I bring up her name? You know, Bruce, looking back, there was something odd about her. The whole time I was with her and through everything we did it was like her mind was somewhere else, always calculating, always planning her next move. She was detached from the moment, as if she was just going through the motions. I mean, I really didn't care because the sex was pretty great. Now I guess it makes sense. But how was I to know?"

"You can't beat yourself up over her, Bob. No one could have predicted it. You were having fun with a nice-looking woman."

"No doubt about that, but it does nag at me."

"You gotta let it go."

"I'll try. I need a shower. My last one was in Lake City, I believe, in a square tub with an empty tube of shampoo. Seems like a month ago."

"Upstairs on the right. She's on the left so give her plenty of space. I guess you're piling in for a few more days. Welcome again."

"Thanks, but I'm leaving soon for Maine. I want cooler weather and I need to get away from this place. The insurance company is already giving me the runaround and I don't feel like fighting right now. How long is she staying?"

"She just got here. I have no idea. She mentioned a memorial service next Saturday in California and I'm already thinking of ways to avoid it."

"That would be just awful. I quit doing funerals years ago. Such a waste of time and money and emotion."

When he was gone, Bruce tidied up the kitchen and left for his next adventure, a trip to the nearest grocery store.

4.

At dusk, Bruce and Polly left his house in the Tahoe and headed north. A few blocks from downtown the island became dark again as they drove into areas still without electricity.

Polly was stunned by the devastation; she had never witnessed firsthand the aftermath of a major storm. Neither had Bruce, for that matter, but after five days he was growing accustomed to downed utility poles, blocked streets, overturned vehicles, front lawns filled with soaked rugs and furniture, and mountains of debris and garbage. They passed a small church where dozens of FEMA trailers were assembled in neat rows in a parking lot and people were waiting quietly, in a long line, to be served dinner brought in by volunteers. They passed a park where a tent city had sprung up. Parents sat in lawn chairs around a fire pit while children kicked soccer balls in disorganized games. Next to the park on a softball field, National Guardsmen were handing out bottles of water and loaves of bread.

Bruce found the street in an old section of postwar tract homes, all of which were damaged and uninhabitable. In most driveways, shiny new FEMA trailers now sat next to cars and trucks. Some had pipes running to the sewage lines; others did not. From the looks of the houses, the trailers would be used for a long time.

Wanda Clary had been Bruce's first employee when Bay Books opened twenty-three years earlier. As the only holdover from the prior owner, Wanda assumed from day one that she knew far more about selling books than her new boss, and though she was right she wrongly tried to assert too much control. They clashed early and often, and Bruce thought about firing her on many occasions, but she was loyal, punctual, and willing to work for the low wages he offered in the early days. As he learned almost immediately, in retail dependable help is hard to find. With time they staked out their own duties and turfs and Wanda held on to her job, if only by a thread. Before her stroke, she was often abrupt with Bruce, short with customers, and rude to coworkers. But after her stroke, which as it turned out was not that serious, not the first one anyway, her entire personality changed dramatically and Wanda became everybody's grandmother. Customers adored her and sales increased. Bruce paid her more and they became friends. But the second stroke almost killed her and forced her retirement. Her husband died shortly thereafter, and Wanda, who was pushing eighty, had been barely surviving on a pension for the past ten years.

She was sitting in a lawn chair beside her FEMA trailer, chatting with a neighbor, when Bruce surprised her. She managed to stand, with a cane, and gave him a big hug. He introduced Polly as a friend from California. Wanda introduced her neighbor, a lady not much younger than her, and offered them seats in her kitchen chairs, which had been arranged in the driveway near the trailer. Much of the rest of the furniture was piled near the street to be hauled away one day.

Wanda said her house had taken eight feet of water that had not subsided for three days. Everything was ruined, same as her neighbors. Most of them had no flood insurance, nor did Wanda, and the future was pretty grim. The FEMA trailer was free for ninety days with a possible extension, which made no sense. What was FEMA planning to do with the trailers when they took them away? Wait for the next Cat 4?

Wanda and her neighbor had survived the storm in a shelter on higher ground, and they managed to find a little humor in their story. It was a frightening experience, one that they would never forget. Both vowed to evacuate the next time. Bruce told a few stories about the storm but said nothing about Nelson Kerr. He doubted if Wanda had met him, though she still read almost everything.

Polly just listened and tried to absorb the surroundings. Twenty-four hours earlier she was leaving the safety of San Francisco. Now she was sitting in a war zone with people who were sleepwalking through a nightmare, people who had lost everything and were happy to have a warm bed in a dark, tiny trailer. For a moment, she almost forgot about her brother.

Across the street a small gas engine came to life, then a light-bulb. Wanda said, "That's Gilbert. His son brought him a gen-erator yesterday and he's showing it off, says he might be able to rig up a small window unit for some cool air."

"Have you talked to your son?" Bruce asked.

"Well, yes, finally. We didn't get phone service until Thurs-

day. Phil called yesterday from St. Louis. Asked if I needed anything. Nothing really, I said. Just a new house, new car, new
furniture, some food might be nice. A bottle of cold water. He
said he'd do what he could, which of course means nothing."

Changing the subject, and ready to leave, Bruce said, "We
brought some water and food." He left and walked to the Tahoe.
Polly followed him and they hauled four cases of bottled water
and three boxes of groceries to the trailer. Bruce took a quick
look inside and was overwhelmed by the thought of living in
such tight quarters for any length of time.

Wanda was crying, and Bruce held her hand for a few minutes. He promised to come back, and made her promise to call
if she needed anything. When they left, a crowd was gathering
around Gilbert's lightbulb, and there was music on the radio.

5.

On the southern end of Camino Island, Curly's Oyster Bar
was crowded with locals looking for comfort food and a cold
drink, and utility crews killing time on a Saturday night. Bruce
and Polly waited half an hour and got a table outside on the
deck. Of course, she did not eat fried foods and had never con-
fronted a raw oyster. They settled on a bucket of boiled shrimp
and waited on beers. She preferred white wine but Bruce steered
her away from the boxed stuff poured at Curly's. The music
from the jukebox was soft and distant, and the conversations
around them were subdued, as if folks had just stumbled out of
the nightmare and were still stunned by the changes. There was
too much work to be done to feel good about life.

In a low voice, Bruce said, "So, you're the executor of Nelson's estate."

"I am. He made a new will last year and named me as executor, or executrix, to be more precise. The gender thing."

"Who drafted the will?"

"A law firm in Jacksonville."

"Have you talked to them yet?"

"No. Why the interest in his estate?"

"Just curious, that's all. I assume he had some assets."

She sighed, removed her designer frames, and rubbed her eyes. "How much do you know about Nelson's business?"

"Not much at all. Mostly the stuff we've covered—legal career, bad divorce, blowing the whistle. He let it slip once that he paid a million bucks for his condo, but other than that I have no idea what's in the bank."

"And his publishing contracts?"

"Nothing. I never asked, he never offered. As we know, he didn't talk much."

She put her glasses back on as two tall draft beers appeared on the table. She began, "He left the law at the age of thirty-two, eleven years ago. At the time he was making it big but spending a lot too. What he didn't spend his wife did. They saved virtually nothing because the future had no limits. As I said, the government paid him five million in exchange for the scoop on his crooked clients, but he thought it would be a lot more. Half of it went for taxes. We pay a lot in California."

"Another reason to live in Florida. Zero income taxes."

"A bit too red for me. Anyway, he and Sally were at war, and not long after the money arrived she filed for divorce. After

fees and such, he walked away with about a million. A lot of
that went for therapy. Then he started writing and made some
money, I guess. Again, Nelson rarely talked about his business."

"Who inherits?"

"A third to me, two-thirds to our parents. A pretty simple
will. I'm also the administrator of his literary estate, whatever
that means."

"It means you'll handle all the rights to his novels—
hardback, paper, digital, U.S., foreign, maybe even TV and film.
Plus you'll sell the latest novel, if it doesn't get you killed."

"Thanks."

"One good thing about dying young is that it usually means
a spike in royalties."

"Are you trying to be funny?"

"Yes."

"Well don't."

"Sorry."

The waitress placed the bucket of boiled shrimp between
them and disappeared. They peeled and ate for a few minutes,
then slowed down for a little beer. She asked, "So what's up
tomorrow?"

"Our friend from the state police called. He wants us to
gather at the station and spend a few hours going over what we
know and what they've found. Should be interesting."

"And the thumb drive?"

"They may ask us what we know about his last novel, especially if the hard drive is missing. I want to truthfully say that
I've never seen it."

"I feel like I need a lawyer."

"You gotta hire one sooner or later to probate the estate, here in Florida."

"Do you know a good one?"

"One or two, but it might be hard to find them right now."

"Okay, if you're playing dumb, then I'm playing dumb. For now."

"We'll be fine. These cops are not the sharpest ones you'll ever meet."

"Am I supposed to be comforted by that?"

"No."

6.

The Santa Rosa Police Department was housed in the rear of city hall, a sprawling mix of add-ons and afterthoughts situated two blocks from the harbor and thus deluged by Leo. The complex had been soaked, was still wet, and all its systems would remain inoperable for a long time to come. Temporary police quarters were in the process of being established in a middle school gymnasium a mile inland. When Bruce, Polly, Bob, and Nick arrived punctually at ten on Sunday morning, the school's parking lot was crowded with patrol cars, city vehicles, and contractors' trucks. Inside the gym, crews were working to erect temporary walls and doors. No one knew where anyone else was, so Bruce used his cell phone to find Wesley Butler somewhere in the rear, near the boys' locker room. They followed him down a hallway to an empty classroom where Carl Logan, the chief of police, and Hoppy Durden, ace homicide detective, were waiting with two technicians from the crime lab.

Quick introductions were made, with Butler taking charge.

First, they wanted to videotape the statements from Bruce, Bob, and Nick, so a camera and lights were set up in one corner. Bruce and Nick went first. While they answered the same questions, Bob walked across the hall with the two technicians. Using a fourteen-inch laptop, they began working on a composite photo of Ingrid. Butler interviewed Polly and quizzed her about the family and as much of Nelson's background as possible. He did not ask her about the current novel. When she asked if they found the hard drive, he wouldn't answer. Half an hour later, the technicians printed a color rendering of Ingrid, and Bob was amazed at the likeness. He warned them, though, that the blond hair was fake.

The woman, whoever she was, looked to be around forty, as Bob had been saying, with high cheekbones, twinkling hazel eyes, long blond hair on the darker side, a comely smile that would invite men of all ages to sit right down and buy her a drink. Gawking at the composite, Bruce found it hard to believe that this lovely creature was capable of such a vicious murder. Poison, maybe, but not a beating with a blunt weapon.

Polly was asked if she wanted to view any of the photographs of her brother on his patio. She said no, she was not ready for that. Butler briefly reviewed the autopsy findings with Bruce and Polly, and downplayed the gruesome parts. Not surprisingly, they had so far found no witnesses, no neighbors who saw anyone coming or going during the storm.

All the neighbors were gone, Bruce thought, but said nothing. He listened as he and Nick were fingerprinted. Because Bob was a felon, his were already on file.

When the videotaping was finished, they gathered around a folding table littered with files and reports. Butler summarized what was already known and what they expected to soon learn. They'd found blood on two walls, on the bathroom vanity, and in the rugs. All samples were at the lab to be matched against Nelson's. They had also lifted many fingerprints but analyzing those would take time. They were trying to get information from the Hilton—registration records, surveillance footage, and so on, but for obvious reasons that was being delayed. As life returned to normal, they would gather info from other nearby hotels and condo rentals in an effort to identify Ingrid, but Butler spoke as though he knew that effort would be fruitless.

Before the meeting, Bruce had decided that the best tactic going in was to say as little as possible. The police didn't know much anyway, and asking a dozen questions would a) yield few answers, and b) only alienate Butler and Logan. They were tired and irritated to be working on a Sunday morning, and it became obvious that the review session was only a formality. Butler made his biggest mistake when he said, "We've examined the golf clubs and fireplace hardware and everything else in the condo that could've been used as a murder weapon, and so far nothing. Assuming, of course, it was a murder."

Polly quickly asked, "You think it was something other than murder?"

"Perhaps. There was a lot of stuff in the air, Ms. McCann."

Logan jumped in with "Having now survived a Category 4, Ms. McCann, I can assure you that the amount of debris and junk falling and blowing around in all directions is hard to imagine. You have to see it to believe it. We think it's possible that your brother got hit more than once with limbs, pieces of the roof, or maybe bricks, who knows?"

Bruce took a deep breath, as did Bob and Nick. Polly gritted her teeth and said nothing.

Butler knew they were not happy with this and said, "But we're not sure, and we'll investigate everything. It'll take some time, as always."

Bruce cleared his throat and asked, "What about the hard drive from his computer?"

Butler glanced at Logan, who looked at Hoppy, who appeared to be on the verge of a quick nap. Butler said, "We have the hard drive, but it's encrypted. Our guys in the lab will play with it again tomorrow, but it looks pretty secure."

Bruce had heard enough. He stood and said, "Anything else?"

Everyone suddenly stood and began the forced ritual of shaking hands, saying thanks, and promising to keep in touch. As Bruce walked out of the room, he wondered if he would ever see Wesley Butler again.

Driving away, he glanced to his right and saw Polly wiping away a tear, but she said nothing, not for a long time. In the rear seat Nick and Bob were just as quiet, both angry at the police, but also mentally packing their bags. Bob was now cleared to leave the island and would do so within hours. Nick was needed at college where he would party for a week to celebrate the end of summer, and then head to Venice for a rough semester abroad.

7.

Monday morning, Bruce followed Polly to the Jacksonville airport where she returned her rental. They drove to the funeral home where she finished some paperwork and wrote a check.

Nelson's body would be transferred to the airport for the flight home, with his sister riding above him in coach. Back at the airport, Bruce walked her inside and they found a coffee shop in the main terminal.

Nelson's condo was still guarded by police tape, and Butler wasn't sure when it would be released. Bruce knew the best mover on the island and agreed to oversee the removal of Nelson's furniture and possessions. He would get it cataloged and stored, and in a few weeks Polly would return to deal with it. Bruce knew several of the good realtors on the island and would arrange for them to look at the condo and discuss a listing, but cautioned her that the market would be soft for some time. He had a friend who dealt in German imports and could probably sell the car at a fair price.

They sipped coffee and watched the foot traffic. She said, "Nelson's memorial service is this Saturday. I don't suppose you could be there."

Bruce had been contemplating several ways to avoid a trip to the West Coast for what would be a dreadful event, but in the split second he had to come up with a believable response he completely choked. Whether he wanted it not, he was the Kerr family's point man on the scene and they needed him. "Of course," he managed to say with just enough conviction.

"I'll send along the details as they come together. It will mean a lot to my parents. They're so desperate for information."

Can't wait, thought Bruce. How could his presence possibly mean anything to her parents, people he had never met, and, after the service, would never see again?

"Sure, I'll be there. San Francisco?"

"Dublin, east of the city."

"Will there be a crowd?"

"Who knows? He had friends in the area, and the old gang from Stanford, but they've scattered. Could you possibly say a few words?"

The dreadful event just got a lot worse. Bruce, though, was suddenly quicker. "I can't do it, Polly. I've tried before and just can't maintain my composure. Sorry."

"No problem. I understand."

"The cops didn't ask about Nelson's manuscript," he said.

"I know. What are you thinking?"

"I'm thinking the book needs to be read, but not by you, not by me. Not by anyone even remotely connected to Nelson."

"I'm listening."

"I want you to send it to a writer named Mercer Mann. She's from the island but didn't know your brother. These days she's teaching at Ole Miss. She can be trusted. She'll read it, share it with her boyfriend, a former journalist and writer himself, then I'll talk to them."

She shrugged as if she would do whatever he asked. "And you think the manuscript will lead the cops to the killer?"

"I wouldn't put too much confidence in the police. It's a tough case to solve and they already have a more convenient theory. Blame it on the victim for wandering around outside in the storm. They'll shuffle papers and ignore our calls and wait for some time to pass, and then one day they'll break the news to you that the investigation has gone nowhere, which is exactly where it's headed right now. They'll promise to keep the file open and hope for a miracle."

She nodded and said, "I'm afraid I agree with you."

"I seriously doubt the manuscript will lead to the killer, but it's the only possible clue we have right now. That, and a pretty good description of dear Ingrid."

"He was killed for a reason, Bruce. Nelson had no enemies. He was a lovely man who enjoyed life and wouldn't harm a flea." Her voice wavered for a second and her eyes watered.

Bruce handed her a folded piece of paper. "Here's Mercer's address in Oxford. She's waiting and will read it immediately."

Polly wiped her eyes and nodded. "Thank you, Bruce. For everything."

They walked to the security checkpoint and hugged good-bye.

8.

On Tuesday, eight days after the storm, Bruce waited all morning at Bay Books for a contractor who didn't show. The insurance adjuster promised to swing by for another look, but he too was busy elsewhere.

Most of the downtown shops were still closed. Some were digging out and tossing spoiled merchandise into dumpsters. Others were locked and dark. The streets were empty. Many of the island's residents had returned, but they were in no mood to shop. All tourists were gone and wouldn't be back for months, maybe years.

On Wednesday, another contractor failed to show. Bruce walked home, changed into jeans, and went to welcome Myra and Leigh. They were working at a reasonable pace, hauling debris and trash to the curb, until he arrived, at which time they found chairs in the shade and poured drinks and supervised his labors. Bruce was expected to move the heavier stuff—moldy rugs, piles of wet books, etc. He strained and sweated as they drank and talked about the horrors of surviving Leo. When he was soaked, he finally asked for a break and a drink.

Inside, in the cool air, they gathered in the den. The television was on mute. Myra walked in front of it, stopped as if frozen with fear, and said, "You gotta be kidding." She moved away and on the screen a weatherman was pointing to a mass in the Atlantic. Hurricane Oscar was still days away, but one projected path, one of many, had it heading their way.

"I can't take it," Leigh said.

By Thursday morning, Oscar was a bit closer and even more menacing. Its cone of possible targets had narrowed slightly, but another direct hit on the island was a possibility.

That afternoon, Bruce drove to Jacksonville, boarded a flight to Atlanta, and from there flew to San Francisco.

9.

He was sitting in the elegant Regency bar of the Fairmont Hotel downtown when she walked in. Noelle had been gone for a month, off to Europe to see friends in Switzerland and family in France, and to get away from the Florida summer heat. She had watched with horror as the hurricane pummeled the island, and she had reluctantly followed his advice to stay away. There was little to do at the moment.

She looked like a model, and Bruce embraced and kissed her. That she had spent the last month with Jean-Luc was of no consequence. They had known each other for years, since long before Bruce came along, and their relationship was not going to change. She needed both men and they adored her.

They ordered a drink and talked about Nelson Kerr, a friend she had liked immensely. Bruce brought her up to date with his death, the possibility of murder, Polly's visit, and so on. In Bruce's opinion, as well as Bob's and Nick's, there was no doubt that it was murder. Noelle was shocked by this. Bruce told her about Nelson's novel and the thumb drive.

There were no secrets between the two. A wide-open marriage makes secrets unnecessary. The couple trusted each other implicitly and shared everything.

Noelle liked the idea of Mercer reading the manuscript first. No one would suspect her. "Did you and Mercer spend any time together?"

"No. She has a new boyfriend, Thomas, and he was in the way. You'll like him. Cute boy."

"Can't wait. So you have a trip planned. Let's hear it."

"Well, we'll do the service tomorrow, then leave Sunday morning for a little road trip through Napa. Lunch with Rodney on the mountain. There's a new winemaker, remember that Lance cab that blew us away?"

"Of course."

"We're pen pals now and I promised him a visit. Then we'll make our way to Oregon and the Willamette Valley to taste some new pinots. Sound okay?"

"Sounds marvelous. Sounds like you're happy to be off the island."

"Yes, and I'm happy you're here. The island's a mess and it won't improve much while we're away. It's quite depressing, Noelle. It'll take years."

"We'll survive. Poor Nelson."

"I know. We'll give him a proper send-off tomorrow."

CHAPTER FIVE
THE MIRACLE DRUG

1.

Two more storms followed Oscar, both frightening early on but ultimately duds. Both fizzled over the Atlantic and turned north to places ignored by the storm trackers. Oscar himself brought heavy rains to the Bahamas before breaking up and limping away as a mere tropical depression. When he was gone, the satellite maps were clear for the first time in weeks. Maybe the season was over.

By the end of August, the island was busy again, though the routines were different. Early morning brought supplies and contractors, as opposed to hotel employees, and throughout the day the eastbound traffic over the bridge was diesel trucks, more FEMA trailers, more machinery for debris removal. Westbound traffic was a steady caravan of large industrial vehicles hauling an endless collection of storm damage to bulging landfills on the mainland.

School openings were delayed for two weeks, then a month. One by one, the downtown shops and cafés opened. On Satur-

day, August 31, almost four weeks after Leo, Bay Books reopened
with a flashy party that lasted the entire afternoon, even into
the night, and included clowns and stories for the kids, caviar
and champagne for their parents, a jazz band, and a late afternoon barbecue on the upstairs veranda with a bluegrass combo
and two kegs of beer.

Over its twenty-three-plus years, the bookstore had become
the center of downtown Santa Rosa. Bruce opened the doors
himself each morning at nine and offered coffee and pastries to
the early customers. It stayed open until ten each night, long after
all other retailers had called it a day. On Sunday mornings, there
were homemade biscuits to go with the newspapers from New
York, Washington, Chicago, and Philadelphia, and it was often
difficult to find a seat in the second-floor café. Bay Books hosted
many author and literary events and a crowd was all but guaranteed. The upstairs shelves were on wheels, and when they were
shoved back the floor could seat a hundred. Bruce used it primarily for author readings, but also for book clubs, children's hours,
lectures, student groups, art exhibits, and small concerts. It was a
rare day when there was not a gathering of some sort.

The store's reopening, with its atmosphere of worn rugs
and saggy shelves and neat stacks of books in every corner, was
soothing to its loyal customers. "Bay" had survived unscathed
and was ready for business, so life goes on. The worst was behind
the island.

2.

The investigation proceeded at a languid pace that surprised
no one who was concerned with it. After several attempts, Bruce

managed to get Captain Butler on the phone for an update, but learned little. There were a lot of fingerprints to compare, and that process was moving along with nothing important to report. The Hilton had finally responded with the unsurprising news that no one named Ingrid Murphy had been registered there before the storm. In fact, no one with that name had ever stayed in a Hilton on U.S. soil. Its surveillance footage had either been lost or destroyed, but the company was still searching. Beyond that, Butler had nothing to offer, at least not to Bruce. He implied that he knew more than he could report, but, as always, his vagueness sounded phony. Bruce and Polly conferred by phone. She had not heard from the authorities and was frustrated by the lack of communication.

Bruce talked to Carl Logan, the chief of police, but he was unconcerned. As usual, there was immediate friction between the locals and the state boys, and since the state had assumed jurisdiction there was little Logan could do. He seemed to prefer it that way. Besides, he was trying to run his police department from temporary quarters and all nerves were frayed. During a second call, Logan said, "Come on, Bruce, this is going nowhere."

"You think it was murder, Carl?" Bruce asked.

"What I think doesn't matter. If it was a crime it'll never be solved, not by Butler anyway."

"*If it was a crime,*" Bruce repeated to himself afterward. He was mumbling a lot by late August because his two co-sleuths had left the island. Bob was on a lake in Maine waiting for the leaves to turn, while Nick was back at Wake chasing coeds and counting the days until he pursued serious studies in Venice.

3.

The day before Bay Books reopened, Mercer and Thomas had arrived on the island eager to examine the cottage. Larry met them there and gave a quick rundown on the damage, which was slight. A new roof was a good idea, though the current one was good for another year or two. He had already replaced the gutters, one shutter, one window, and a screen door. He had met with the insurance adjuster and they had lined up a contractor to replace the boardwalk to the beach. All in all, the cottage had survived in good shape. A half a mile to the north, a four-story rental had partially collapsed and would soon be razed.

A tourist had been killed there, one of eleven, Leo's final toll on the island. As Mercer and Thomas drove around, taking in the aftermath, they found it difficult to believe that so many people had died. Camino was a laid-back resort community, a tourist attraction, a wonderful place to live and retire, with little thought ever given to sudden, unexpected death. But then, Tessa had died in a horrible storm less than a mile off the beach.

Bruce wanted her to stop by the store for the reopening and autograph books for the crowd. She and Thomas had lunch in a downtown deli and roamed the streets of Santa Rosa, just like in the old days, before the storm.

4.

Sunday brunch was on the veranda, with Noelle in charge of the details and lively with chatter about her shopping excursions throughout southern France. The morning was overcast

but the stifling heat had broken, if only for a day or two. It was
the first of September, and only four weeks earlier they had
gathered in the same place to toast Mercer and her wonderful
new novel, with Nelson still alive and Leo a distant threat.

That crowd was not invited this morning because of the
delicate subject at hand. The four of them sat at a round glass
table Noelle had found somewhere deep in the Vaucluse, and
they ate chocolate waffles and duck sausage while relishing the
fact that the bookstore was now open again and life was returning to normal.

Bruce had been adamant that nothing about the novel was
to be put in writing. The book report would be an oral one.

Mercer began, "It's five hundred pages, a hundred and
twenty thousand words, dense at times, and I'm not sure if it's
a mystery, a thriller, or science fiction. Not really my cup of tea."

"More up my alley," Thomas said as he took over the narrative. It was immediately obvious that he liked the book far more
than Mercer did. "Here's the basic plot. A bad company, privately
owned by some bad people, operates a string of low-end nursing
homes scattered around the country. Three hundred or so, and
not the nicer assisted living places or retirement homes you see
advertised. These are the depressing places where you stick your
grandparents when you just want them to go away."

"There are two on the island," Bruce said.

"And a couple of nice ones as well," Noelle added. "After all,
it is Florida."

"There are over fifteen thousand nursing homes, rest homes,
retirement villages, call them whatever you want, from coast to
coast. About a million and a half total beds, and almost all are
filled, demand is constant. Many of the patients suffer from

various forms of dementia and are out of it, completely. Any experience with advanced dementia?"

"Not yet," Bruce said as Noelle shook her head.

Thomas continued, "Well, I have an aunt who checked out ten years ago but is still alive, barely, still breathing, shriveled up in a bed with a feeding tube and not a clue about what day it is. She has not uttered a word in five years. We would've pulled the plug years ago, but the law does not recognize the right to die. Anyway, my aunt is one of half a million Alzheimer's patients put away in nursing homes, waiting for the end. The care may not always be good but it's always expensive. On average, a nursing home charges Medicare between three and four thousand dollars a month per resident. Its actual cost—a few meds, the bed, the nutrients in the tube—is much less, so it's a profitable business. And a booming one. Six million Americans suffer from Alzheimer's and the number is increasing rapidly. There is no cure in sight, in spite of billions being spent to find one. In Nelson's novel, the bad company is expanding in anticipation of future demands."

"And that's not fiction," Mercer said.

"Nelson's writing about nursing homes?" Bruce asked.

"Hang on," Thomas said. "As you know, the disease is hideous and degenerative with no way of predicting how fast a patient will wither and die. It's usually several years. For my aunt, as I said, it's ten years and counting. But once they completely black out, go unresponsive, and live through a tube, they can still hang on for a long time. At three thousand bucks a month. The nursing home operators have an obvious financial incentive to keep them alive, regardless of how nonresponsive they are. Keep the heart going and the checks roll in. This is an enormous business. Last year Alzheimer's cost the federal government close to three hundred billion in Medicare and Medicaid payments."

"Does the novel have a plot?" Bruce asked, tapping his fingers.

"We're getting there," Mercer said. "It's sort of a legal thriller with female characters who leave a lot to be desired."

"I didn't write it," Thomas said with a laugh. "I'm just the messenger. Anyway, the protagonist is a forty-year-old corporate lawyer, male, whose mother is stricken with the disease, and he's forced to put her in a nursing home where she steadily worsens and is soon out of it. The family is torn and goes through the right-to-die debate and all that."

"Ad nauseam," Mercer said. "He really beats it to death, at least in my opinion."

"Your opinion is of the highbrow literary variety," Bruce said. "Right now it doesn't count."

"All you want to do is sell books."

"And what's wrong with that, young lady?"

"Here we go," Thomas said. "The lawyer's mother weighs ninety pounds but her heart keeps going. And going. It gets as slow as thirty beats a minute, and the lawyer is monitoring this rather closely, then it begins a slow but unmistakable increase. Thirty-two beats, then thirty-five. When it gets to forty and stays there, the lawyer starts asking questions of the doctors. He's told such a rise is unusual but not unheard of. His mother is totally unresponsive and that won't improve, but she won't die because her heart keeps beating. Month after month her rate fluctuates between forty and fifty and she hangs on."

Thomas paused for a bite of duck sausage and a sip of coffee. Bruce ate too but asked, "And so, what's the backstory?"

"There's a drug called Daxapene that no one knows about. Totally fictional of course, because this is a novel."

"Got that," Bruce said.

"Daxapene is not on the market. It is registered, has a trade name, but will never be approved. It's not exactly legal, not exactly illegal. Not much of a drug, really, because it's not a stimulant, not a barbiturate, not anything really. It was discovered by accident in a Chinese laboratory about twenty years ago and sold only on the black market here in the U.S."

Another bite. Bruce waited, then asked, "And what's the purpose of Daxapene?"

"It extends life, keeps the heart beating."

"Then why isn't it a miracle drug? I'd like to invest."

"It has a rather limited market. It's not clear if scientists and researchers understand how it works, but it stimulates the medulla, that section of the brain that controls the heart muscle. And it works only in patients who are basically, as they say, brain dead."

Bruce and Noelle chewed on this for a moment, then she said, "Let me get this straight. There is very little brain activity but enough to pump the heart."

"Correct," Mercer said.

"Any side effects?" Bruce asked.

"Only blindness and severe vomiting, but these were discovered by accident in China. There are no clinical trials for patients with advanced dementia whose heart rates steadily increase. Why bother?"

Bruce was smiling and said, "So, the shady company buys the Daxapene from the shady Chinese lab, pumps it into all of its dementia patients on their last leg, keeps 'em alive for a few more months so it can collect a few more checks."

"Gotta love fiction," Thomas said.

"Oh, I do. In the novel, how much money is on the line?"

"The bad company owns three hundred facilities with forty-five thousand beds, ten thousand of which are occupied by Alzheimer's patients, and all of them get a dose of Daxapene each morning either in their feeding tube or in their orange juice. The drug is packaged like it's just another vitamin or supplement. Most patients in nursing homes get a handful of pills every day anyway, so what's another little vitamin."

"The staff has no clue?" Noelle asked.

"Not in the novel. At least in fiction the culture is 'When in doubt, give 'em another pill.'"

"Back to the money," Bruce said.

"The money is vague because everybody eventually dies. That's why the drug has never been tested. One patient might hang on for another six months with the help of Daxapene; for another it might be two years. In Nelson's fictional world, the average is twelve months. That's roughly an extra forty grand per patient, and he plays around with the figure of five thousand anticipated deaths per year, so something like two hundred million in extra cash from the government."

"And the company's annual gross?"

"Three billion, give or take."

Noelle asked, "If the drug extends life, what's illegal about it?"

Mercer replied, "Well again, in the novel, the bad guys take the position that they're doing nothing illegal. But the good guys say it's fraud."

"Let's get back to the plot," Bruce said. "Assuming there is one."

"Oh that," Thomas said with a laugh. "Well, the corporate lawyer has a road-to-Damascus conversion, chucks his high-end career, sues the bad company for keeping his poor mum alive, almost gets killed several times, and eventually wins a big verdict to bring down the bad guys."

"Predictable," Bruce said.

"Thoroughly," added Mercer. "I had it figured out halfway through. Does he really sell?"

"He did, yes. Nelson had some talent but he was a bit on the lazy side. I don't think he wrote for the female audience."

"And that's more than half the crowd, right?"

"Sixty percent."

"I'll stick with the girls. And don't call it chick lit."

"You've never heard me say that."

Noelle interrupted with "Okay, back to the book. We're supposed to believe that this novel is responsible for Nelson's death, right? Seems like a stretch to me."

Thomas said, "I've been digging for two weeks and can't find anything even remotely touching this story. Nelson is accurate enough with his numbers regarding dementia patients and nursing home beds and the vast sums of money and all that, but from the drug angle there's nothing. It looks like pure fiction."

"So who killed him?" Noelle asked.

There was a long gap in the conversation as the food kept their attention for a few moments. Mercer broke the quiet with "And we're all convinced that it was murder, regardless of what the police might think?"

They all looked at Bruce, who nodded slightly and offered a smug, tight smile, as if he had no doubt.

"I agree," Thomas said. "But I'm not sure this book will help. His first novel, *Swan City,* was about arms trafficking, and a much better book, by the way. His second, *The Laundry,* was about a Wall Street law firm that laundered billions in narcotics money for Latin American dictators. His third, *Hard Water,* dealt with Russian thugs peddling spare parts for nuclear weapons. It seems like he would have made much scarier enemies with those books."

"But he really didn't expose anyone, as I recall," Bruce said.

Noelle asked, "Was there anything in Nelson's past that involved pharmaceuticals?"

Bruce shook his head and said, "I don't think so. His clients were tech firms selling sophisticated software abroad."

"What happens in the novel?" Noelle asked.

"The bad guys get caught, pay up, go to jail. The Daxapene disappears and old folks start dying."

"What an awful ending."

"Thank you," Mercer said. "I didn't like the ending, the beginning, or anything in between."

"What happens to it now?" Noelle asked.

"I'm sure his family will try to sell it," Bruce said. "It's worth something on the market. Nelson had a lot of fans. Dying young is usually a good career move."

"I'll try to remember that," Mercer said.

Bruce chuckled and poured more coffee. He looked at Thomas and said, "There must be some bad actors in the nursing home business. Look at all these billboards and TV ads from law firms begging for abuse cases."

"And the patients are pretty vulnerable," Noelle said.

Thomas said, "There are eight major players and they control ninety percent of the beds. Six are public, two privately owned. Some get high marks for care, others stay in trouble with regulators and the courts. Nursing home litigation is lucrative in most states, especially here in Florida. Lots of old folks, lots of hungry lawyers. I found a bunch of blogs with horror stories of neglect and physical abuse. There's even a publication, *Elder Care Abuse Quarterly,* published by some lawyers in California. But, as I said, the business is so lucrative, because of Medicaid and Medicare, that plenty of companies want a piece of the business. And costs are projected to go through the roof."

"That's comforting," Noelle said.

Bruce said, "Well, dear, you're not sticking me in one of those places. I've always said that when it's time for the diapers it's time for the black pill."

"Let's talk about something else," Mercer said.

5.

Nick claimed to be in the library but there was soft music in the background. After being sworn to secrecy, he listened intently as Bruce summarized Nelson's last novel. Nick had just reread his first three books but did not believe they were revealing enough to get the author killed.

When Bruce finished, Nick said, "Nelson wouldn't know beans about the nursing home industry."

"I agree."

"So he probably had an informant, a whistleblower who found him, probably someone who read and admired his work."

An informant? Once again, Bruce was a step behind Nick.

"Okay. I'm listening."

"I don't think there's anything in his first three books, Bruce. Therefore, it has to be number four. And since he stepped outside his field, then someone approached him with the story. An insider. That's the guy you have to find."

Bruce reminded himself that this kid was only twenty-one. A well-read twenty-one, but still a kid nonetheless. "And how do we go about finding this person?"

"He'll probably find you. What if Nelson promised him something, like a slice of the pie, or maybe some cash up front and the rest on the back end? If you had a really juicy story and wanted to spill the beans, wouldn't you want some money?"

"Why not go to the FBI like Nelson did?"

"I don't know. Nelson got screwed by the FBI, didn't he?"

"He allegedly got five mil. Wanted more but he took what they offered."

"But he wasn't happy with the deal. Plus it's taxable income, right?"

"Right."

"So maybe this informant had his reasons to stay away from guys with badges, but he wanted the story told and he wanted to get paid. He cut a deal with Nelson and now Nelson got whacked. He'll probably come sniffing around looking for his money."

"There is no money. The book hasn't been sold to a publisher."

"Maybe he doesn't know that. Will it get sold?"

"Probably. But according to my secret readers it's not very good."

"Do I know these readers?"

"I can't answer that."

"Why can't I read it?"

"Because you're headed to Venice for a semester of hard work."

"Let me read it and I'll figure it out."

"I'll think about it. When do you leave?"

"Next week. Do the cops know about the book?"

"I don't know. They have his computer, but, knowing Nelson, they won't be able to turn it on."

"Are they pushing hard?"

"What do you think?"

"Sorry. I saw online that the store has reopened. Congratulations. I already miss the place."

"We're open but nothing is selling. The locals aren't thinking about books, and the tourists have disappeared."

"Sorry, boss. I'll send you a postcard from Venice."

"We might get over there. I've never seen those canals."

"Please come see me. I'll need cheering up."

"Right."

Two hours later, as Bruce and Noelle were sipping wine on the veranda, Nick called back. "What is it now?" Bruce asked.

"Been thinking about this latest conspiracy. Is it safe to assume that Nelson's murder will not be solved by the state police?"

"Probably."

"Then go to the FBI. Murder for hire is a federal offense. A somewhat famous writer gets taken out with a contract. The FBI will be all over it."

"So you're a lawyer now?"

"No, but one of my roommates is in law school."

"Can he find the nearest courthouse?"

"Probably not. But he's a great guy."

"No doubt. Look, Nick, I had lunch with my lawyer last week, and he can usually find the courthouse. On a good day. He says you have to be careful because fights between the locals and the Feds are easy to start and hard to stop. He thinks it's best to wait a few weeks and see where the investigation goes. Fortunately, you'll be out of the country and preoccupied elsewhere."

"No doubt. Here's the real reason I called. You know I really dig this stuff, and so I spend far too much time surfing the Internet. I ran across an interview with a retired super-sleuth who spent forty years investigating famous crimes. Specialized in murder. Ex-FBI and all that. He sort of let it slip that he also worked for a mysterious firm that did nothing but solve big crimes after the cops gave up. I kept digging and I found the firm, just in case you need it."

"Why would I need it? He ain't my brother."

"Because I know you, and you're about to spend whatever it takes to find Nelson's killer. Because you care, Bruce."

"Right, right. Shouldn't you be studying?"

"Ha. Not this semester. I will not open a book. Or at least not a textbook. Please let me read Nelson's manuscript."

"I'm thinking. How's your Italian?"

"I can say *pizza* and *birra*."

"You'll be fine."

6.

After a week on the island, Mercer was ready to leave. The cottage was intact and Larry had its repairs under control. With no tourists, the beach was deserted, and while this was usually desirable she now found it sad and depressing. The beachcombers were gone because the island was a wreck and it would be months or years before the allure of coastal living returned. She missed the laughter of children playing in the sand and wading in the surf. She missed the friendly "Good morning" from every single person she encountered. She missed the dogs straining at their leashes to say hello. The storm had disrupted the natural cycle of egg-laying by the greenbacks, and in her long solitary walks she found no trails left by the turtles. She found plenty of debris, though, and cleaning up the beach would take a long time. If she walked to the north she saw the damaged cottages and condos and family-owned motels. The gossip was filled with stories of owners who had no or inadequate flood insurance, and thus could not begin to clean up or rebuild.

Mercer decided to leave and come back in six months. Maybe then things would be better. Or maybe a year.

She and Thomas hosted a small dinner party on her deck, with Bruce and Noelle, and Myra and Leigh. Bob Cobb was still away pursuing cooler weather. Jay Arklerood, the poet, didn't answer his phone. Amy was too busy with her kids. Summer was over and the gang was scattering. The gang was also burdened by the aftermath and fearful that life might never be the same. Bay Books was practically deserted these days, and that was enough to worry all its writers.

As Mercer packed her car early the next morning, she was delighted to be leaving the island. Her teaching duties at Ole Miss were calling, she had a novel to start, Thomas was bored with the beach, and they sped away wonderfully unburdened because it wasn't really their home. When they came back in six months, perhaps there would be no trace of the storm and the island would be perfect again.

7.

A month after burying her brother, Polly McCann returned to the island to assume her official capacity as executrix of his estate. Because he had little else to do and was bored hanging around an empty bookstore, Bruce met her at the airport and they drove to the state crime lab in Jacksonville.

Wesley Butler had agreed to pry himself away from his other urgent duties and give them half an hour of his time. That proved far too generous. Even with coffee served in paper cups, the meeting could have ended ten minutes after it began.

Butler said the investigation was proceeding nicely, though he provided few details and nothing new. Fingerprint analysis showed matches for Bruce, Nick, Bob Cobb, and Nelson himself, but that was expected. There were two prints that could not be matched. One probably belonged to Maria Peña, a housekeeper who cleaned each Wednesday afternoon. They were trying to coax her into providing prints, but she was undocumented and not cooperating. No sign of Ingrid Murphy or any blonde resembling her. The surveillance footage from the Hilton was gone. They were plowing through the digital records of dozens of rental units in the area, but it was the old needle-in-a-haystack routine. Nelson's hard drive was impenetrable. Its encryption scheme had tied their experts in knots.

Not once did Butler think to ask Polly if she knew anything about Nelson's last work in progress. The meeting was all about himself and his efforts, lame as they were. Driving away, Bruce and Polly were convinced that the state had all but closed the file. Butler and his "team" probably considered Nelson's death an accident because they had no chance of solving a crime.

Bruce said, "I have a summary of the novel."

"From Mercer Mann?"

"Yes."

"She sent the thumb drive back. Let's hear it."

8.

They had lunch at the Blue Fish, Bruce's favorite seafood place in Jacksonville, and they arrived early enough to get a table in a quiet corner. The waitress brought Polly an herbal tea. For Bruce, a glass of sauvignon blanc. He ordered the crab salad and she asked for some raw tuna dish.

She said, "The initial appraisal of his condo is nine hundred thousand, and there's no mortgage. I'm inclined to sell it because I don't have time to play landlord."

"I agree. But it might take a year or so for the market to rebound."

"No other real estate. There is eight hundred thousand in cash—CD's, Treasurys, a checking account. In Nelson's will he leaves behind a hundred thousand in trust to each of my sons, his only nephews. That was a nice surprise because he never told me."

"Who gets the rest?"

"Me, Mom, Dad, split three ways. And since the estate is under three million we shouldn't worry about estate taxes. However, there is one complicating factor, an issue that may cause problems. Nothing with Nelson was ever easy."

"He buried some money?"

"How'd you know?"

"It's a common theme in his books. Someone is always funneling money through offshore accounts. In real life he was a lawyer who understood international trade. I'm not surprised. Did he hide it from his ex?"

"Apparently. When he got the reward for blowing the whistle, he bought a hundred thousand dollars' worth of stock in a new tech venture in Silicon Valley, but he did it through a shell company in Singapore. His wife and her lawyers never found it."

"How'd you find it?"

"Two years ago he whispered to our father. I've reviewed his divorce papers and the stock was never mentioned."

"What's it worth?"

"Eight million."

"Nice investment."

"Brilliant. Now what do we do with it?"

"You need a lawyer."

"I've hired a firm here in Jacksonville. My lawyer thinks we'll have to deal with the ex-wife. A really unpleasant person. She's already divorced number two and is living with number three."

"But there'll be a lot left over, right?"

"All of it. It's tax-free under current law."

"Congratulations."

"I suppose," she said softly as their plates arrived.

Bruce said, "I'm sorry. That was crude. There's nothing to celebrate here."

She smiled and glanced away. Ignoring the tuna, she sipped her tea and said, "It doesn't seem fair. The money was invested eleven years ago and Sally, the ex, had nothing to do with the transaction. She never knew about it. Nelson was smart enough to pick the right stock and to keep it away from her. Otherwise, she would have blown through it. She got more cash and assets in the divorce than he did, and now I'm supposed to contact this dreadful woman and inform her that she gets a few more million."

"I wouldn't do it," Bruce said with certainty. "I'd leave the stock right where it is and not say a word. Probate the estate, close the estate, let the clock tick away."

"You're serious?"

"Dead. I know a little about offshore banking."

"I'm all ears."

A long pull on the sauvignon blanc. A glance around the empty dining room. "Well, you see, from time to time I deal in rare books and manuscripts. Occasionally, I'll look at one with a provenance that's a bit shady and the seller might want to do the deal offshore."

"Is that legal?"

"Let's call it a gray area. It's certainly illegal to steal a rare book, or any book for that matter, and I've never done that, not even close. But it's also impossible to look at an old book and say for certain that it has been stolen. I never ask the seller or his broker if the book was stolen because the answer will always be 'No.' Sometimes I'll get too suspicious and back away. There's a lot of thievery these days in the business and I'm very careful."

"This is pretty interesting."

"That's why I do it. I love the business. The bookstore keeps me busy and pays the bills, but if and when I make money it's in the old stuff."

She sliced a thick wedge of tuna and shoved it around her

plate. Bruce was working on his crab salad and ordered a second glass of wine.

She said, "So, I'm intrigued. Can you give me an example?"

He laughed and said, "No, but let's try a hypothetical. Let's say a dealer I know in Philly contacts me and says he has a client whose wealthy parents have died off and he's in charge of the estate. The old man collected rare books and the client has his hands on a few of them. Books are like jewelry, very portable and not always accounted for. They can be walked right out of one's estate. Let's say the client has a first edition of *Ulysses* by James Joyce, and that it's in extraordinarily fine condition with a dust jacket. He'll send me photographs of the book. At auction it would fetch around half a million, but auctions also attract a lot of attention. The client does not want attention. We'll negotiate, and let's say we agree on three hundred thousand. I'll meet the dealer somewhere in the Caribbean and he'll have the book. I'll transfer the money into a new account at an old bank, and everybody is happy."

"What happens to the book?"

"Hypothetically, it stays in a vault in another old bank down there. I'll sit on it for a year or so and put out feelers to potential buyers. Time is always on our side. Memories fade. The authorities lose interest."

"Sounds dishonest." She finally took a small bite of raw tuna.

"Maybe, maybe not. The client might have included the book with the estate's inventory. How am I supposed to know?"

She took another bite, had some tea, and seemed suddenly bored with the conversation. "And you would not include this stock in Nelson's estate?"

"Oh, I'm not sure what I'd do, really. Who knows about it?"

"Just me and Pops."

"And he's in bad health, right?"

"Quite bad. He won't last a year."

Bruce took a drink of wine and watched as four business-men were seated at the table next to them. He lowered his voice an octave or two and said, "Me, I'd leave it alone, but then I'm willing to take more risks than most people."

She ate another small bite, took another sip. "This is over-whelming, Bruce. I didn't ask for this job."

"Most executors don't. And the pay is lousy."

"Why don't you do it? You're here, much closer to the court-house and the lawyers and his condo, and you know more about this stuff."

"What stuff? Offshore accounts and contract killings? No, thanks, Polly. I'll help when I can but Nelson chose you for a reason. And the lawyers do most of the work anyway. Aside from the hidden stock, it's a pretty simple estate."

"Nothing seems simple, especially his death."

"You can do it."

"Wouldn't it be easier to simply go along with the police and close the file? Who needs to waste the emotional energy worry-ing about an unsolved murder? Nelson's dead. I can accept that. He's gone. Does it really matter how he died?"

"Of course it does."

"Why?"

"Because he was murdered, Polly. We can't simply walk away from that."

"We?"

"Yes, those of us who knew Nelson, his family and friends.

Somebody out there paid a pro to kill your brother. I can't believe you want to go back to the West Coast and forget about it."

"What am I supposed to do?"

"I don't know. For now, we wait for the police to either finish whatever they're doing or close the file. After that, we'll have lunch again and decide what to do."

9.

By the end of September, Bruce had figures to support what he already suspected—Bay Books was down 50 percent from a year ago. During an average year, almost 40 percent of its sales were to tourists, and there were none to be found on Camino Island these days. The locals were loyal but many were still cleaning up and watching their money. He canceled all author events for the rest of the year, laid off two part-time employees, convinced Noelle to lock up her antiques store, and together they fled the country.

They flew to Milan and took the train to Verona where they roamed the old city and took in its gardens, museums, piazzas, and restaurants. They drove deep into the Dolomites and spent four nights in a rustic, family-run outpost twenty miles from the Slovenian border. During the day they hiked the spectacular mountains until they were exhausted, and at night they consumed large meals of Ladin cuisine—dumplings and schnitzel—with local wines, grappa, and even homemade schnapps.

Late on their last afternoon at the lodge, they cuddled under thick quilts on the patio, sipped hot cocoa, and watched the sun disappear behind the mountains.

"I don't want to go back," Bruce said. "It's still hot in Florida and there's still trash in the trees."

"Where do you want to go?" Noelle asked.

"I don't know. I've had the store for twenty-three years and retail takes a toll. We have enough stashed offshore to quit working forever."

"You're forty-seven years old, Bruce, and you're not wired to stop working. You'd go nuts in retirement."

"Oh, I'll always trade rare books, and you'll always trade French antiques. But we can do that anywhere. It'll take years for the island to recover from the storm, and I'm not sure I want to grind it out waiting for the good old days. Let's at least talk about a change."

"Okay. Where do you want to go?"

"I want to keep the house, not sure about the store. What if we lived there when the weather is nice, then go north? Six months at the beach, six months in the mountains? A small town in New England, or maybe out west. I don't know, but it might be fun looking around."

"Europe? What's wrong with this view?"

Bruce thought for a long time before saying, "You belong to someone else in Europe, and I'd rather stay away."

"Things are changing, Bruce. There is bad news. Jean-Luc has cancer and the prognosis is not good."

She watched him closely for a reaction but he revealed nothing. Not sympathy, because he cared nothing for her French boyfriend. Not relief, because Bruce knew the rules when he fell in love with her. She and Jean-Luc had been together long before Bruce entered the picture, and, being French, she was perfectly willing to balance the two men, but only with complete disclosure up front and brutal transparency. She couldn't marry Jean-Luc because he was married to an older woman with money. His wife knew the score, as did Bruce, and for almost twenty years the two open marriages had survived without major conflict. The open door gave Bruce the green light to spend time with any of his favorite authors who stopped by on tour.

"I'm sorry," he said.

"Don't say that."

"What do you want me to say?"

"Don't say anything."

"That doesn't work either. When did you find out?"

"Back in the summer. Right before the storm. It's pancreatic cancer, Bruce, he has only weeks."

"Do you need to go?"

"No. He's at home and Veronique is taking good care of him. There's nothing I can do. We said goodbye, Bruce. We said goodbye." Her voice cracked and her eyes watered.

"You should've told me before now," he said.

"Why? It's only a matter of time. I spoke to Veronique last week and he's going down pretty fast."

Bruce suddenly felt incredibly guilty because he wanted Noelle all to himself. He was tired of sharing, tired of being jealous and wondering which man she preferred to be with. He believed he would get the nod, but he had never been certain.

"We're almost middle-age, Bruce."

"Speak for yourself. When does that start?"

"At fifty, so say the experts. Fifty to sixty-five."

"What's after that?"

"Something about seniors."

"This is depressing. What's your point?"

"My point is that I think it's time that we grow up a bit and recommit ourselves to the marriage."

"Monogamy?"

"Yes. Let's say the games are over and we learn to trust each other."

"I've never distrusted you, Noelle. I've always known exactly what you were doing, just as I was open with my adventures."

"Games, adventures, see what I mean, Bruce? I love you and I'm tired of sharing. Do you love me?"

"You know I do. Always."

"Then let's change the rules."

Bruce took a deep breath, then another sip of hot cocoa. He was tempted to offer the opinion that Noelle was suddenly interested in a monogamous relationship because her boyfriend was dying, but he let it pass. He was not going to lose Noelle, because he adored her and had for twenty years. He loved her beauty, grace, easy disposition, chicness, intelligence.

But old playboys don't exactly fade away. As a general rule, they go down swinging.

Carefully, he said, "Okay, let's agree to start the conversation about a new set of rules."

She nodded in agreement, but she knew it would be a challenge.

They left late the following morning and drifted toward Venice, stopping for lunches in picturesque villages and sleeping wherever they could find a room at an inn.

CHAPTER SIX
THE CONSULTANT

1.

Three years earlier, when Mercer returned to Camino Island for the first time in many years, she did so under the pretense of taking a sabbatical to finish a novel. She settled into the cottage built by her grandmother, Tessa, which was still owned by the family. She hung around the bookstore, met Leigh and Myra, Bob Cobb, Andy Adam, and the rest of the gang, and quickly ingratiated herself with the island's literary mafia, of which Bruce was the unquestioned leader.

She made little progress with the novel, though she claimed otherwise. The writing was part of the act, the ruse, the smoke-screen to divert attention away from her real motive: she was being paid a handsome sum by a mysterious security firm hired by an insurance company that was desperately searching for some stolen manuscripts. A lot of money was on the line, especially for the insurance company, and the security firm had come to believe that one Bruce Cable had the manuscripts hidden somewhere on the island.

And they were correct. What the firm didn't know was that Bruce was suspicious of Mercer from day one, and as she got closer and closer, and indeed all the way to his bedroom, he became even more convinced that she was working for the enemy. Her presence prompted him to ship the manuscripts overseas and eventually sell them for a fortune in ransom.

Though the elaborate ruse had failed, in the end all parties were happy, especially Bruce. The owner, Princeton's library, got the priceless manuscripts back. The insurance company took a hit but the damage could have been far worse. Of the actual thieves, little need be said. Three were in prison. One was dead.

Since then, Bruce had marveled at the security firm's elaborate scheme. It was nothing short of brilliant and had almost worked. He became convinced that he needed to know more about the people who had almost ruined him. He leaned on Mercer, who reluctantly made the phone call and established the contact. Her handler had been a shrewd operator named Elaine Shelby, and Bruce was determined to meet her.

2.

The building was one of half a dozen tall, new, gleaming structures near Dulles Airport, twenty-four miles west of the U.S. capital and in the sprawl of northern Virginia. From the moment Bruce parked his rental car underground, he felt as though he was being monitored. At the front desk, he was photographed, body-scanned, and asked to stare into a camera to record forever his facial features. As he was led to an elevator he searched in vain for a directory on a wall, but didn't see one. Evidently the folks who leased these offices did not favor publicity.

A security guard was waiting when he stepped off on the fourth floor. No smile, no pleasant greeting, no meaningful word. Just a grunt and a motion. There were no work pods with multiple desks, no pools of secretaries. From the time Bruce stepped off the elevator until he walked into the office of Elaine Shelby, he saw no one else except the guard.

Elaine was coming around her desk with a smile and handshake as the guard closed the door.

"I feel as though you should frisk me," Bruce said.

"Bend over," she snapped and Bruce burst out laughing. She waved to a sofa and said, "Might as well laugh, Cable, you beat us fair and square."

They took seats around a low table and she began pouring coffee.

"You got the manuscripts back," he said. "Everybody's happy."

"Easy for you to say."

"It was a brilliant idea, Ms. Shelby."

"Drop the formal stuff. I'll be Elaine and you'll be Bruce, okay?"

"Fine with me."

"You call it brilliant, in our business we call it a failure, which, I hate to say, is not that unusual. We are dealt the toughest cases and we don't always win."

"But you always get paid."

"Damned right we do. Don't you just love Mercer?"

"I tried my best. Great girl, wonderful writer."

"Did you guys make it all the way to bed?"

"Oh, I never kiss and tell, Elaine. That's very unprofessional."

"You have a horrible reputation for chasing the young female writers."

"Why is that horrible? I assure you it's all consensual. These liberated women are on the road and looking for fun. I just try to accommodate them."

"We know, we know. That was our plan."

"Almost brilliant. Was it your idea?"

"We have teams, no one works solo around here. It was a joint effort."

"Okay. What can you tell me about this outfit?"

"I understand you want to hire us."

"I'm interested, but I need to know more."

She took a sip of coffee and recrossed her legs. Bruce refused to notice. "Well, for lack of a better description, we are a security firm."

"Do you have a name?"

"Not really."

"So, if I eventually write out a check for payment, it will be 'pay to the order of . . . '"

"Alpha North Solutions."

"How wonderfully bland."

"And you came up with 'Bay Books'?"

"I did. Much sexier."

"Is it really that important for you to like our name?"

"I guess not."

"May I proceed? You did inquire."

"I did. Please. Sorry."

"Anyway, we provide security for companies and individuals, we investigate crimes for insurance companies and other clients, we subcontract with the federal government to consult on security matters. We operate around the world, with head-quarters here."

"Why here?"

"Why does it matter?"

"It doesn't, I guess. It's just that you're stuck out here in the middle of nowhere with nothing but eight-lane roads running in all directions."

"It's convenient. Dulles is right there and we travel a lot. Virtually every employee here is former FBI or CIA, and this area is home."

"And you?"

"FBI for fifteen years, worked primarily in recovering stolen art."

"And manuscripts."

"Among other items. I've looked through the materials you sent, interesting reading, and you're smart to avoid email. I assume the locals down there have not made much progress."

"Not much at all, I'm afraid."

"And you realize this will be expensive?"

"Yep. I wouldn't be here if I were looking for a bargain."

"Okay, so I suggest that we walk down the hall to visit my colleague Lindsey Wheat, one of our homicide investigators and, until five years ago, one of the FBI's finest. She was also one of the first female African American agents in the field."

"Why would she, or you, leave the Bureau?"

"Money and politics. The pay here is about four times that of the Bureau, and most of us are women who got sick of the internal politics and sexism." She stood and motioned toward the door.

Bruce followed her down the empty hall. Ms. Wheat was at

her desk and rose with a big smile when they walked in. Last names were discarded as first names were assumed. She was about fifty and as slender and stylish as Elaine. She walked them over to a similar sitting area and inquired about coffee. All declined.

Bruce had already gone through one round of preliminary chitchat and wished to avoid another. He said, "So, you specialize in old murders?"

Lindsey smiled and said, "Or recent ones. It doesn't matter. I began on the streets as a homicide detective. Houston, Seattle, five years in Tampa. It's a thick résumé, if you'd like to take a look."

"Maybe later." Bruce had already accepted the fact that these people were eminently qualified. For a second it made him even prouder that he had outfoxed them three years earlier.

Lindsey asked, "Have you talked to the FBI down there? If it's a contract for hire then it's likely to be federal."

"That's what I've been told. But no, I have not talked to the FBI. Not sure how one does that, really. I'm just a simple bookseller who knows little about the law." He smiled at Elaine, who rolled her eyes.

"So you've read the materials too?" he asked Lindsey.

"Yes."

"Look, before we wade in too deep, I'd like to clear the air about your fees. I know this won't be cheap and we—Nelson's sister, who is his executrix, and me—are willing to step up, but we have limits. Nelson was my friend and he deserves justice, but I'm only willing to pay for so much of it. His sister feels the same way."

"What's in the estate?" Elaine asked.

"It's complicated. About two million, cash and assets, no

debts. But he buried some money offshore years ago and kept it away from his ex-wife. It's in the common stock of a company and worth around eight million, for a total of ten. The state and federal exemptions this year are eleven million and change, so the estate is free and clear. The ex-wife has lawyered up and is deeply wounded because she got the shaft several marriages ago, but Nelson's sister thinks her feelings can be soothed with a couple of million. Bottom line, the estate is in good shape and is willing to write a check. The obvious question is: How much will this cost before it's all over?"

"We don't guarantee a win in this business," Elaine said.

"I understand. It's a long shot."

"Three hundred thousand," Lindsey said. "From soup to nuts. All up front. No hourly billing, no monthly statements, expenses included."

Bruce nodded and stared at her pretty eyes without blinking. Polly had predicted half a million, but then she was in California. Bruce was hoping for two hundred or so and refused to flinch at three hundred. He would pay half, as would the estate. He could afford it, and Ms. Shelby sitting across from him with a smirk damned well knew it. What she didn't know was where his ransom was buried.

He shrugged as if it grew on trees and said, "Deal. Now what do we get for the money?"

"Hopefully, the killer," Lindsey said with a smile.

3.

Elaine shook Bruce's hand goodbye and left them to their business. Bruce followed Lindsey down the hall to a larger room with screens on all four walls and a long table filled with laptops and other devices. They sat across the table from each other and she opened a file of some sort. "Let's start with the woman," she said as she pushed a button on something and Ingrid's computer-generated face appeared on two of the wide screens.

Lindsey said, "Of course, we don't know this woman, nor anyone who might be her, but we'll begin the search."

"The search for what?"

"A contract killer. We know of several, but it's a fairly nebulous group. They don't convene annually for parties and they don't have a registry."

"You know the names of contract killers?"

"Of course. The FBI has monitored them for years. Back in the old days most were Mafia boys who killed each other in turf battles, but today there are a few who are known."

"How? How do you know about them?"

"Mainly through informants, snitches, rats. Almost all contract killings are done by dumb criminals who need a few bucks to knock off a spouse or hubby's secret girlfriend. Family stuff, usually. Bad business deals are not uncommon. Most of the hit men are caught and convicted by forensics."

"Where might one find a good hit man?"

"Well, you can actually start online, believe it or not, but those guys cannot be trusted."

"Imagine that. A dishonest hit man."

"Right. If you wanted to knock off, say, a business partner, you'd probably start with a local private investigator, someone you might know and trust. He'll know someone who's done hard time and lives around the fringes. He might also know an ex-cop or maybe a former Army Ranger, someone accomplished with weapons. Guns are used nine times out of ten. About sixty percent of the time word leaks out, the police get a tip, and everybody gets arrested before there's a killing."

"But we're not dealing with a dumb criminal here," Bruce said, enjoying the discussion.

"No, we are not. There are a few contract killers who are referred to in the trade as 'masters.' They rarely get caught, and they are well paid."

"How much?"

She pressed a button and Ingrid disappeared. Six names were listed in one column. Beside each was the year of death, and to the far right was an amount of money. The largest sum was $2.5 million; the lowest, $500,000. Lindsey said, "None of these figures can be trusted, but ten years ago a retired hit man wrote a long tell-all piece for an online crime magazine, anonymous of course. He claimed responsibility for the first three murders. His command of the details convinced the FBI he was there. The last two are from other sources."

"Why did he retire?" Bruce asked.

"He turned sixty-five, Social Security kicked in, or so he said. Had a real sense of humor. He wrote that he almost got caught during his last job when things got messy. A young teenage boy got in the way and took a bullet. The hit man found a conscience and hung up his Glock."

"And none of these five killings were ever solved?"

"No. The cases are still open."

"So, our little venture is indeed a long shot?"

"Absolutely. I thought we were clear. No?"

"Yes, quite clear." Bruce kept staring at the numbers. "The pay's not bad," he said.

"The average job is about ten thousand bucks, but, as I said, the average hit man is not that bright. Most get caught because somebody talks too much. And most of the people handing over the cash aren't that smart either. You're going through a nasty divorce and your spouse is suddenly murdered. Don't you think the police might have some questions?"

"I don't recognize any of the victims."

"None are from Florida, and none involved divorces. Most were bad business deals. The last one was an inheritance issue."

"Do you have photos or composite sketches of other contract killers?"

She punched some keys and another computerized face flashed on the screen. Male, age forty, Caucasian, flat nose, beady eyes, bushy hair, and so on. It was only a sketch. She said, "Four years ago, this guy was seen leaving a marina in Galveston just seconds before a yacht burst into flames. Three people died, not from burns but from bullets to the head. Probably a bad business deal."

"And a bad sketch. This guy could be one of a million."

"Yes, but it's not one of our cases. Luckily."

"May I ask how you got the sketch?"

"We have a lot of contacts, some within law enforcement, some on the outside."

"Nice to know. So our girl is a master killer."

Lindsey hit a key and Ingrid returned to the screens. "Not so sure about that. She allowed herself to be seen by a number of people. She slept with your friend several times. They had lunch and dinner out, and so on. That's highly unusual for a killer at the master level. Normally, these guys are never seen. But, on the other hand, hiding in plain view is often a smart move."

"Maybe she had no choice. Sleeping with Bob led her to her target."

"Any chance she slept with Nelson?"

"Who knows? He was single and close by. A nice-looking gal, great body, ready to hop in the sack for other reasons but eager nonetheless. Surely you've seen this before."

"Not really. It's not unusual in the world of espionage but we've never seen it. The elite spy services have always recruited beautiful women who know how to seduce. As you know, men can be quite weak at times."

"So I've heard. But this is not exactly the Mossad, right?"

"Highly unlikely. A trained spy would not run the risk of being caught on video around the hotel."

"How many contract killers are female?"

"Zero, in my experience. Ingrid would be the first."

"So how'd she do it?"

"I've read your summary and I think you're pretty close. She arrived on the island with a colleague, probably a man. Posing as a couple, they leased a condo near Nelson's. I assume there are plenty available."

"Only about a million. It is Florida."

"She hooked up with your friend Bob and that's how she met Nelson. She got lucky when the storm appeared, and that virtually eliminated her chances of being caught. She's gone."

"No chance of finding her?"

"Always a slight chance. I'll meet with my pals at the FBI and have a chat. They'll be excited to see Ingrid here, to add her to their rather short list of professional killers. Who knows? This is a murky world and there's often a potential informant looking for money. It's a long shot but there might be someone out there who knows a thing or two and needs a buck. Doubtful, though."

"What's your theory on his computer?"

"After she killed him, she would not have left without his hard drive. However, if she simply stole it, then she would have left behind a massive clue for the police."

"She replaced it?"

"That's my guess. Replaced it with a hard drive that contains nothing useful but is heavily encrypted. The police can't scratch its surface."

"So she knew the specs of his desktop."

"Again, we're guessing at this point, but my answer would be yes. She and her pal had probably been inside Nelson's condo. Did he have home security?"

"Yes, there was an alarm system. There was a camera at the front door and another looking at the rear patio. Both were destroyed in the storm. The police think they may have been disabled beforehand."

"Where is his computer?" she asked.

"Police. They're supposed to hand it over, along with other personal effects, next week. Polly McCann will meet with them and take possession. I've been pushed out of the investigation, which is fine with me."

"What day next week?"

"Wednesday."

"I'd like to be there."

"Come on down. I'll give you the grand tour."

"We really need to look at the hard drive. If it's a dummy left behind by the killer, that's a clue, though I'm not sure what we can do with it. If it's the real hard drive, then it could be a treasure trove of information."

"Assuming it can be accessed."

"Yes, but didn't you say in your notes that his sister has the passcode for the thumb drive?"

"She does."

Lindsey flashed a knowing smile and said, "That's all we need. Our guys can get in with that."

"I'm drowning here. This is way over my head."

"Mine too. We'll let the experts worry about it."

"So you'll need the thumb drive?"

"Of course. I want to read the novel, and we'll use it to try to penetrate Nelson's hard drive."

"I'll bet you don't find much. He was secretive and didn't trust the Internet, hated the cloud, refused to shop online, said nothing important in emails, ignored all social media, paid cash for most of his purchases. I doubt if Nelson left too many footprints behind."

"And the condo is on the market?"

"Oh, yes. It's been scrubbed, painted, emptied, as good as new. The police released it three weeks ago. The market is very soft, though."

"And you can arrange a meeting with Polly McCann?"

"I'd be delighted. I have nothing else to do. No one's buying books on the island and I'm bored to death."

4.

The middle-aged man had the jaded and shaggy look of a veteran reporter. He stopped by the bookstore, found Bruce bored at his desk, and helped himself to a chair. He said he was a freelancer for *Newsweek* and tossed over a card that was supposed to verify this. Bruce examined the card. Donald Oester. Washington address.

Oester was sniffing around trying to put together a story about the death of bestselling author Nelson Kerr. He had done the legwork that one would expect. He had examined the file in probate court but found little. The inventory of assets and liabilities wasn't due for several months. He had pestered Carl Logan, Santa Rosa's police chief, but got nowhere. He had made contact with Captain Wes Butler of the state police, but was told that there was nothing to discuss because it was an ongoing investigation.

"Aren't all homicide investigations ongoing until they find the killer?" Oester asked with a laugh.

Bruce talked, cautiously, about Nelson and his time on the island, and his books, but he was careful not to say anything about the crime scene or anything else. Several days after Nelson died, there were brief stories in a few newspapers about his death during the hurricane. An online publishing magazine mentioned the police involvement but revealed nothing. The Jacksonville daily ran a short obituary, then followed it with a slightly longer article about the investigation. Before Oester, no reporter had contacted Bruce.

"Was he working on a novel?" Oester asked.

"Don't know about that," Bruce replied. "But most writers are usually working on something."

"I chatted with his ex-editor at Simon and Schuster, guy said Kerr was jumping ship, looking for a new house, and working on something big."

"I believe he was still looking. To my knowledge, Nelson was not under contract when he died. He was also between agents."

"How much do you know about his past, his old days as a lawyer?"

"How much do you know?"

Oester laughed again, nervously. "I tracked down a former colleague out there but the guy said it was ten years ago. Not much, really. I tried his ex-wife, a tough one."

"Never met her."

"Is it fair to call him a 'bestselling author'? I mean, I know that gets thrown around all the time, but did he really sell that many books?"

"He did. All three of his novels hit the lists, the *Times* and *Publishers Weekly*. And each book did better than the last. I encouraged him to write more, but he enjoyed travel, sportfishing, life on the beach."

"A hundred thousand copies each time out?"

"I'd guess. You can find his numbers online."

"I've looked, and I've been told those numbers are not that accurate. Did you sell his books?"

"I did. Nelson had a following."

"You think he was murdered?"

"I'm not saying anything that you might want to print. The state police are investigating, that's all I can say."

"Fair enough. Do you know his sister, Polly McCann?"

"I do."

"Would you ask her to talk to me? She's hung up twice."

"No, sorry. Don't know her that well."

Oester jumped to his feet and headed for the door. "I'll be back. Give me a call if you hear something."

Don't bet on it. "Sure."

5.

The boredom ran on unabated as the days finally cooled. The week after his trip to D.C., Bruce welcomed Lindsey Wheat and Polly McCann to Bay Books. They met in his newly renovated office on the first floor, in his First Editions Room, the walls lined with hundreds of autographed books. It was a Saturday morning and for a change the store was busy as young mothers brought in their children for story time upstairs in the café. Normally, Bruce would have been up there among them, sipping cappuccino and flirting with the ladies, but he had important business at hand.

The day before, Polly had met with Wesley Butler at the crime lab and received yet another useless update. Little progress had been made. Indeed, so little that she could not remember anything new. Butler did hand over Nelson's laptop, desktop, cell phone, and two leather briefcases. He admitted that their tech people had been unable to penetrate the encryption codes Nelson had used. Again, he did not have the presence of mind to ask Polly if she knew anything about her brother's novel-in-progress. He gave every indication that he wasn't sure what to do next and was generally not that concerned with solving the crime. And, he made a point of letting her know that he did not want Bruce Cable calling again and sticking his nose into the investigation.

Bruce took this news well. As far as he was concerned, the state police were not a factor and he had already wasted too much time with them.

Lindsey took the thumb drive from Polly, plugged it into her laptop, entered its encryption passcode, and sent its data to her technicians at the home office. She gave it to Bruce and asked him to print three hard copies of the manuscript for their evening's reading. They were in agreement that it was time to read Nelson's last masterpiece. The ten-page treatment written by Thomas and Mercer had been useful, but the full story was now needed.

An hour later, Lindsey received a phone call from her office with decoding instructions. She opened the desktop, entered the codes, and, to no one's surprise, found the two hard drives secured by another layer of encryption. As she expected, Ingrid had stolen the two real ones at about the same time she murdered Nelson and had replaced them. She and her gang had no way of knowing that Polly had a thumb drive with a passcode and the finished novel. They rightfully assumed the police would be unable to log in to Nelson's computer and the search would end there.

As for his laptop, there were no passcodes and all access was blocked. Lindsey agreed to take it back to the office and let the techies have a go, but she was not optimistic.

They spent two hours, with endless cups of black coffee, plowing through Nelson's notebooks and random files. At lunchtime, Bruce ordered takeout and they continued working in his office. A clerk delivered sandwiches and iced tea, and as she left Bruce asked if she had seen any customers that morning.

"Only the kids," she said with a laugh.

Lindsey, the professional and the one being paid by the other two, had gently assumed control of the conversations. Bruce and Polly were happy to trust her and follow along. As they ate, she said, "I have an idea for a plan that we have discussed back home at the office. We can agree that Nelson showed no interest in nursing homes at any point in his life, until the end. So, someone approached him. Someone with the story. Someone on the inside. An informant, a whistleblower, though whispering to an author is not exactly blowing the whistle the way the FBI sees things, but you get the picture. This person chose not to go to the police for whatever reason, so he found Nelson. He read his books and knew that he wasn't shy about using his fiction to expose some nasty people and their businesses. All names changed to protect the guilty, of course. This person is crucial to our success."

Bruce was nodding along as he ate his sandwich. He'd heard this before. Nick Sutton had predicted months ago that an informant was involved.

Lindsey continued: "We have to make it easier for this person to come find us. This person is probably watching the probate file, it's all public and online, and looking for a way to contact us. Step one of the plan is to appoint Bruce as the executor of Nelson's literary estate. Step two is to sell the novel to a publisher and make sure it's reported. Bruce, this is your territory and you'll do a better job at it than Polly can do out in California."

Bruce said, "I'm not sure I want Ingrid back on the island."

"You can forget her. She's gone."

Polly said, "We discussed this, months ago. Remember, Bruce, I asked you to handle his literary affairs?"

"Yes, of course I remember. Do you remember why I said no?"

"No. Things were a blur back then."

"It makes perfect sense," Lindsey said. "You know the agents and publishers and you can get a good deal for the book. Plus, you're more knowledgeable about the backlist and what to do with it."

"The backlist?" Polly asked.

"His old titles, all in paperback," Bruce replied.

"Will they still earn royalties?" Polly asked.

"Oh yes, especially with a new book out. The estate will earn royalties for a few more years, then they'll trickle away, I guess."

"What about film interest?" Lindsey asked.

"Nelson's had that in the past, though nothing happened. Almost every bestseller gets its share of attention from film and television. But I'm not sure I want the attention from the bad guys. We're laboring here under the assumption that Nelson was killed for a reason, right? If I'm the one pushing his books, you might find me with a gash or two in the skull."

Lindsey waved him off. "They're done and they're not coming back. No way they'll risk another job like this. It was a pretty stupid move in the first place. They wanted to stop Nelson from publishing the book, but they didn't know that he had finished it. Now it will be published anyway."

Polly said, "We're assuming it's good enough to publish, right?"

"Right," Bruce replied.

"I've told you this, Bruce. I can't read his stuff. I've tried many times and it just doesn't appeal to me. I can't imagine having to deal with his literary estate for years to come. I'm out of my league with the rest of his estate. I really want you to take the job."

"Okay, that's one reason," Bruce said. "But the other reason is to attract this informant person who we think might actually exist but we're not sure."

"Correct," said Lindsey. "We think it could be a crucial part of our plan."

"And who's 'we'?"

"My people, Bruce. My team. This is what we do, what you're paying for. We lay the traps, create the fiction, put the right people in place, and hope it all works. Just like three years ago. You said yourself our plan was brilliant."

"It was, but it didn't work."

"What happened three years ago?" Polly asked.

Bruce smiled and said, "Let's save it for dinner."

A clerk walked in with three bulky manuscripts, all four inches thick. He dropped them on Bruce's desk, handed him the thumb drive, and left the room.

Lindsey said, "Well, I guess we have our work in front of us."

Polly said, "I really don't want to read that. The summary was tedious enough."

Bruce said, "I'm afraid you have no choice. You are both welcome to retire to my home and read on the porch, the veranda, in a hammock, or wherever. Noelle is there and she would enjoy having you around."

"Where are you going to read?" Polly asked.

"Right here. I'm fast and I need to keep an eye on the store just in case a lost customer stumbles in."

6.

Early reviews for *Pulse* were mixed. When they gathered for cocktails at dark on the veranda, the three weary readers compared notes. Bruce claimed to be almost finished, though he admitted he often skimmed as he blitzed through books. He was enjoying the story, said he was hooked. Lindsey professed to be no literary critic and her tastes ran to nonfiction and biography, but she was enjoying the story. The writing wasn't that great. Polly was hardly halfway through the pile of five hundred typewritten pages and seriously doubted if she could finish.

"Can you sell it?" she asked.

"Of course," Bruce replied. "Given Nelson's track record, some publisher somewhere will give us a contract. It's very commercial and the pages turn." Bruce did not miss Polly's use of the word "you," as if the probate court had already substituted him as Nelson's literary executor. He waited for her to ask "How much?" but she did not.

Noelle appeared with a bottle of white wine and refilled the glasses. She was certainly welcome to sit and join the conversation. Bruce had made it clear that he told her everything, but she left to check on dinner.

Bruce said, "I keep asking myself as I read how much of this can really be true. Is there really a drug that can prolong life in the sickest of old people? A drug whose true side effects are really unknown because the patients are comatose and dying anyway?"

Lindsey said, "It's bizarre, but right now we have to assume it's real. Nelson was murdered for a reason and until we know otherwise, we are assuming it's because of this novel."

"Which makes the informant all the more plausible," Polly said. "Because there was no way Nelson knew anything about this story. I've been on the Internet for two months and have found nothing even remotely similar to this scenario."

"Same here," Lindsey said. "If it's true, it's a deeply guarded secret."

"With billions on the line," Bruce said.

"So let's speculate," Polly said. "You're Nelson Kerr and you've written three bestsellers, none dealing with drugs, healthcare, the like. You're approached by an informant, probably someone working for the drugmaker or the nursing homes, and this informant wants to talk. He wants to expose the bad guys."

Bruce said, "And he also wants some money. He's sticking his neck out and he wants to be compensated."

"Why not just go to the FBI?" Polly asked.

"Because he's not sure it's a crime," Lindsey said. "The drug is prolonging lives, not killing people."

"But it's fraud, right?"

"Don't know. It's never been litigated, never been heard of. The informant isn't sure he'll get anything for blowing the whistle. He has a conscience. He's frightened. He needs his job. So he decides to approach Nelson Kerr, an author he admires."

Bruce said, "And Nelson started digging and asked too many questions. The bad guys realized they might have a problem, and they were probably watching him. When they realized what he was doing, they panicked and decided to take him out."

"A really stupid move," Lindsey said. "Think about it. It has already been reported that he died under suspicious circumstances during a hurricane. He had just finished a novel, his last one, and it's about to be published. Can you imagine the media frenzy when word leaks that the author was murdered? If you're the guy who ordered the hit, publicity is the last thing you want. There will be more people digging into the murder while the book is flying off the shelves. A really stupid move by someone."

"Agreed. But who?" Polly asked.

"We'll find out," Lindsey said.

"I'd like to hear your plan," Bruce said.

"We are paying for it," Polly added.

Lindsey relaxed in her chair and kicked off her sandals. She took a sip of wine and seemed to savor it. Noelle appeared in the doorway and said dinner would be ready in five minutes if anyone wanted to wash up.

Lindsey finally said, "Initially, we're moving on two fronts. The first one we've discussed and it calls for Bruce to become the literary executor, sell the book, and generate as much buzz as possible over the author's death. We hope that this will attract Nelson's informant. The second front involves the infiltration of the industry. There are eight companies that control ninety-five percent of all nursing home beds. Six are publicly traded, and because they answer to shareholders they generally comply with regulations and stay out of trouble. The other two are privately owned and both are bad actors. They get sued all the time and are notorious for health violations, shoddy recordkeeping, pathetic facilities, it's a long sad list. You wouldn't want anyone you know staying in one of their homes. Both are billion-dollar corporations. So, we go in."

Bruce and Polly were left hanging and waited for more. Finally, Bruce said, "You used the word 'infiltrate.'"

"Yes. We have methods. We're not the government, Bruce, and, as you know, we have ways of gathering information that some might consider in the gray areas. We never break laws, but we're also not bound by such legal niceties as probable cause and valid warrants."

Polly said, "Excuse me, but what are we talking about?"

"I'll explain it over dinner," Bruce said. "But you're working for us, Lindsey, and it's fair for us to ask if you operate outside the law."

"No. We know the gray areas. As do you, Bruce."

7.

Noelle was an excellent cook and her lobster ravioli was well received. The conversation was about flood insurance, or lack thereof, and how many people on the island were realizing that their losses were not covered. As with all storms, the early responders and aid groups were crucial and much appreciated, but with time they had moved on to the next disaster.

Bruce filled his wineglass and shoved his plate a few inches away. "So, Polly, I don't know if you recall, but three or four years ago some valuable manuscripts were stolen from the Firestone Library at Princeton. Though they were considered priceless, they were insured for twenty-five million. Princeton didn't want the money. It wanted the manuscripts. The insurance company didn't want to write a check, so it decided to track down the manuscripts. It hired Lindsey's firm."

Lindsey smiled and went along like a good sport.

"At the time, I was a pretty serious dealer in the rare book trade, a dark and murky world on the best of days, and I was even suspected at times of handling stolen rare books. Don't ask if I did that because I will not answer, and if I do answer I have been known to dabble in fiction, like my favorite writers."

Noelle said, "I'm not sure you should tell this story, Bruce."

"I will not tell everything. So, in the course of events, some people came to suspect me of having possession of the Princeton manuscripts. Again, don't ask. A very talented operative working for Lindsey's firm set up this elaborate plan to infiltrate my home, business, and circle of friends. The plan was to get really close to me, and snoop. They zeroed in on Mercer Mann and offered her enough money. She was broke and a good target. She also had a history with the island. Mercer showed up at her grandmother's cottage on the beach, said she would be here for six months to finish her novel. It was a great story, a great cover, and it worked perfectly. Until it didn't. She became a delightful friend of ours and she sat at this table many times. We adored Mercer, still do. A writer with enormous talent."

"Did she find the manuscripts?" Polly asked.

"No, but she got close enough to send in the FBI. They were a bit late. Barely. Some money changed hands and the manuscripts eventually made it back to Princeton. In the end, everybody was happy."

"And that's enough of that story," Noelle said.

"Indeed it is."

"Am I supposed to be impressed, or comforted?" Polly asked.

"Impressed," Bruce said. "Lindsey's firm is not cheap and it's worth the money we're paying."

8.

Jean-Luc finally died the week before Thanksgiving. Noelle seemed to take it well, though Bruce left her alone. If she was grieving he certainly didn't want to know about it. She was subdued for several days but put on her game face and did not mention her longtime boyfriend. Bruce had some business in New York and left the island for a week.

The more he left home, the more he thought about escaping. The island was frazzled and his neighbors were weary. Leo hit three and a half months earlier and with time it was becoming apparent that the recovery would take years. It was there every day, staring you in the face. A stretch of fence to mend or replace. An old tree with debris still stuck in the limbs. A leaky roof that no contractor had time to fix. An abandoned house too damaged to repair. A drainage ditch choked with garbage. A city park filled with FEMA trailers and desperate people sitting in lawn chairs around them, waiting for something. In the woods nearby, people even more desperate still living in tents.

For a spell, Bruce considered closing the store, taking a year off, running away to some exotic place with Noelle and doing nothing but reading all the great books he had neglected. He had no debts, plenty of money in the bank. He could call it a sabbatical or whatever and reopen at some time in the future when the island was whole again and the tourists were back. But the moment passed. Bay Books was too important to the island, and Bruce could not imagine life without it. That, plus he was loyal to his employees and customers.

The Christmas season was at hand, and one-third of all book sales took place during the holidays. He and his staff decided to decorate the store even more than usual, and keep longer hours, and offer more discounts and giveaways, and throw some parties. The island needed its bookstore to hold things together and remind everyone that life was returning to normal.

Bruce spent most of December at his desk reworking *Pulse*. He had always enjoyed editing the works of other writers, and he read so many popular novels that he could always tweak here and there and improve them. For the first and perhaps only time in his life, he now had the chance to fiddle with an entire manuscript. Bruce paid a typist to produce a clean draft, and when it was finished he coerced Bob Cobb into reading it. Bob was not that impressed with the writing or the story, but then he was often too critical of other writers. Nick was home from Venice, and Bruce shipped him a hard copy in Nashville. He read it in two days and said it would sell.

The first week in January, Bruce went to court with the probate lawyer and got himself appointed as the executor of Nelson's literary estate. The old judge had never heard of such a position, but was happy to sign the order nonetheless.

The following day, he sent the book to Nelson's former editor at Simon & Schuster. They had been discussing it for a month and its arrival was no surprise. Nelson had become unhappy with the editor for some vague reason that no longer mattered. Bruce, on behalf of the estate, was not looking for a fat contract. The book did not deserve one, and no publisher would be willing to overpay a dead writer who couldn't promote the book, let alone follow it with a sequel. And money was not an issue. Nelson's estate would eventually be a windfall to Polly and her parents, and they were not greedy people.

Left unsaid was the fact that Bruce didn't want a big contract. More money meant more publicity, especially when the word "murder" got tossed around, and Bruce was not looking forward to the attention. Ingrid was out there somewhere, and if not her then probably someone else. Lindsey Wheat was adamant in her belief that those responsible for Nelson's murder were not that smart and would not strike again, but then she worked in the shadows and few knew her name. Mr. Cable had been appointed by the court, with all the details available online.

A week later, the editor called and offered $250,000 for all rights—hardback, e-book, paperback, and foreign. The money was about half of what the book was worth, and had Bruce been a tough literary agent he would have stormed off and threatened an auction. But he was not, and since he was earning nothing from the transaction he pondered it for a day, pushed for $300,000 and got it.

In fact, the contract was perfect. It was generous enough to be fair to the estate but low enough not to raise eyebrows. Bruce emailed the editor a press release he had worked on for hours. It read:

THE LAST NOVEL OF POPULAR SUSPENSE WRITER NELSON KERR HAS BEEN PURCHASED BY SIMON & SCHUSTER, HIS LONGTIME PUBLISHER. THE NOVEL, *PULSE*, WILL BE RELEASED NEXT YEAR WITH AN ANTICIPATED FIRST RUN OF 100,000 COPIES. MR. KERR'S THREE PREVIOUS NOVELS—*SWAN CITY, THE LAUNDRY,* AND *HARD WATER*—WERE ALL PUBLISHED BY SIMON & SCHUSTER AND BECAME BESTSELLERS. HIS EDITOR, TOM DOWDY, SAID: "WE ARE DELIGHTED TO RECEIVE NELSON'S LATEST, THOUGH WE ARE STILL

DEVASTATED BY HIS DEATH. HE TALKED ABOUT THIS NOVEL FOR YEARS AND WE ARE CERTAIN HIS MANY FANS WILL ENJOY IT."

MR. KERR WAS A RESIDENT OF CAMINO ISLAND, FLORIDA, AND DIED UNDER MYSTERIOUS CIRCUMSTANCES LAST AUGUST DURING HURRICANE LEO. HIS DEATH IS STILL BEING INVESTIGATED BY THE FLORIDA STATE POLICE. HIS FRIEND AND BOOKSTORE OWNER BRUCE CABLE HAS BEEN APPOINTED AS HIS LITERARY EXECUTOR AND HANDLED THE SALE TO SIMON & SCHUSTER. MR. CABLE WAS NOT AVAILABLE FOR COMMENT.

THE ESTATE IS OFFERING A SIZABLE REWARD FOR INFORMATION REGARDING MR. KERR'S DEATH.

CHAPTER SEVEN
THE FICTION

1.

For the ambush, Lindsey Wheat wore a pair of loose-fitting jeans, white sneakers, and a beige blouse under a navy jacket. Dressing down was not easy for a woman who cared about her appearance, but slumming as she was, she still felt overdressed for the early morning crowd eager for chicken biscuits. She recognized Vera Stark the moment she walked in the door and glanced around as if guilty of something. She was twenty-six years old, black, married, a mother of three, and for the past four years had worked as an orderly at the Glinn Valley Retirement Center. Her husband drove a truck. They lived in a neat trailer in a park just outside the town limits of Flora, Kentucky, population 3,600.

Lindsey had called her cell phone an hour earlier as she was dropping her kids off at her mother's house for the day. Quite naturally, Vera was suspicious and didn't want to talk to a stranger. Lindsey, using an alias, had offered her $500 cash for ten minutes of her time, plus coffee and a biscuit.

She coaxed her to the table with a huge smile and a firm handshake, and they sat across from each other. The fact that Lindsey was also black helped ease the introduction. Vera glanced around again, certain there was trouble coming. Her older brother was in prison and the family had a history with the police.

Lindsey handed over an envelope and said, "Here's the money. I'm buying breakfast."

Vera took the envelope and shoved it into a pocket. "Thanks, but I'm not hungry." It was obvious she had not declined too many biscuits. "You a cop or something?" she asked.

"Not at all. I work for some lawyers out of Louisville and we're investigating nursing homes throughout the state. We sue a lot of them for neglect and abuse, and, as you probably know, Glinn Valley does not have a great reputation. I need some inside information and I'm willing to pay for it."

"And I need a job, okay? What I got ain't much, but they ain't no jobs around here."

"You will not get in trouble, I promise. Nothing is illegal, okay? We just need a set of eyes inside to make our cases stronger."

"Why me?"

"If not you, then we'll simply find someone else. We're offering two thousand a month cash for the next three months."

So far, Lindsey had left no trail. If Vera suddenly bolted, drove to work and told her boss about the meeting, they would never find her. She would disappear from the sad little town and never come back. But Vera was thinking about the money. She earned just over ten dollars an hour for a forty-hour week with no benefits. Her husband was about to be laid off. They lived from paycheck to paycheck, and if they missed a single one there was nobody to help.

Lindsey, of course, knew all of this. She pressed on with "It's easy money, Vera, and we're not asking you to do anything wrong."

"Well, it sure smells wrong."

"I assure you."

"And I'm supposed to trust you? Hell, we just met. You call me out of the blue and say meet me for a biscuit."

"We're offering a lot more."

"What am I supposed to do? Be a spy?"

"Something like that. The lawyers I work for are experts in the field of nursing home abuse. You've seen the cases."

"I ain't going to no courtroom, no ma'am."

"We won't ask you to. That's not part of your job."

"And so what happens if these lawyers bring all these cases to court and Glinn Valley goes bankrupt? What am I supposed to do then? Like I said, lady, there ain't no jobs around here. They pay me minimum wage to clean bedpans and you think I like it? No, I don't, but my kids also like to eat, now don't they?"

Lindsey was always quick to admit defeat. She would leave and go to the next name on the list. She raised her hands in mock surrender and said, "Thank you for your time, Ms. Stark. I've paid you. Have a nice day."

Vera said, "Three thousand a month for five months. That's fifteen thousand total, in cash, more than I clear after taxes for the year. First month in advance."

Lindsey smiled and studied her eyes. A hard life had sharpened her edges and made her nimble. Quietly, she said, "Deal."

Vera smiled too and said, "I don't even know your name."

Lindsey pulled out a business card with little accurate data on it. The name was Jackie Fayard. The phone number was for a burner with a monthly plan. The law firm's address was in downtown Louisville at a corporate registry, along with a hundred others. She said, "Don't bother calling the firm, because I'm never there."

"When do I get the advance?" Vera asked.

"Tomorrow, but let's meet at the Food Center on Main, by the produce, same time."

"I don't shop there. That's where the white folks go."

"All the more reason to go there. The meeting won't last five minutes."

"Okay, what am I looking for?"

"Let's start with the names of the patients with advanced dementia. Those who can't get out of bed."

"That's easy."

2.

On the other side of Flora, a colleague of Lindsey's, one Raymond Jumper, walked into a redneck dive and took a stool at the bar. Though the WHITES ONLY signs had long since been removed, their policies were still in effect. The blacks had their honky-tonks, the whites had their beer joints, and for everyone in town the nightlife was as segregated as ever. Jumper ordered a beer and began surveying the crowd. Two large young ladies were shooting pool. One of them was his target, a Miss Brittany Bolton, age twenty-two, single, no kids, a high school graduate currently taking night classes at a community college an hour away and living with her parents. For the past two years she had worked at Serenity Home, a facility in Flora that was marketed as a "retirement village" but was nothing more than a low-end nursing home operated by a company with a long history of cutting corners.

Jumper watched them butcher the game while laughing and talking nonstop, then he bought two bottles of beer and sauntered over. He was thirty-two, divorced, and knew his way around a pool table. He offered them fresh refills and talked his way into the game. An hour later they were in a booth eating nachos and drinking a pitcher of beer, courtesy of his expense account. His story was that he was in town for a couple of days investigating an accident for a law firm out of Lexington, and he was bored and looking for someone to talk to. The motel walls were closing in, so he'd headed for the nearest honky-tonk. He fancied neither woman and was careful with his flirting. Brittany in particular seemed eager for any of his advances.

Her friend, April, had a boyfriend who kept calling. Around 9:00 p.m., she finally had to go, leaving Jumper all alone with a thick young woman he had no desire to leave with. He asked about her job and she said she worked at a terrible place, a nursing home. Jumper seemed fascinated by this and asked questions. The alcohol kicked in and Brittany rambled on about her job and how much she hated it. The nursing home was always understaffed, primarily because it paid slightly more than minimum wage to orderlies, cooks, janitors, everyone but nurses and management. Patients were neglected in more ways than she wanted to talk about. Most of them had been forgotten by their families, and while she was sympathetic, she was just sick and tired of the place. She had bigger dreams. She wanted to become a nurse in a large hospital, a real job with a future, somewhere far away from Flora, Kentucky.

Jumper explained that he did a lot of work for a law firm that specialized in nursing home neglect, and finally asked the name of her employer. They drank some more beer and it was finally time to leave, either together or separately. Jumper claimed he had a long phone call to make and begged off after swapping phone numbers.

The following day, he called Brittany at work and said he wanted to talk. They met after hours at a pizza place and he bought dinner again. After a couple of beers, he said, "Serenity has fifty facilities in the Midwest and a lousy reputation in the business."

"I'm not surprised," she said. "I hate the place, hate my bosses, can't stand most of my coworkers, but that's no big deal because most will be gone in three months anyway."

"Has the facility here ever been sued?"

"Not sure. I've only been there for two years." She set down her beer mug and wiped her eyes. Jumper was surprised to realize she was crying. "Are you okay?"

She shook her head no as she wiped her cheeks with a paper napkin. He glanced around, hoping no one had noticed. No one had. There was a long gap in the conversation as he waited for her to say something.

She said, "You say you work for a law firm."

"I'm not on their payroll but I consult, primarily in nursing home cases."

"Can I tell you a story?" But it was not a question. "No one knows this but everyone should, okay?"

"Okay, I guess."

"There's this patient on my wing, a girl, we're the same age, twenty-two, so she's not really a girl, you know."

"A twenty-two-year-old woman in a nursing home?"

"Hang on. She was in a bad car wreck when she was a kid and has been brain-dead since she was four. She can breathe on her own, barely, and we keep her alive with a feeding tube, but she's been gone for a long time. Weighs less than a hundred pounds. You get the picture. Just pitiful. Her family moved away and forgot about her, and who can blame them? Not really any reason for a visit, you know. She can't open her eyes. Anyway, I have this coworker named Gerrard who's probably forty years old and is making a career there. A real loser who enjoys being the senior bedpan handler. Loves our patients and is always doing fun and games with them. You gotta worry about a man who's content making minimum wage with no benefits, but that's Gerrard. He's been there for fifteen years and just loves the place. However, I think he hangs around for another reason."

A pause. "Okay?" Jumper finally said.

"Sex."

"Sex? In a nursing home?"

"You'd be surprised."

"I've heard of it," Jumper said, though he had not.

She wiped her cheeks again with another paper napkin and took a sip of beer. "Gerrard likes to hang around this girl's room. I got suspicious a few months back but said nothing. There is no one to trust at the place, and everybody is afraid of getting fired. So one day I left my wing to go to lunch in the cafeteria. I passed Gerrard and told him a fib, told him I was going to Wendy's to pick up lunch and did he want anything. He said no. Ten minutes later I circled back. Her door was locked, which is against policy and very unusual. But her room adjoins the next one, with a bathroom in between. I had left the other door unlocked and Gerrard didn't check it. I peeked through the bathroom door and that son of a bitch was on top of the girl, raping her. I started to scream but couldn't. I started to pick up something and attack him, but I couldn't move. I don't remember backing away, don't remember anything until I got to the ladies' restroom where I sat on a toilet seat and tried to stop crying. I was a mess. I wanted to vomit. I couldn't think straight. I couldn't do anything but cry."

She wiped away some more tears.

"I made it through the day without seeing the creep. I checked on the girl and bathed her, something I still do every day. I managed to swab her vagina and I think I collected his sample. Still have it. That poor child, just lying there, dead to the world. I wanted to tell someone. I thought about my parents but they're not much help and wouldn't know what to do. I thought about talking to a lawyer but those people scare me. I can't imagine being on the witness stand in a courtroom with lawyers yelling at me and calling me a liar. So I waited. At one point I was determined to march into the manager's office and tell her everything, but I can't stand the woman. She always protects the company, so she can't be trusted. About a week later I saw Gerrard enter the girl's room and I followed him. I pointed my finger at him and said, 'Leave her alone.' He ran like a scared puppy. He has no spine. Anyway, time passed and here we are."

Raymond Jumper was fascinated by the tragic story but also stunned by it. It was not part of the plan. He had been hired by Lindsey Wheat and her mysterious company out of D.C. to bribe employees to turn over confidential patient records and, hopefully, medications. They had selected Brittany Bolton as their first prospect at Serenity Home. Now, Brittany had chosen him as her confidant. His brain spun as the story went off script. "And that's all?" he asked.

"One small late-breaking item," Brittany said. "The girl is pregnant. Imagine. Brain-dead for eighteen years, alive because of a tube, and now she's pregnant."

"Are you positive?"

"Almost. I bathe her every day, okay, and I'd say she's about six months along. No one else knows it. When she gives birth a quick DNA test will nail Gerrard. Since consent is out of the question, the company will be liable for . . ."

"Millions."

"That's what I thought. Millions. And he'll go to jail, right?"

"I would think so. Probably for a long time."

"Such a creep."

"And the company has insurance, so the matter will be settled quickly and quietly," Jumper said as he sipped his beer. "It's a gorgeous lawsuit."

"It's a killer. I've buried myself online and read a thousand cases of nursing home abuse. You know what, Raymond?"

"What?"

"I haven't found one nearly as good as this. And it's mine. I want a piece of it. I'm an eyewitness and I have his semen. And more importantly, I want out of this job and this town. I'm tired of bathing ninety-year-old men who want me to touch their privates. I'm tired of old saggy flesh, Raymond. Tired of bedpans, and bedsores, and tired of trying to make forgotten people feel good when they have no reason to feel good. I want out, and this is my ticket."

Jumper was nodding, already on board. "Okay, what's your plan?"

"I don't have one, but I'll bet some lawyer would pay me some money for what I know. What about the lawyers you work for?"

They don't exist, Jumper thought, but said, "Oh, I think they'd kill for this case. Assuming all the facts are in place."

"Facts? You doubt me?"

"No, but her pregnancy hasn't been confirmed yet. Gerrard hasn't been tested for DNA."

"The facts are there, Raymond, trust me. I like to think of myself as the whistleblower, the insider who gets paid for what she knows. Is there anything wrong with that, Raymond?"

"Not in my book."

Each took a bite of pizza and tried to sort things out. There were issues, scenarios, unknowns, and a lot at stake. Jumper washed his down with beer, wiped his mouth with the back of a sleeve, and said, "This could take months or years, and I'm on board. But right now I have a more pressing matter. The lawyers I work for need information from Serenity."

"What kind of information?"

"It's sort of vague right now, but they're concerned with the patients with advanced dementia, the poor folks who are bedridden, gone far away and not coming back. What's the slang for them?"

"'Nons,' 'veggies,' there are a number of nicknames for the nonresponsive. Call them anything you want because they don't care."

"And there are some at Serenity?"

"The place is full of them."

"Can you give me their names?"

"That's easy enough. I know a lot of them. We're down to a hundred and twenty-three patients and I could almost rattle off all the names."

"Why are you down?"

"Because they're dying like crazy, Raymond. It's the nature of the place. It'll fill up soon enough. I can't wait to get away."

"How many have advanced dementia?"

"A lot of them, and we're seeing more all the time. I have nineteen patients on my wing and seven of them haven't spoken a word in years. Feed 'em with a tube."

"What's in the tube?"

"Gunk. Geezer formula. We feed them four times a day and load 'em up with about two thousand calories. Usually we add the meds with the meal."

"How difficult would it be to get a list of their meds?"

"Is this illegal, Raymond? Are you asking me to do something that's illegal?"

"No, of course not. If you know what meds a patient is getting, and you tell me that over a beer, then no law is broken. But if you copy the file and hand it over, then we could be in trouble."

"Where's all this going?"

"It's headed for the courtroom eventually, but you won't be involved in that part of it."

"Is there any cash for this intel?"

"Yep. We'll pay two thousand bucks a month in greenbacks for the next few months."

"That's more than I clear at ten bucks an hour."

"Is the answer yes?"

"Sure, I guess, but you gotta promise me I won't get into trouble."

"I can't promise anything, Brittany. But if you're careful we'll be okay. I'm assuming security is not that tight."

"Are you kidding? Patients are getting raped by the staff. I could walk into the pharmacy tomorrow and walk out with anything I want, not that the good stuff is there. The manager forgets to lock her door half the time. The only guard is an old fart who should be a dementia patient down the hall. No, Raymond, security is not a priority at dear ole Serenity. Security costs money and that company cares about nothing but profits."

Jumper was amused. He offered his right hand across the pizza and she shook it.

3.

Glinn Valley was in a chain of ninety nursing homes owned by a private company called Barkly Cave, which was in turn owned by a private company called Northern Verdure. Layered above that were several other corporations in various states. Thankfully, through a federal investigation two years earlier, it was known that the entire and intentionally dense ownership structure came down to a group of investors in Coral Gables, Florida. Their front was called Fishback Investments, and it owned and operated 285 nursing homes in twenty-seven states. It was a shamelessly private corporation that was constantly at war with regulators about how much financial data it should reveal. It had been caught lying many times, with blame always pinned on some junior accountant who was immediately paid off and terminated. Its compliance history was pathetic. Its facilities habitually racked up some of the worst violations in the country, and lawsuits were common.

Even worse was the Serenity Home chain, owned by another shadowy group domiciled in the Bahamas and run by investors who'd never been to the islands. Its parent, Grattin Health Systems, ran 302 nursing homes in fifteen states, and ran them well, judging by the bottom line. According to a quite unflattering article in *Forbes,* Grattin had grossed just over $3 billion the prior year and netted 11 percent after taxes. The company stayed in hot water with every state where it did business because of shoddy facilities, third-rate medical care, inadequate staffing—the list was long and ugly. Lawsuits were a way of life, and another article in a legal magazine profiled two national firms that did nothing but stalk Grattin facilities and file suits. Grattin always settled quickly and quietly, but did little to improve its care. Because of the advanced ages and limited abilities of its patients, the lawsuits were not worth much. One of the lawyers was quoted as saying, "Most of our clients cannot physically or emotionally go through a challenging lawsuit, and Grattin knows it. You can't get those guys near a courtroom. They always settle."

No one from Grattin was available for comment, which was apparently the company's policy. The research painted a picture of a silent, spooked, even mummified outfit hiding bunker-like on the top floors of a high-rise in south central Houston.

Lindsey Wheat met with both law firms that stalked the company but was unable to obtain anything of value. The firms admitted they had little because there had been, over the years, almost no discovery. She wanted the names of the medications prescribed to dementia patients, and neither firm would budge. In return for settlements, the law firms had signed many confidentiality agreements with Grattin and the files remained protected by the company.

4.

With both Vera Stark and Brittany Bolton on the payroll, the fiction was playing out as planned. The only hitch was the rape allegation, and Lindsey and Raymond were still kicking it around.

For the fiction, Lindsey had rented a small, thoroughly nondescript house on the outskirts of Lexington, an hour north of Flora. The den had been converted into an office-like war room with folding tables and maps tacked to walls. The largest was an enlarged highway grid of Kentucky, with colored pinpricks scattered about the state. Fishback Investments had thirteen facilities in the state; Grattin, nineteen.

If her first two informants delivered, Lindsey and her team might be able to avoid moving into another town. But if Vera and Brittany got cold feet, or otherwise fell flat, she would have to go back to the map and start over. So far, Vera had provided the names of eighteen patients with dementia so advanced they were bedridden, tube-fed, and thoroughly nonresponsive. At the moment, there were 140 patients at Glinn Valley in Flora, so it was about the same size as Serenity. From there, Brittany had identified twenty-four patients.

Lindsey's experts were predicting a nonresponsive number of about 25 percent for both companies' facilities in Kentucky. Her legal advisers had analyzed the rape case from all angles and had arrived at the obvious conclusion: It was a massive law-suit that would be difficult to lose, but also difficult to handle. It would have to be brought by the rape victim's family, one that appeared to be unsettled, even chaotic. Money might soothe a lot of tension, but the case would be high-maintenance. And then there was the issue of the unwanted baby. There was not a single stable marriage in either the victim's close or extended family, so the potential for a lot of nasty infighting was high.

But none of that really mattered, at least not to Lindsey Wheat and her project. Her priority was building trust with Vera Stark and Brittany Bolton, and somehow getting her hands on the medications. The labs were waiting.

She met Vera on a cold Saturday morning in January at a laundromat just off Main Street in Flora. The place was crowded and they couldn't talk. Vera slipped her a piece of yellow folded paper and said, "Four more."

Lindsey insisted that they do nothing by text or email because everything leaves a trail. Phones were to be used only to arrange meetings.

She thanked Vera, left Flora, and drove to the small town of Harrodsburg. Promptly at 10:00 a.m., Raymond Jumper walked into the omelet shop and took a seat across from her. A waitress poured coffee as they looked at the menus.

An attractive black woman in her early fifties sitting with a nice-looking white guy in his early thirties. It should not have been a problem, and it wasn't, really. But why were they getting more looks than normal? Both chose to ignore the locals.

Raymond said, "Any luck with Vera?"

Lindsey laid her menu on the table and said, "Four more names. You?"

"Three, up to twenty-four, and Brittany thinks that might be all. Saw her last night in a bar. The girl loves her beer, nachos, and pizza."

"I don't think Vera is ready to raid the pharmacy. What about Brittany?"

"We talked about it. To answer an earlier question, she routinely handles the feeding tubes, but the food and meds are prepared by someone else. They bring her the syringe filled with a mixture of formula and meds, and she inserts it into the feeding tube. She doesn't see the meds but she thinks some are liquid, some are ground-up pills, others are capsules that have been opened and crushed. As she has said, security is not tight at the pharmacy and she's not afraid to go in, but she has no idea what to look for."

"Is she willing to try?"

"I don't know. We discussed it. Verbally giving us names is one thing. Stealing meds is another. She's not so sure about it. Of course, all she wants to talk about is the lawsuit. I strung her along, told her I would discuss it with some lawyers whenever she's ready."

"I like the idea of you advising Brittany about the lawsuit. It builds trust and familiarity. Caution her, though, that it's not her lawsuit. She could well be the most important witness, but she's not entitled to a pile of money."

"She read somewhere, and she is reading far too much, that in some cases the whistleblower gets twenty percent of the settlement. You know anything about that?"

"I only know that every case is different, so the rewards vary greatly. Keep her talking about it. Also, ask her how difficult it would be to walk out with a loaded syringe. We could give her a substitute filled with food and water but no meds. She swaps it, feeds the patient, everything is fine. Our lab technicians are confident they can identify the medications."

"What kind of medications?"

"You got a couple of hours? It's a long list. Diuretics and beta blockers for high blood pressure. Antibiotics for bedsores and infections—almost all have bedsores and they can be fatal. Protein supplements for healthier skin to fight the bedsores. Metformin or any one of a hundred others for diabetes. Coumadin for blood clots. Something for the thyroid. Aricept for dementia. Antidepressants. I could go on."

"These people have been in comas for years and they're getting antidepressants?"

"Happens all the time. Approved by Medicaid and Medicare."

"Is the nursing home in the business of selling pills?"

"Not really. The drugs and their prices are tightly regulated. But if one is approved, you can bet it's being used."

A waitress finally made it over and poured coffee. Lindsey ordered an omelet and Raymond asked for pancakes. When she was gone he said, "Brittany told me something interesting last night. She said that the nonresponders, she calls them Nons, get the best treatment of all. They are fed on time. They get the best meds. Their beds are cleaner. They get more attention from the staff. The care for the other patients is pretty lousy, even abusive at times, but not the Nons."

"They're more valuable," Lindsey said. "The longer they live, the more money they draw." Raymond Jumper was just a freelance investigator who had never heard of Nelson Kerr and didn't have a clue as to who was behind the fiction. He was being paid a hundred dollars an hour to do a job and was discouraged from asking questions.

Lindsey said, "I want Brittany to swap syringes. See if she can borrow an empty one, give it to you so we'll know the make and model, then she can take it back. No crime there. Ask her if she can get the name of the formula. Our plan will be to load up one of ours, hand it to her in exchange for a real one. She'll make the swap. I doubt if anyone will be watching."

Jumper grimaced and shook his head. He said, "I don't know, might take some time. She's not ready yet. How about your girl?"

"She's not ready either. I think Brittany is our best bet."

"I'll get it done. I may have to sleep with her, but I'll get it done."

"Attaboy."

Jumper's phone rattled and he yanked it out of his pocket. Lindsey picked up hers, and for ten minutes they returned texts and emails. The food arrived and they finally put down their phones. Jumper said, "Got a question."

"All right."

"Why not just hack into the nursing home's records and get all the information you want? Its security is lousy. Any decent hacker could do the job overnight. I got some friends."

"It's against the law, plain and simple." Lindsey realized she sounded a bit too pious. The truth was that they had hacked before and would do so again. Their hackers were far better than anything they faced. But the real truth was that the mysterious drug they were looking for would not be in any patient's records.

CHAPTER EIGHT
THE INFORMANT

1.

On a warm breezy day in early March, Bruce was sitting at his desk and enjoying his coffee as he opened the daily mail for the store, something he still insisted on doing after almost twenty-four years. He also insisted on opening each of the countless boxes of new books that arrived three times a week. He loved the smell and feel of each new book, and he especially enjoyed finding the perfect place on the shelves for each one. And he habitually boxed up all the unsold books and sent them back to the publishers as returns, acts of defeat that still depressed him.

A plain envelope, light lemon yellow in color, was addressed to him at Bay Books on Main Street in Santa Rosa. The address was typed in all-caps on a label, and there was nothing for the return. It was postmarked in Amarillo, and at first glance it looked like nothing but junk mail, and he almost tossed it in the wastebasket. Then he opened it. On a plain yellow sheet of paper the sender had typed:

THE LAST PERSON I TALKED TO ABOUT THIS WAS NELSON AND WE
KNOW WHAT HAPPENED TO HIM. DO YOU THINK WE SHOULD HAVE
A CONVERSATION?

Attached to it was a yellow index card with the message:
*Crazy Ghost is a chat room for anonymous mail. Costs $20 for a month,
credit card. The address there is: 3838Bevel.*

Bruce placed the letter and the card on his desk, took his
coffee cup and went upstairs to the café and rinsed it out. He
dried it, poured another cup, stared out the window, spoke to no
one because the place was deserted, and went back to his office.
He went online, couldn't find anything, and walked to the front
cashier and asked a twenty-year-old tattooed part-timer about
the site. In less than three minutes the kid, without looking
up from his screen, said, "It looks legit. One of the private chat
rooms from overseas, either Singapore or the Ukraine, there
are a bunch of them, and they burn the messages five to fifteen
minutes or so after they're put up. Twenty bucks a month."

"Would you use it?" Bruce asked.

"You don't pay me enough."

"Ha ha. In other words, what do you do when you want
complete privacy?"

"I use sign language. Seriously, I assume nothing is private
on the Internet so I post only what I don't care about. Texting is
a bit more private."

"But you wouldn't be afraid of this?"

"Probably not. You laundering money again?"

"Ha ha." This, from a twenty-year-old kid. No respect.

Bruce went to the site, paid with a credit card, and said hello
to 3838Bevel.

Bay Books here. Anybody home? Got the message.
    050BartStarr.

Fifteen minutes passed, there was no answer, and his message vanished. He waited half an hour and tried again with the same result. With meaningful work now impossible, he puttered around his First Editions Room and tried to appear busy. He got a response on his third attempt.

Bevel here. What was Faulkner's last novel?
The Reivers.
And Hemingway's?
Old Man and the Sea.
Styron's?
Sophie's Choice.
Did Nelson's last one have more than one title?
Don't know.
"Pulse" is a nice title.
The book is pretty good too. What's our risk here, on this site?
Are you a techie?
No, a cave man.
We're safe. But you can assume some nasty folks are watching
    you.
Same ones who got Nelson?
Yep. Put nothing in writing. Assume they're listening to your calls.
This is pretty intense.
So are they. Look at Nelson. Gotta run. 2 pm tomorrow.

Bruce stared at the screen until the entries faded. When it dawned on him that they were indeed gone forever, he scrib-

bled down as much as he could remember. He left the store and
walked to a wine bar where he ordered a seltzer water and pre-
tended to read a magazine. He decided he would not tell Noelle
until later. It could be a significant moment in the Nelson mystery, or not.

No, it had to be significant.

Little progress was made the following day during their second exchange. Bruce asked:

Why the letter?
We need to talk but not sure if we can.
About Nelson?
You catch on fast.
Look, if you want to talk, then let's do it. So far we're just
     dancing.
That's probably safer.
Do you know who killed him?
I have a pretty good idea.
Why keep quiet?
Oh that's much safer, believe me. Now there's another dead
     body.
Am I expected to respond?
A young lady in Kentucky.
Again, I'm treading water.
Better go. Same time tomorrow.

Bruce tried to print the exchange but the site wouldn't allow
it. He quickly scribbled down the words.

The following day, Bevel was a no-show. Same for the day
after. Bruce did not want to alarm Noelle, so he didn't tell her.

2.

Two days later, Bruce flew to Washington Dulles and went to his hotel room near the airport. Three hours later, Nick Sutton arrived by car and brought a girl with him, which Bruce had not anticipated. Nick assured him she would not get in the way and had family in the area.

After a leisurely semester abroad in Venice, Nick was drifting through his final weeks at Wake Forest and claimed to be in a funk at the prospect of leaving college. Bruce had little sympathy and told the kid it was time to get off his ass and find a real job, not the usual summertime bookstore gig where he split his time between reading crime novels and stalking college girls on the beach. Nick wanted to write fiction for a living and do it the old-fashioned way, with a big advance that allowed him to work at a leisurely pace of a few pages a day before long lunches and plenty of booze. His dream was to become a famous writer and hell-raiser at a young age, much in the tradition of Hemingway, Faulkner, and Fitzgerald, though he planned to put aside literary aspirations and write mysteries that would sell. Bruce thought he had talent but was already worried about his work ethic.

They quickly retired to the hotel bar and ordered sandwiches, without the girl. Bruce summarized the developments in the state's investigation, of which there were few, and described his own efforts to solve the crime with Alpha North Solutions. Nick loved the idea of hiring a secretive security outfit to handle an investigation that the police were in the process of botching.

Bruce wanted him in the room because, so far, his instincts had been near-perfect. And because he was only twenty-one, he was far tech-savvier than Bruce could ever hope to be.

Bruce showed him the transcript of the two exchanges with 3838Bevel.

"A huge step in the right direction," Nick said with a satisfied smile. "This is our guy, the snitch who knows it all and contacted Nelson with the goods. Beautiful."

"But he's gone silent. How do we get him back in the loop?"

"Money. That was his motivation to begin with. How much did you get for the novel?"

"Three hundred thousand."

"Has that been reported?"

"No, but the sale has. Bevel certainly knows there's a book deal."

"And Bevel wants the cut that Nelson promised. He's not going away, but he's also afraid of his shadow."

"So what's our next move?"

"We wait. He'll contact you because he needs you, not the other way around. Your goal is to solve Nelson's murder. If you fail, your life goes on unchanged. He ain't your brother. But Bevel here wants the money Nelson promised. For him it's a definite game changer."

3.

Promptly at nine Friday morning, Bruce and Nick entered the nameless mirrored tower where Alpha North Solutions hid itself. Lindsey Wheat met them at the elevator and Bruce introduced Nick, who drew a look with his faded jeans, battered sneakers, colorful T-shirt, and oversized sports coat with tattered elbow patches.

"Nick here was a friend of Nelson's and was with me when

we discovered his body," Bruce said, almost apologetically, though he didn't care if she approved or not. He was paying her.

They followed her to her office, with Nick soaking up all of the surroundings, what little there were. The interior designer who outfitted the place had apparently been ordered to avoid all color and warmth.

They gathered around a small conference table and prepared their coffees. Bruce cared little for chitchat, and when Lindsey asked Nick for his plans after college, Bruce said, "Look, let's skip the preliminaries. You have news. I have news. Let's get on with it."

She smiled and said, "Indeed." Then she picked up a report, adjusted her reading glasses, and began, "We infiltrated three nursing homes in rural Kentucky. One owned by Fishback, one by Grattin, one by Pack Line Retirement. As you know, Fishback and Grattin are privately owned and have deplorable compliance histories. Pack Line is the worst of the publics. More about them later. We started in Flora, Kentucky, a backwater little town of three thousand, and quickly managed to sign up a couple of employees. The first was Vera Stark at Glinn Valley, the Fishback facility. I handled Vera myself and slowly brought her along. She provided the names of the advanced dementia patients, the nonresponsive ones, more commonly referred to by staff as 'Nons,' as I have learned, along with several other nonflattering nicknames. After she gave us the names, I convinced her to research the types of formula and meds that are tube-fed to the patients. Because the place is perpetually understaffed, Vera began volunteering to handle the feedings, something that is not unusual. The syringes are usually loaded in the pharmacy and given to the staff on duty, but security is not tight. Rules and procedures are not always followed. She lifted a new syringe, brought it to me, and I ordered a box of the same. We loaded a substitute with the same formula and Vera agreed to swap it with a real one. Over the course of two weeks, she made about three dozen swaps from four Nons, giving us plenty of samples to analyze. The bottom line is that there is nothing suspicious being administered to these patients, not at Glinn Valley. As far as Vera could tell, the meds are always given with the feedings, three or four times a day. She also noted that the Nons receive much better care than the other patients. Plenty of calories and water, cleaner beds, hourly turnings, and so on. Gotta keep 'em alive, you know.

"Meanwhile, a colleague named Jumper was handling a young lady named Brittany Bolton, an orderly at Serenity Home, a Grattin facility across town. Brittany's story became far more complicated because she planned to be a star witness in an abuse case. Seems she saw one of her coworkers raping a young lady who's been brain-dead for a long time. Brittany claimed the girl was pregnant and she was probably right. Brittany did the same syringe swap and gave us over forty samples from seven different patients. Our lab technicians here in D.C. found the usual concoction of various formulas and meds for blood pressure, diabetes, dementia, blood clotting, blood thinner, blood thickener, pretty much the entire menu. Plus some vitamins. And then they found something they could not identify. A mysterious ingredient that was neither food nor vitamin. And it appeared in all forty samples Brittany lifted from Serenity. Our scientists ran test after test but got nowhere. So Jumper went back to Brittany and said we needed more, we needed to get inside the pharmacy.

"This would take time. I moved on to the third facility, a Pack Line Retirement home in an even more rural area about an hour from Flora. I made contact with a twenty-year-old newly-wed father with a kid, working for thirteen dollars an hour. Because Pack Line is a public company its pay scale is slightly better. He needed cash and took the deal. We eventually got samples from five Nons, and all checked out. Nothing suspicious.

"Back to Brittany. She volunteered to work double shifts so she would be on the floor late at night. We gave her a list of every medication and vitamin that the labs had identified so far, and she memorized it. She already knew most of the meds anyway. Without creating suspicion, she managed to learn her way around the pharmacy and realized that she could leave with certain over-the-counter items—aspirin, cough drops, Band-Aids, and so on—almost any time she wanted. Because of staffing issues, she told her supervisor that she was willing to learn how to handle the food and meds for the feedings. Eventually, she walked out with a jar of something called vitamin E3, a generic-looking capsule that could pass for almost any supplement. Don't know how much you know about vitamins but there is no such thing as E3. It sent off alarms in the lab and went through every possible test. The bottom line is that it's an obscure drug called Flaxacill, one that's never been on the market. It's never been approved anywhere because no one has tried to get it approved. The story is that it was accidentally created as some by-product in a Chinese lab twenty years ago and was tested on a few human guinea pigs over there. It was dropped immediately when they realized that the drug causes vomiting and blindness."

"That would pose a challenge for marketing, even for a drug company," Bruce quipped, but it fell flat.

"Apparently it's an easy drug to make and is produced only on demand."

"So what does the drug do?" Bruce asked.

"Keeps the heart beating, barely, but only in people who are practically brain-dead anyway. It stimulates the medulla, the lower half of the brain stem that connects to the spinal cord and controls our involuntary functions like breathing, heart rate, swallowing, blood pressure. Pretty important little area."

Nick added, "It also causes vomiting, which explains that side effect."

"Correct."

"And no one knows the patients are blind, because they can't open their eyes, right?" Bruce added.

"Exactly."

Nick said, "So Nelson was on to something."

"He certainly was. He knew about this drug, and the only way he could have possibly learned of its existence was through an informant, someone with deep connections at Grattin."

"Thought so," Nick said, almost under his breath. He shot a quick smug smile at Bruce, who could only shake his head.

"And what happened to Brittany?" Bruce asked.

Lindsey slowly took a sip of coffee while staring at Bruce. "Do you know what happened?"

"Yes, I do, and the question is whether you planned to tell me."

"Yes, I was going to tell you. She's dead."

"Opioid overdose, according to the newspaper over in Kentucky. You believe that?"

"No, not really. It got real complicated and it's far from over. We're done, but the plot thickens. Evidently there was a surveillance camera in the pharmacy that Brittany did not notice. She was seen lifting the vitamin E3 along with other medications. Maybe pain pills, maybe not. We really don't know. They kept a fair amount of the heavy stuff in the pharmacy but usually under lock and key. If Brittany lifted the opioids, we didn't know about it. There are a few cameras around the facility but hardly anyone to monitor them. A colleague named Gerrard, a real character, had access to the cameras and he had noticed Brittany's new and sudden interest in the pharmacy. It appears that Gerrard doesn't miss much. He kept the footage for future extortion. He and Brittany despised each other. Not long afterward, she caught him in the room with the pregnant patient and they had a huge fight. She accused him of getting the girl pregnant and threatened to tell a lawyer. He accused her of stealing meds and said he had the video to prove it. He showed the video to the director and Brittany was fired on the spot. Two days later, the pregnant girl died 'of complications.' Brittany was certain that Gerrard juiced her with a mix of drugs. Her body was immediately sent to her mother in Ohio and buried quickly. The lawsuit was gone. The company then knew that Brittany had lifted some E3, although at the time our lab work wasn't finished and we didn't know about the drug. Neither did Brittany. Jumper suggested that she leave town for a spell and we even offered to send her away. She was thinking about this when she died."

"And, she died how?"

"She was in a crowded bar last Saturday night, drinking heavily, and apparently someone spiked her drink. From there

we don't know. Her body was found in a ditch behind the bar.
Official cause was too much oxycodone, which is hard to believe
since she was drinking and partying with friends and not swallowing pain pills. My guess is that someone grabbed her as she
was fading, injected her with a massive dose, and left her for
dead."

"The same people who killed Nelson," Nick said.

Lindsey nodded in agreement but said nothing. Bruce said,
"So, in a way, we're responsible for her death."

"I disagree," she said. "No more so than Nelson's. The people doing the killing are running scared and trying to hide dirty
secrets. They knew Brittany filched the E3 and they could take
no chances. They also knew that Nelson knew, and they wanted
to silence him."

"I'm sorry," Bruce said. "But I feel some level of responsibility. You assured me that you do not break laws."

"Look, Bruce, in this line of work we often operate in the
gray areas. We didn't steal the bottle of E3, rather, we borrowed
it and then took it back."

Bruce exhaled in frustration, stood, and walked around the
room, obviously bothered. Lindsey watched him with a tight,
smug smile as if she had no concerns. He would come around
because he had no choice.

Finally, Bruce said, "I don't buy it, Lindsey. I'm sorry. Those
two girls are dead because of our, what do you call it, 'infiltration.'"

"Our hands are clean, Bruce," she replied coolly, completely
unruffled. "The patient had been brain-dead for years. If she
was raped and impregnated, that's hard to pin on us. As for
Brittany, we had nothing to do with her murder."

"How can you say that? We had everything to do with it. Under your scenario, she was murdered because she swiped a bottle of their secret drug, one that they are, evidently, quite touchy about. And she 'borrowed' the E3 at your suggestion and direction. You were paying her. That implicates the hell out of us."

"She was sloppy, Bruce. Jumper warned her repeatedly about surveillance cameras, especially around the pharmacy. She got herself caught on video—"

"While she was stealing for you, for us. I can't believe this. Nick, help me out here."

Nick shrugged and raised his hands in mock surrender and said, "I'm just a college boy and right now I'd love to be back on campus. What am I doing here?"

"Thanks for nothing," Bruce shot back.

"Don't mention it."

Lindsey, eager to control the narrative, said, "We are not implicated because we committed no crime, and nothing we did in Kentucky can be traced to us. As I promised you up front, we are very careful and we know what we're doing. Brittany was handled in a proper fashion and she simply missed a surveillance camera."

"So let's blame her for getting herself killed," Bruce said.

"If she had noticed the camera she would probably be alive."

"I'm not believing this." Bruce was standing in the window, peering through the blinds, talking over his shoulder.

Nick cleared his throat and asked, "Is her death being investigated?"

"Yes, sort of. There was an autopsy but I don't know the results. If they find traces of club drugs they'll know they've got a problem."

"Club drugs?" Bruce asked.

Nick said, "Roofies, GHB, Ecstasy, Special K, the usual date rape stuff."

"Jumper says there's a rumor that a witness saw her outside the bar with a stranger. Who knows? It's hard to have confidence in the local boys in rural Kentucky."

Nick said, "Well, we got the Florida State Police on the ball and they haven't made it halfway to first base."

"We had nothing to do with Brittany's death," Lindsey said defensively.

"You keep saying that," Bruce said, still talking to the blinds. "Who are you trying to convince?"

"You know, Bruce, I'm a bit perplexed by your tone and attitude. We are in a gray area here and that's often where we are forced to go. Need I remind you of where you were three years ago when our company first met you? The stolen manuscripts? You were so far out of bounds you weren't even near a gray area."

"What happened three years ago?" Nick asked.

"None of your business," Bruce snapped.

"Just thought I'd ask."

Bruce suddenly turned around and took a few steps toward Lindsey. He glared at her, pointed a finger, said, "Your company is fired as of now. Close the file and keep the change. Don't lift another finger on behalf of me or the estate of Nelson Kerr. Send me a termination letter."

"Come on, Bruce."

"Let's go, Nick." Nick jumped to his feet and followed Bruce through the door. Lindsey Wheat kept her cool and took another sip of coffee.

4.

Nothing was said as they drove the seven minutes to their hotel. Nothing was said as they entered it and walked through the lobby and went straight to the bar. Both ordered coffee, though both really wanted a drink. Nick managed to keep quiet and knew that Bruce should speak first.

When the coffee arrived, both ignored it. Finally, Bruce rubbed his eyes and said, "You think I'm wrong?"

"No. There's something about her I don't like and I'm not sure she would ever tell the whole story."

"We don't need her anymore, Nick. That's one reason I walked out. We know the name of the company, the name of their secret drug, and the informant has made contact with me. We never told Miss Lindsey about the secret messages. We debated that and thankfully we didn't say anything. She'd probably screw it up or get someone else killed. Probably me. They almost got Mercer hurt three years ago."

"Then why'd you hire them?"

"Because they're good. They found the drug, Nick. Who else could have done that? The Florida State Police? The yokels in Kentucky? Not even the FBI, because they have to play by the rules."

"Are you going to tell me the story?"

"I'll tell you part of the story and if you ever breathe a word I'll take away your employee discount."

"It's only twenty percent. At Barnes and Noble it's forty."

"I can't do this over coffee. I need a drink."

"Me too."

Bruce walked to the bar and brought back two beers. He

took a mighty gulp and smacked his lips. "You remember when the Fitzgerald manuscripts were stolen from Princeton, about four years ago?"

"Sure. Big story. Somebody paid a ransom and the thieves returned the manuscripts."

"Something like that. The stolen loot was on Camino Island. It's a long story."

"For this, I have all the time in the world."

5.

In the normal scheme of things, Camino Island came to life each year in the middle of March when students on spring break headed in droves to Florida. They took over the beach hotels and condos and summer rentals, and they drank and danced and frolicked on the beaches because they were nineteen years old and weary from the rigors of study. Daddy could afford it. Daddy was told it was simply part of the entire college experience. And Daddy himself had probably been drunk and sunburned for an entire week back in the day.

But the island was still wounded, so the parties went farther south. A few hotels had reopened but there was construction everywhere. The last thing the recovery needed was twenty-five thousand young idiots loose in the streets. Quietly, the island advertised that it was not yet open for business. Come back next year and we'll be ready.

When Ole Miss turned them loose, Mercer and Thomas packed up the dog and their shorts and headed for the island. Larry had finished the repairs to the cottage and Mercer was eager for a week away from the classroom. She was also excited about her first book party since Leo had ruined her last one. For weeks, Bruce had insisted on throwing a "major author event" and wouldn't take no for an answer. The paperback of *Tessa* had just been released and Mercer had signed on for another grueling summer tour to promote it. Bruce insisted that the first stop be at Bay Books and harangued the publisher into underwriting half of it.

The party began on Saturday afternoon with barbecue and a bluegrass band on the sidewalk and street in front of the store. The locals needed some fun, and the crowd was large and continued to grow. At 3:00 p.m., Mercer took her spot downstairs behind a table, with stacks of books all around her, and greeted her admirers.

She chatted them up, posed for dozens of photos and selfies, autographed the paperbacks and some hardbacks as well, held a couple of babies, signed the cast on a broken arm, answered questions from people who claimed they knew Tessa, did a quick interview with the island's newspaper, and all in all had a delightful time being the popular author with a long line of fans snaking out the front door.

When Bruce wasn't working the crowd and selecting other titles for certain preferred customers, he and Thomas and Bob Cobb sat outside on the balcony and sipped tequila. The music switched to reggae late in the afternoon and the air was filled with soothing music and plenty of laughter. Benny's Oyster Truck arrived at five and a crew began shucking on the side street. Two kegs of beer materialized from somewhere and attracted the faithful.

It was springtime and the weather was perfect.

At six, Mercer moved upstairs where a hundred folding

chairs had been arranged for her reading. Three years earlier during her brief sabbatical on the island she had attended several author talks in the same space, and at the moment she couldn't help but remember the twinge of jealousy she had felt for those touring writers who were publishing, selling, and drawing crowds. Now, it was her turn at the podium.

Leigh and Myra were in the front row, as always, and they beamed at her like proud grandparents. Leigh appeared ready to cry. Next to her was Amy Slater, the vampire girl, present with her husband and all three kids. Andy Adam stood in a corner with a diet drink and smiled at Mercer. Jay Arklerood, the sour poet, was in the second row and looked out of place, as always. Mercer was certain that Bruce had threatened him to compel his attendance. His last book, a thin collection of incomprehensible free-verse poems, had sold only a thousand copies across the country. Bay Books was responsible for half of them. If Bruce wanted a favor, Jay couldn't say no.

Back in the good old days, before Leo, the store hosted several author events each week. Some of the writers were popular with large followings that made for easy draws. But others were the rookies or mid-list authors wanting desperately to sell more, and for them Bruce guaranteed a crowd. He did so by calling, cajoling, charming, and strong-arming his friends and loyal customers. To him, a small turnout was a crushing defeat, one he simply couldn't tolerate.

And he was determined to make Mercer Mann a success. He admired her as a writer and adored her as a person, and with her he dreamed of doing something he had never fully accomplished: to make her a literary star, one who could slay the critics while selling books. He, Bruce Cable, wanted to be responsible for her greatness. No one knew this, not even Noelle, though she knew he was quite fond of Mercer. She had the talent, but he wasn't sure about the drive, the ambition.

She smiled at Bruce and Thomas near the back and began her talk. She was delighted to be back, as always, and impressed with the resiliency of the island. It had been six months since her last visit and she marveled at the recovery. She was grateful for the thousands of volunteers and hundreds of nonprofits who had rushed down to help. She switched gears and talked about her summers on the island—every summer from the age of seven through nineteen she stayed with Tessa, her beloved grandmother. Her parents were divorced. Her mother was ill. For nine months she suffered at home in Memphis with a father who had no interest in her. She begged him to let her live with Tessa permanently, but he wouldn't yield.

Thomas watched and listened with enormous pride. He had accompanied her the previous summer on her thirty-four-stop book tour, and he had heard these stories at least as many times. Her transformation, though, had been remarkable. Never timid, she had gone from being a chatty speaker who ran out of things to say after thirty minutes, to a seasoned raconteur who could tell the same story three different ways and draw tears with each telling. By the end of the tour, no audience wanted her to stop after only an hour.

And Thomas knew a deep secret that one day soon everyone else would know. Mercer was hard at work on her next novel. She had written half of it, and it was brilliant, by far her best work to date. Bruce, of course, had, over drinks, already tried to pry out anything to do with the next novel, and Mercer had warned Thomas about this. So he admitted only that she was working but keeping it all to herself.

She opened up the discussion with questions from the floor, and when it became obvious they might go on for hours, Bruce pulled the plug at 7:30 and said Mercer needed dinner. He thanked her, hugged her, and made her promise to return soon with the next novel. The crowd stood and applauded loudly. Both Leigh and Myra were in tears.

6.

They walked as a group to the Marchbanks House, four long blocks from the store. Noelle, who had sort of enjoyed the first five hundred or so book signings but had long since stopped attending them, was fussing around the kitchen and veranda, waiting for her guests. All went straight to the bar, where Bruce and Noelle fixed drinks. Andy Adam finished another diet soda, gave Mercer a hug, and drifted away. After a round or two, Noelle called them to order and got them seated.

For a second, Bruce flashed back to last August when his little literary mafia had gathered at the same table. It was their last gathering before Leo, and his friend Nelson Kerr sat right over there to his left and seemed to enjoy the evening. Twenty-four hours later he would be dead.

It was Mercer's day and all talk revolved around her, though she was weary of the attention. Salads were served, wine was poured. The spring air turned chilly and Bruce lit an outdoor heater. Hours passed as everyone seemed to talk at once.

After dessert, Bruce abruptly stood and reached for Noelle.

As they held hands, he said, "Attention please. I have an important announcement. Tomorrow evening at exactly six p.m., you are invited to a wedding on the beach. Your attendance is not voluntary, but rather mandatory."

"Who the hell's getting married?" Myra blurted.

"We are."

"It's about time."

"Hang on. You see, many years ago Noelle and I got married in the South of France. We were in a small, rustic village near Avignon, and we walked into this gorgeous little church that was five hundred years old. The place was so beautiful, so awe-inspiring, that we decided, on the spot, to get married there. So we did. No priest, no paperwork. Nothing official. We made up some vows and declared ourselves husband and wife. So for the past twenty years we've been—"

"Living in sin," Myra blurted.

"Something like that. Thank you. And so now we have some paperwork, and we'll have a real minister, and we'll do it the right way. We will pledge our everlasting love, and faithfulness, to each other."

The word "faithfulness" stunned them. Their jaws dropped and a couple actually gasped. Was the open marriage finally coming to a close? Was Bruce Cable, playboy extraordinaire and legendary stalker of lonely female authors on tour, finally growing up? Was Noelle finished with her French-style affairs across the ocean?

Myra, on a roll and fairly well liquored-up, asked, "Did you say 'faithfulness'?" The others laughed nervously as they breathed again.

"I did."

"That's what I thought."

"Now, Myra," Leigh chided.

Bob Cobb looked at Myra and cut his throat with an index finger. *Shut up!*

She did.

"We expect you all to be there. On the beach, so shoes are optional. No gifts, please."

7.

The caterer pitched a party tent not far from the Main Pier, which had been rebuilt and christened with a ribbon cutting only a week earlier. Half the island turned out for the party, and politicians spoke for hours. The new pier was a welcome symbol that the famous twelve-mile stretch of open and wide sand was now clean and ready for a new future.

Under the tent, two clerks from the store, earning double time, poured champagne while soft jazz emanated from hidden speakers. Two waiters circulated with trays of fresh raw oysters and marinated shrimp on skewers. There were about fifty in attendance and everyone felt honored to be included. All friends, no family. Noelle's parents had divorced years earlier and didn't speak. Bruce's father was dead and his mother lived in Atlanta, which was not that far away but dealing with her was not worth the trouble. He was somewhat friendly with his sister but she was too busy for an impromptu wedding.

Noelle was stunning in a white linen pantsuit with the cuffs rolled halfway up to the knees. Bruce, true to form, wore a brand-new white seersucker suit with shorts instead of pants. No shoes for either. At 6:30, as the sun began to fade, they gathered in a semicircle at the water's edge. The officiant was a young Presbyterian minister from the island who had worked in the store through high school. In bare feet, he welcomed the friends and offered a prayer, followed by a verse from Second Timothy. Bruce and Noelle exchanged vows they had written, the crux of which was that they were renewing their love and devotion, and basically dedicating themselves to a new lifestyle, one in which they were completely committed to each other.

It was over in fifteen minutes, and, once pronounced husband and wife, Bruce pulled out a sheet of paper, the marriage certificate, for all to see as proof that this time they were properly hitched.

The wedding party then returned to the tent for more champagne and oysters.

8.

The second yellow envelope arrived with Tuesday's mail. Bruce stared at it for a long time. No return. A preprinted mailing label was addressed to him at the store. And, remarkably, a postmark dated yesterday from the Santa Rosa post office across the street.

"So he was here," Bruce said under his breath. "And probably in the store."

He thought about taking a quick photo of the envelope, but then changed his mind. Everything was hackable, right? If the bad guys were watching and listening with sophistication far beyond his comprehension, then why couldn't they steal his photos?

He slowly opened the envelope and removed one folded sheet of paper, the same color yellow. The typed message read:

LOVELY CEREMONY SUNDAY AFTERNOON AT THE BEACH.

YOUR WIFE IS VERY PRETTY. CONGRATULATIONS.

SNAIL MAIL, EMAIL, IT ALL LEAVES A TRAIL.

THERE ARE SERIOUS PEOPLE WATCHING YOUR EVERY MOVE.

THEY KILLED NELSON. THEY KILLED BRITTANY.

THEY ARE DESPERATE MEN.

BULLETTBEEP, A CHAT ROOM, TOMORROW AT 3 PM. YOU'LL BE
    88DOGMAN.

SO LONG, HOODEENEE36

Bruce was certain that in his forty-seven years he had never felt as though he was being watched or followed or observed, especially by people whose interests he did not share. He left the store, something he did at least four times a day, and stepped onto the sidewalk along Main. He could almost feel the lasers of someone's surveillance locking in on his back. He stood straighter, walked with a purpose, tried his damnedest not to cut his eyes in all directions, and after fifty yards called himself an idiot for being so paranoid. What could anyone gain by watching Bruce Cable walk down Main Street in Santa Rosa, Florida?

He ducked into his favorite wine bar and ordered a glass of rosé. He sat in his favorite corner with his back to the door and studied his notes. Why would "he" mention Noelle? Was it a way of threatening Bruce? It certainly felt like a threat. Was "he" friend or enemy? No one outside Bruce's circle knew about the wedding, right? How would "he" know to be at the beach at the right moment? Bruce had not mentioned the ceremony to anyone in an email or text. And how could "he" get close enough to Noelle to know she was "very pretty"? Bruce had been occupied with his bride and the party at hand, and had not bothered to glance around at the beachcombers. There were always people on the beach, but not many on a cool late afternoon in mid-March. He didn't remember seeing anyone.

If they were listening to his phone calls and reading his emails, for how long had they been at it? He recalled when he first contacted Elaine Shelby, he did so by phone. She immediately warned him against using emails. He then flew to Washington and met Lindsey Wheat. Was it possible that "they" knew he had hired a private security firm to find Nelson's killers? It seemed doubtful, but then with technology what was not possible?

He puzzled and pondered and took pages of notes, none of them revealing or helpful. He ordered another glass of rosé, and the second one proved as ineffective as the first.

9.

With Nick away at school, Bruce's favorite employee was Jade, a thirty-year-old part-timer with two college degrees and two toddlers at home. She was still looking for a career but in the meantime thoroughly enjoyed the flexible hours Bruce offered. She was a tech whiz, addicted to social media, knew the hottest and latest apps, and was contemplating a graduate degree in computer science. Without getting too specific, Bruce asked her to walk him through the scenario of corresponding through anonymous chat rooms. He fibbed and said such activity was a subplot in Nelson's novel and he wanted it to be accurate. He knew it was quite unlikely Jade would ever read it.

She took a seat in his office and said, "BullettBeep is just another secret chat room, based in Bulgaria. Most are in Eastern Europe because privacy laws are tighter there. Crazy Ghost is based in Hungary. I found three dozen of these sites in half an hour. They're legit, for a fee. Most are around twenty bucks for thirty days."

"Can they be hacked?" Bruce asked.

"In my opinion, it would be very difficult for someone stalking you to read your messages on one of these sites."

"Why not? Let's assume I've been hacked as of now and they're reading my mail. When I log in and go to BullettBeep or whatever, they're watching, right?"

"To a point. Once you pay up and become a 'member,' for lack of a better term, your messages are instantly encrypted and protected. They have to be or these sites couldn't work. They have to guarantee complete anonymity."

"And they're popular?"

"Who knows? It's all secret. I mean, I never use them and I don't know anybody who does, but then I'm not having an affair or selling arms or doing whatever Nelson was up to in his novels."

"Thanks."

She left and Bruce waited, and waited. At exactly 3:01, he went to BullettBeep, followed instructions, paid with a credit card (which was also being watched, he presumed), and said hello as 88DogMan. He was already tired of the silly names.

Hello HooDeeNee36. I'm here.
Good afternoon. How's married life?
The same. Why did you mention my wife? I don't like that.
I shouldn't have. Sorry.

Friend or foe? I'm not sure.

Brittany was murdered. Would the enemy tell you this?

Yes, if the enemy was trying to scare the hell out of me.

You need to be scared. So am I. May I suggest a destination
    for the honeymoon?

Oh go ahead.

New York City. I'm there on business next week. We really
    should meet face to face. There is so much to cover.

And what will we cover? And where is this going? What's the
    endgame?

You want Nelson's killer?

Only if no one else gets hurt, including me. I can walk away
    right now.

Don't do that. They will not walk away. They don't want his
    book published.

They being Grattin, right?

There was a long pause as he waited and gawked at the
screen. He took a deep breath and tapped his fingers beside the
keyboard. Finally,

I think you just gave me a heart attack.

Sorry, didn't mean to. Look, I know some things.

Obviously.

And I'm tired of these little chat rooms and silly names. Are
    we going to meet and have a serious discussion?

New York, next week, honeymoon. I'll be there on business.

Any particular hotel?

The Lowell, on 63rd. I'll find you.

10.

After two days and nights at the Lowell with no contact, Bruce was privately bitching about Manhattan hotel prices and thinking of leaving. To make matters worse, Noelle was shopping out of boredom. Whatever the reason, the prices were high and the boxes were piling up. Bruce had lunch with Nelson's editor, and he had drinks with an agent, and he hung out in a couple of his favorite bookstores, but he was tired of the city. On the third day, Noelle was having tea in the hotel bar when an attractive brunette stopped at her table and said, "You're Noelle, right?"

The "i" was flat, as in North Florida.

"I am."

She handed over a small envelope, yellow. "Please give this to Bruce." And she was gone.

Bruce read the note: *Meet me in the second floor bar of the Peninsula Hotel on 55th at 3:30 p.m. I'll be alone.*

They arrived early and the bar was empty, and dark. Noelle took a table close to the counter, ordered a seltzer, and began reading a newsmagazine. Bruce went to the rear with his back to the mirrors and a full view of the bar. At 3:30, the same brunette sauntered in like a fashion model, noticed the couple was not together, and walked to Bruce's table and sat down. Without offering a hand, she said, "I'm Danielle."

"Also known as Dane?" Bruce asked calmly, and she couldn't conceal the shock. She exhaled as her shoulders dropped and all pretense of being cool and in charge vanished. She flashed a fake smile and glanced around. Perfect teeth, high cheekbones, lovely brown eyes, a bit too much padding in the forehead, but all in all one good-looking woman. Tall, slender, decked out in designer stuff. Very classy.

"How'd you know?"

"A long story, one of many. I'm Bruce. We weren't expecting a woman."

"Sorry to disappoint. Look, I'd feel better if we had more privacy. I have a room on the fourth floor."

"I'm not going to your room, because I'm not sure what I'd find there."

"You'll find nothing."

"If you say so. Noelle and I are happy to invite you to a room we have on the sixth floor."

"Very well."

They rode the elevator with three strangers so not a word was spoken. Once safely inside the room, they managed to relax as they sat around a small coffee table. With a flair, Bruce began with "Well, I'm Bruce Cable, small-town bookseller from Camino Island, Florida. This is my wife, Noelle, peerless importer of antiques from the South of France. And you are?"

"Danielle Noddin, Houston, Texas, and I have a lot of questions."

"So do I," Bruce said. "How did you know about our wedding ceremony on the beach?"

She flashed a warm smile and Bruce almost melted. "I was on the island with a friend, just a few days at the beach. I wanted a closer look at you and your turf. When we were in the store we overheard a conversation about the ceremony, so we just happened to stop by. It's a small town and I guess people talk too much."

"That's certainly true," Noelle said.

"I'm sorry. I didn't mean to frighten you. I mentioned it so that you would take my letter seriously."

"Oh, I did," Bruce said. "We're not playing games here."

"No, we're not. Why did you know I'm called Dane?"

"We went through Nelson's stuff after the police were finished. There wasn't much. Virtually all of his notes and research were, evidently, in his computer and heavily encrypted. But there were three notebooks with all sorts of random chicken scratch. Notes on the best dive lodges in Bermuda; restaurants in Santa Fe; a three-page story idea for a novel, one that went nowhere because the idea was not good; a few phone numbers that the police checked out and got nowhere. That sort of stuff. But there were four references to a 'Danielle,' who was also called Dane. I take it you guys met once in San Antonio."

She shook her head in disbelief. "We did."

"The police paid no attention to it. No surprise there."

"Where is their investigation?"

"Still open, but they've found little. Coffee, anyone?"

Noelle nodded and Dane said, "That would be nice."

Bruce stepped to the phone and called room service. Noelle asked her softly, "You're in the city often?"

"Twice a year. The usual, shopping and Broadway and a new restaurant or two, with some girls from Houston."

It was obvious Dane had expensive tastes and lived well. Noelle pegged her age at forty-one, max.

Bruce returned to the sofa and asked, "Now where were we?"

"How much do you know about Grattin?" Dane asked.

"Well, everything that has been written about a company that works extremely hard at revealing nothing. Basic corporate structure, sales figures, number of facilities, a few names of the big boys, and a lot of bad press about nursing home abuse. The company seems to relish staying in trouble."

"The company relishes making money, and it's very good at it. Does the name Ken Reed ring a bell?"

"It's his company, CEO and chairman."

"When Ken was about thirty years old, his father died in a plane crash and he inherited a string of cheap nursing homes in Texas and Oklahoma. He learned the business, spruced up his facilities, and began expanding. He was and still is very ambitious. Now he's sixty-two, rich, and still works seven days a week."

"Do you work for him?"

"I sleep with him. I'm wife number three. First I was his secretary slash assistant slash girlfriend. He got tired of wife number two and I got the big promotion. Now he's looking for number four. The man will never have enough money or women. He's more than happy to get me out of town. It's never been a healthy marriage and it will soon be over."

"*Forbes* puts his net worth at six hundred million."

"No one knows. He buries it here and there, does a lot of offshore banking, runs money through a maze of corporations. He's paranoid about his privacy and cheats like hell on his taxes. Not your typical rich Texan who can't wait to show off his money. There's always somebody richer down there so he doesn't play that game."

"Why will the marriage soon be over?"

She smiled again and looked out the window. "We don't have enough time."

"You brought it up. We can talk about something else."

She offered him a soft gaze but the beautiful eyes were

focused, almost glaring. "When I was twenty, I got a job as a secretary with a company in Tulsa that owned some nursing homes. Ken bought the company and came through one day. I caught his eye, primarily because his eye is always roving. I got a promotion I didn't deserve and was transferred to Abilene, where I got another lucky promotion and a one-way ticket to Houston, where his company was headquartered. It was called West Abilene Care back then. Later merged with Grattin, and Ken liked that name better. His name is on nothing but his car titles and land deeds and not all of them. Anyway, when I got to Houston he was waiting. He offered me the job as his executive assistant, at a generous salary, and before long we were companions. This went on for about five years. He finally paid off number two and I became number three. That was fourteen years ago. I worked hard, took my job seriously, learned everything about the company, most of which I'd like to forget, by the way, and kept up with the technology. Over time, Ken began to worry that I knew too much, so he forced me into retirement, to get me out of the office. But I was quite unhappy sitting around the house—I refused to have children with him, which has proven to be a wise decision—and I insisted on a job, something meaningful. He resented this but finally agreed. Not long after I returned to work I learned that he had a serious new girl in Dallas. This was no surprise, really, because he has never stopped philandering. So, I've played the game myself. Not exactly an open marriage but it's kept me sane."

Bruce looked uncomfortably at Noelle, who ignored him. The term "open marriage" brought back memories.

"And you met Nelson?" Bruce asked.

She smiled seductively at her own memories. "I did. I liked him a lot. Obviously, you've read his last novel."

"Read it, edited it, sold it."

"Well, folks, the novel is true, and the story is about Grattin and its secret drug. When I decided to squeal, snitch, blow the whistle, call it what you want, I decided to go to Nelson Kerr. I had read an interview with him in which he talked about his work and his research into shady conspiracies and such. I reached out, we met, hit it off in a fine way, and began a relationship."

"Go, Nelson," Bruce said.

"Come on, Bruce," Noelle scolded.

"It's okay," Dane said. "We were very fond of each other. And, I feel responsible for his death. If he hadn't met me he would still be alive."

"We're leaving out entire chapters here," Bruce said. There was a knock on the door and Bruce opened it. A porter set the coffee service on the table, and Bruce signed the check. Noelle poured as Bruce locked the door.

They fiddled with their sugar and cream for a while. Dane said, "A question. Can the novel be stopped?"

"No way," Bruce said. "That's where they screwed up. They didn't know that Nelson was finished with it when they took him out. I've sold the book and it's coming next year. In a big way. If we can prove he was murdered because of it, they won't be able to print 'em fast enough. A question for you. How did they know about Nelson and his research?"

"He went to China and found the lab. I told him not to go, just as I told him not to dig too deep. Just take the story, fictionalize like crazy, and write a novel. That wasn't good enough for Nelson. He wanted to know all the dirt. Somehow, somewhere in the underworld, word got out that Nelson Kerr, a bestselling author, was writing about a nursing home company and its mysterious drug."

"Was the Chinese lab involved in his death?"

"I doubt it. It's a huge pharmaceutical over there that makes all manner of illegal and semi-legal drugs. They don't care and they're immune from prosecution and liability. They make fentanyl, even meth. How much do you know about the drug?"

With a bit of showmanship, Bruce pulled a small plastic bag out of his pocket and tossed it on the table. Inside were three clear capsules filled with a brown substance. "There is the mysterious vitamin E3. Guaranteed to keep you ticking even though you can't see a damned thing and you're puking up your guts."

Dane's jaw dropped as she gawked at the pills in disbelief. They watched her as she tried gamely to be stoic while her mind went crazy. She breathed deeply and said, "I've never seen the drug. How on earth did you get it?"

"It's a long story that we don't need to discuss. But, Grattin has three hundred facilities in fifteen states, so there's a lot of this stuff in the pipeline and in play. It wasn't that difficult to lift a few capsules."

"How'd you know about the side effects?"

"We ran it through some high-end labs where it was finally identified as Flaxacill. We've done some work, Dane."

"Indeed you have. Was this by chance found in Flora, Kentucky?"

"It was. By Brittany, who is no longer with us. You feel responsible for Nelson's death. We feel responsible for Brittany's."

"Don't. Brittany was killed by the same people who took care of Nelson."

"The boys at Grattin?"

"Yes. I wasn't in the room, but I'd bet that when Ken Reed and his circle found out that a ten-dollar-an-hour orderly in Flora, Kentucky, had lifted a bottle of E3, they went into a panic."

"These guys kill all the time?" Noelle asked.

Dane tried to relax with a sip of coffee. She gently set down her cup and took two deep breaths. "These guys, and there are four of them, began as decent men. The money ruined them. They started making millions and figured out ways to make millions more. They provide substandard care at expensive rates, courtesy of the taxpayers. If there's a way to screw Medicare, Medicaid, Social Security, Ag, Defense, pick another one, then these guys know how to do it. Have they killed before? Probably, but nothing has ever been proved. Roughly ten years ago a federal meat inspector in Nebraska died under suspicious circumstances. One of Reed's offshore corporations owned several meat-processing plants in the Midwest, low-end beef and pork they peddled to fast food chains, school lunch programs, even the military. An inspector surprised them with a visit and found plenty of violations. He shut down two plants. The company ran to Washington, lined up the politicians on its payroll, and got them reopened. The inspector would not go away and kept inspecting. He shut them down again, and again. He eventually died in a car crash, late at night, on a lonely road."

"Who are the four?" Bruce asked.

"Ken Reed; his cousin Otis Reed, a lawyer; Lou Slader, head of security and bribery; and an accountant named Sid

Shennault. Slader is the one to worry about. Ex-FBI, ex–Army Ranger, a smooth operator who always carries a gun. He runs all security, at least around the headquarters. There's not much at the facilities, costs too much. He also handles the political side and doles out huge sums of money to politicians, above the table, and to regulators, under the table. Grattin operates on a large scale, so there are a lot of inspectors and bureaucrats to keep at bay. It's far cheaper to pay bribes than to provide quality care."

"And these four men make all the decisions?"

"No, not at all. Ken Reed is the dictator. The other three are like sycophants. They do what he says, make him look good, and never cross him. He demands complete loyalty."

"Is there a weak link?" Bruce asked.

"I doubt it, but then they've never been threatened. Ken pays them a fortune and keeps 'em happy. I think they would take a bullet for him."

"Who's the youngest?"

"Sid's about forty-five, happily married with five kids still at home. Clean-cut, devout Baptist, a country boy from somewhere around Waco. Last time I checked, his salary was almost a million bucks a year. That buys a lot of loyalty."

"How much access do you have?" Noelle asked.

"More than they know. When I was Ken's executive assistant I knew virtually everything. He became uncomfortable with that and I realized it. I know their computers and systems. I don't hack anything but I still see a lot of stuff they don't know I'm seeing."

"And you're still on the payroll?"

"Vice President in charge of marketing, of which there is almost none. You don't have to advertise in this business."

"Do they suspect you?" Bruce asked.

"No. If they suspected me of talking to Nelson I wouldn't be here now."

They let those words settle around them. Softly, Dane said, "And it's time for me to leave now. Nelson was killed in August, and since then there has been a real change in Ken's moods around me. I don't think he feels guilt over the killing, and, as I said, I don't think he suspects me. But he is worried sick about being exposed. Sure, Flaxacill is not an illegal drug, and, sure, it actually extends life, but he fears a massive federal investigation into Medicare fraud, with indictments likely. And look at the lawsuits, tens of thousands of them by the families of the victims, families whose misery was prolonged by the drug. And no insurance company will step forward to save Grattin, not for illegal acts. I need to get out while I can. I hate what the company does and I despise most of the people who work there. I want a new life."

"What's your endgame?" Noelle asked.

"Nelson promised me half the royalties from the book. Nothing in writing. In fact, he made the promise in bed. But for me, it's still binding."

Bruce was shaking his head. "It'll be tough to collect from his estate. Alive, he could honor his commitment, but I'm not sure his executrix and the probate judge will go for it. Besides, you can't exactly file a claim in court and expect it to go unnoticed."

"That's what I figured. Do you know much about the whistleblower statutes?"

"Me? I'm just a small-town bookseller."

"I doubt that. I need some help. I can't tell the entire story myself because I'm married to Ken Reed, the chief conspirator. I mean, there's no law prohibiting one spouse from ratting out the other, but I just can't do that."

"Get a divorce," Noelle said. "Sounds like you're ready."

"I plan to, but it's complicated. Ken would not agree to it right now. He's too paranoid and afraid of my lawyers digging through his dark world. Anyway, there's a prenup in the way, one I signed practically under duress. I get a million bucks cash and nothing else. I could probably attack it based on his net worth, but that's another huge lawsuit that would drag on for years. There's also an element of fear involved here. These are dangerous people, obviously. I want to get out and get away."

For the first time her voice cracked, but just slightly. Then she collected herself, offered them a lovely smile, and drank some more coffee.

Noelle asked, "How much is all this worth, this huge scam they've been running for, how many years?"

"At least twenty."

"So, in the past twenty years, how much money has Grattin made off its vitamin E3?"

"Have you read Nelson's novel?"

"Half of it."

Bruce said, "He puts the number at two hundred million per year in extra Medicare payments."

Dane smiled and nodded. "I'd say that's close. Keep in mind that no one really knows because it's impossible to know how long these patients will survive with the drug. One might get an extra six months, another might hang on for three years."

"That's four billion total," Noelle said.

"Give or take. And there's no one to complain. It's a brilliant scheme, until it's discovered. I have a hunch that Ken Reed might be ready to stop it. He's made enough and he might feel some danger."

"Because of Nelson's book?" Bruce asked.

"That, and now a sample has gone missing. All he has to do is snap his fingers and the E3 disappears. No one will know about it. The staff has no idea what the drug is anyway. The patients will die but that's what they're supposed to do. Their poor families will be relieved. No one will ask questions."

She glanced at her watch and seemed surprised that she had been there for almost two hours. "I need to go. My friends will be waiting. Can I make a suggestion?" She was opening her large purse. She withdrew two small boxes.

"These are cheap phones, burners, bought 'em at a Walmart in Houston. Let's use them only for each other, okay?"

"Sure," Bruce said. "When shall we talk again?"

"Soon. The walls are closing in and I want to get away from these people."

She stood and everyone shook hands. Bruce escorted her to the door, closed it behind her, then fell onto the sofa. He rubbed his eyes, then closed them and threw an arm across his forehead. Noelle found a bottle of water in the minibar and poured two glasses.

She finally asked, "Do you ask yourself why you're doing this? Couldn't we just as easily go home and close this little chapter, let the police down there do their thing, or not, and just forget about Nelson? Why are we expected to solve the murder? As you like to say—he ain't your brother."

"Only about five times a day." He sat up and said, "Look, Noelle, I don't have to tell you that this is not sustainable. I can't live with one eye in the rearview mirror. Can you believe that we're going about our routines with the belief that someone is listening to our phone calls and reading our emails? I'm just not cut out for this. I'm tired of losing sleep and sick of worrying about who killed Nelson."

"Can you walk away?"

"Of course not. I'm his literary executor and his novel will be published next year. I'll be dealing with that and his backlist for years."

"I get that. But no one appointed you as his private detective."

"True, and it was a mistake to hire that firm in D.C. and get so involved."

"But it's done. So what's next?"

"We're going to D.C."

11.

They left the Lowell in a cab headed for Penn Station, not LaGuardia. Their two seats on the flight would go unoccupied. Instead, they took the Acela Express and three hours later rolled into Washington's Union Station where they hopped in a cab for the long haul to Dulles. Near the airport, they walked into the unmarked building just after 1:00 p.m. and Lindsey Wheat was waiting. Elaine Shelby joined them and they gathered in a conference room and kept things polite. Less than three weeks earlier, Bruce had stormed out of the building with Nick in tow.

Bruce handed over a document and said, "This is your termination letter, which I did not sign."

"Excellent," Lindsey said with a generous smile. "Nice to keep you as a client."

"Maybe. We need some help, and of course you have been paid in full."

"Indeed we have."

"One rather significant condition. You do not 'infiltrate' or organize any other scheme to collect information without first notifying me. This is not negotiable."

Lindsey looked at Elaine, then looked at Bruce. "We don't usually make this concession because it can handcuff us later. You see, Bruce, we don't always know exactly where the truth might take us. We have to be flexible and we often are forced to adapt on the fly."

"You also get people hurt. Brittany being one. Three years ago you came within minutes of getting Mercer hurt, or worse. You make me this promise or I'm leaving. Again."

Elaine said, "Okay, okay. You have our word."

Everyone took a deep breath, then Bruce plowed on. "We have met the informant, and the informant has confirmed everything we suspected about Nelson, about Grattin, and about its use of Flaxacill, or E3. Nelson's math was close—about two hundred million a year for the past twenty years. They desperately want to stop the publication of *Pulse*, and they murdered Nelson. And Brittany Bolton."

Lindsey nodded along as if this was what she expected. "Okay, tell us the story."

12.

When he finished, Elaine said, "You insist on referring to the informant as 'the informant.' Meaning that you don't want to reveal his or her gender. But if he was a man, you'd have no problem referring to him simply as he. Therefore, the informant is obviously a woman." She smiled at Lindsey who smiled back. Aren't we smart.

Noelle was thinking the same.

Bruce said, "Okay, it's a woman, and she's Ken Reed's former executive assistant who's now his third wife. She knows a lot. But because she's married to the guy, she is not willing to blow the whistle. She is also scared. You cannot reveal her identity until I say so."

Noelle said, "She thinks there's an urgency here. The company could simply stop using the drug and no one would ever know the difference."

"You didn't hire us to bust the company. You hired us to find Nelson's killer, right?" Lindsey asked.

"Right."

Elaine said, "The question is: Does one lead to the other? We can't answer that, but we do have a very rough plan, one we put together before the, uh, termination."

Bruce asked, "You wanna share it with us?"

"It involves going to the FBI," Lindsey said.

Elaine said, "We have contacts in high places within the Bureau, and if we can convince them of an epic Medicare fraud, we think they'll take it and run, especially with a factual background as unique as this."

"They'll love it," Lindsey said. "I need to make three phone calls."

Elaine glanced at her watch and said, "I'm starving. Have you had lunch?"

"No. Good idea," Bruce replied.

Lindsey was on her feet, waving them away. "Go eat. Bring me a sandwich. I'll make the calls."

13.

On Lindsey's recommendation, they spent the night at the Willard Hotel on Pennsylvania. The following morning was a perfect spring day, a Friday, and they had been gone for an entire week that they had not planned on spending away from home. They walked five blocks to the main entrance of the Hoover Building and met Elaine and Lindsey. Just inside the door, they were scanned, photographed, ID'd, and told to pose in front of a tiny camera to record their facial features. Once cleared, they were met by two serious young women who escorted them to a conference room on the third floor.

"And who are we meeting with?" Lindsey asked one of the ladies.

"Mr. Dellinger." She closed the door as she left.

Bruce and Noelle had no idea who Dellinger was, but Lindsey and Elaine certainly did. Lindsey said, "Impressive, the Deputy Director."

Within minutes, Dellinger swept in with a SWAT team of five assistants, all in matching black suits, black shoes, white shirts, and a variety of bland ties. Rapid introductions were

made and all names forgotten in a blur. Dellinger swept his arm
at the table and everyone had a seat. A secretary served coffee
as Elaine and Dellinger talked about old friends at the Bureau
back in the day. As soon as the secretary left and the door was
closed, he looked directly at Bruce and said, "First of all, Mr.
Cable, thank you for coming forward. I'm sorry about your
friend, Nelson Kerr." It was a pleasant thing to hear, even if it
was completely devoid of any warmth or emotion.

Dellinger looked to his right and nodded at Mr. Parkhill,
who lifted some paperwork and plunged right in. "I'd also like
to say thanks. This appears to be an historic Medicare fraud,
and we would not have known about it but for you."

Bruce nodded, already tired of their gratitude.

Parkhill continued: "We burned some oil last night and verified a lot of the story that's on the table. Our plans are to begin
immediately, at the lowest levels. We'll pick off a few orderlies
and nurses at various facilities and collect samples. We'll do this
without setting off any alarms in Houston. We'll track down
the drug and figure out its distribution channels. Flaxacill has
never been approved, so its use in such a widespread scam will
probably lead to thousands of violations. That alone could sink
the company. At some point, we'll raid the offices, haul away the
bad guys, and seize their records."

"What about Nelson's murder?" Bruce asked.

"Could be a tough one. Once we get 'em locked up, charged,
indicted, and all that, we'll start squeezing and offering deals.
Usually, someone will cave and try to save his own skin. Sid
Shennault looks especially vulnerable, with five kids at home.
At any rate, we'll figure that out when we get there. We know
how to be effective when dealing with wealthy criminals who

prefer to stay out of jail and keep their toys. Having said that, this company looks to be well run and in the firm grip of a tough cookie. They may not talk."

Dellinger said, "Obviously, Mr. Cable, it goes without saying that this is extremely confidential."

"Of course. Who would I tell?"

"Do you plan to correspond with your informant?"

"Maybe. I don't know. Should I?"

"We really need the name of the informant."

"I can't give that to you without the informant's approval."

"Fair enough. Now, we'd like to ask you a bunch of questions and get your responses on tape, if that's okay?"

"Can't wait. Can I ask a question?"

"Certainly," said Dellinger.

"This appears to be a contract killing, so it's federal, right?"

"Probably."

"Can we get the FBI office down in Florida to take charge of the investigation?"

"It's already done."

"Thank you."

"No, thank you, Mr. Cable."

Two of the suits left with Dellinger. Bruce and Noelle spent the next three hours answering Parkhill's questions about Nelson, his death, his books, his estate, and the stories told by Dane Noddin, the still unnamed informant. When they were finally released at noon, they hustled down Pennsylvania Avenue to 15th Street and the Old Ebbitt Grill, where they enjoyed a long lunch with Lindsey and Elaine.

CHAPTER NINE
THE ROUNDUP

1.

Each of Grattin's facilities was supposed to have its own licensed practical nurse, but the low pay and lousy benefits guaranteed a constant shortage of help at all levels. Laurie Teegue, the current LPN at Madison Road Nursing Home, was pulling duty at two other homes and working fifteen hours a day, with no overtime.

They followed her to work outside the town of Marmaduke, Arkansas, gave her a few minutes to get to her tiny office, then barged in with badges on display. "FBI," they said in unison. One closed the door as the other motioned for her to sit. They wore matching outfits—khakis, navy blazers, white shirts with no ties—as if by dressing down they would not attract attention. Casual as they tried to be, they were still seriously overdressed in this rural outpost.

Laurie fell into her undersized chair behind her disheveled desk and tried to speak. Agent Rumke held up a hand and stopped her. "We prefer that no one knows we're here, okay? We come in peace, though we have a warrant for your arrest."

Agent Ritter whipped out some papers, tossed them on the desk, and said, "One count of dispensing an unauthorized controlled substance known as Flaxacill. Ever heard of it?"

She ignored the papers and shook her head. No.

"Who's the boss of this place?" Rumke asked.

"We don't have one right now. Can't keep one."

"Makes sense. Look, we're serious about keeping this quiet. So, if someone asks just tell them that we're a couple of accountants from the home office going over the books. Got it?"

"Whatever. You're going to arrest me?"

"Not yet. We're going to offer you a deal that will keep you out of jail and all of this quiet. You want to hear it?"

"Do I have a choice?" She took a tissue and rubbed her eyes.

"Sure you do. You can tell us to get lost, at which time we'll handcuff you and give you a ride to the jail in Jonesboro. There, you can call a lawyer to try and get out."

"I'd rather not go that route. I've done nothing wrong."

Ritter said, "That'll be for the jury to determine, if it gets that far. However, the deal we're prepared to offer will allow you to avoid juries, courts, lawyers, reporters, everyone. You don't even have to tell your husband."

"I think I like this deal. What's Flaxacill?"

"An illegal drug made in China and shipped stateside by the U.S. Postal Service. We think that in your company it's commonly referred to as vitamin E3. Ever heard of that?"

"Sure."

"Who gets it?"

"Advanced dementia patients. Do I need a lawyer?"

"Only if you want to go to jail. Listen to us. Here's the deal. You cooperate with us and help us track down the drug. You act as an informant against your employer, and if things go as planned then the indictment against you will be dismissed."

"What happens to my employer?"

"Do you really care?"

"No."

"Good, because they don't care about you. This is a widespread investigation in fifteen states that will uncover a huge Medicare fraud. Your employer may survive, probably not. If I were you I'd stop worrying about the company and cover my own ass."

"My brother's a lawyer in Jonesboro."

"We know. He specializes in bankruptcy and doesn't know beans about criminal law."

She stared at Rumke, then she stared at Ritter. Both were about thirty, cocky, smug, and they knew everything and she knew nothing. They had the power to slap the cuffs on her wrists and march her out the front door, on display for all her patients and coworkers to see. She also had four kids at home, the oldest being eleven, and the idea of their mother sitting in jail was overwhelming. She began to cry.

The following day, Laurie went to the pharmacy during lunch and lifted a bottle of E3 capsules. She chatted with the pharmacist and learned that the vitamins and supplements arrived by overnight shipment once a week from a company warehouse in Texas. The controlled substances were hand-delivered each Wednesday morning by a courier from Little Rock.

Rumke and Ritter alternated their visits to collect the

evidence. They were working eleven other nursing homes in northeastern Arkansas. The task force was targeting a hundred Grattin facilities in fifteen states, and after the first month not a word had leaked up to the headquarters in Houston.

2.

The burner rattled for the first time in a week, and Bruce stepped into his office to chat with Dane. She was in Houston, skipping a yoga class and waiting on a friend for lunch. The big news was that she had seen a divorce lawyer the day before and the first visit went well. She was in no hurry to file, though she was sick of living in the same house with Ken Reed, who was seldom at home. The daunting issue was strategy. Did she have the guts to allege adultery and go through the nightmare of trying to prove it, and risk a long ugly court case? She wasn't sure. If the plans fell into place, Mr. Reed and his company would soon be drowning in all manner of litigation, both civil and criminal.

Bruce knew little about the FBI's investigation and had no idea about when to expect big news. An agent in Washington called once a week with a five-minute update that was a waste of time.

"I really worry about you, Bruce," Dane said. "You're just so vulnerable, just sitting there in your little store where anyone can find you."

"And do what? Gun me down in the streets? What would Reed and his boys gain by coming after me? They can't stop the publication. They tried that with Nelson, which, the more you think about it the dumber it gets. The guy was writing a novel that was complete fiction. Reed finds out about it and assumes that when people read the book they're going to automatically assume he based it on Grattin and their Medicare scam gets uncovered. Kind of a stretch, right?"

"No. Reed didn't know the book was fiction. He thought Nelson was writing an exposé, a real story about his company."

"Still, killing him scored no points for the bad guys. The book was finished."

"They're nasty people, Bruce. And they are desperate. I think Ken sees it all slipping away."

"I don't care, Dane. I've changed phones and email addresses and I'm still being careful, which by the way is tiresome. We're leaving Saturday for a month on Martha's Vineyard. Noelle wants a change of scenery and there's nothing happening here at the store. The island's dead. I'll be okay. And you?"

"I'm fine. Just keep in touch."

Bruce ended the call and stared at the phone. If not for his latest wedding vows, he would really like to see Dane again.

Go, Nelson.

3.

Sooner or later, as they say in the trade, luck swings your way.

The sniper hiked a quarter of a mile uphill, through thick woods and without the benefit of a trail. The perfect spot was deep in the trees. He and his partner had walked it four hours earlier and now knew the terrain. He found his perch, a thick white oak with low branches, and he climbed up forty feet and rose above the tops of the other trees. Down below, three hundred and eighty yards away, was the rear patio door of a sprawling and gaudy country home owned by Mr. Higginbotham, the largest asphalt paving contractor in western Ohio.

Higgs was off to Vegas with the boys, a gambling trip he made several times a year. He was now certain that his younger second wife was seeing one of her ex-boyfriends while he was away. The sniper had never met Higgs and wouldn't know him by sight. Their contract had been arranged by a trusted broker. Higgs had hired some good investigators who had hacked phones and passed along the terrible news that a rendezvous was planned for this afternoon around 4:30, after the housekeeper left.

Once secure and wedged between the trunk and a limb, the sniper slowly opened his case and began assembling his rifle, a military-grade beauty that cost twenty grand. In his business, one could never have enough weaponry. He had never used it before in a live situation, though after hours at the range he was confident he could hit anything at five hundred yards or less. He adjusted the scope, took a close look at the patio door, and shoved in three cartridges. Hopefully he would use only two. Each could be worth a million dollars.

The house was isolated on a paved country road without a neighbor in sight. All the toys were down there: a large, odd-shaped blue pool, a tennis court, a separate garage where Higgs stored his vintage cars, and a small barn where the missus kept her horses. His kids were with the first wife on the other side of the county.

At 4:40, a black Porsche Carrera appeared and slowed and turned into the drive. The sniper embraced his weapon. The driver parked at the rear of the house in such a way that his car could not be seen from the road. Perfect for the sniper, who followed it closely through the scope. Romeo got out—thirty-five years old, plenty of thick blond hair, thin, dressed in jeans. He strode across the patio like a lucky man, stopped at the door for a truly needless but nonetheless nervous glance around, then went inside.

4:41. How long would they last? Under normal circum-stances there would be no hurry, but this was a fling and they couldn't tarry. A proper warm-up, the deed, some pillow talk, perhaps a postcoital cigarette. He'd take the under at forty min-utes.

He lost. At 5:28, forty-seven minutes after entering the house, Romeo emerged, closed the door behind himself—no sign of her—and sauntered, perhaps a step slower, to his car. When he touched the door latch, the sniper pulled the trigger. At about the same split second, a six-millimeter bullet from the .243 caliber rifle entered the target's head just above his left ear and exited through a gaping hole on the right side, taking most of his brain with it. Blood and brain matter splashed against the windows and doors of the car as the target fell hard to the ground.

The sniper extracted the bullet casing from the chamber, reloaded the semiautomatic, and trained his sights on the patio door. With the distance and density of the woods, he had no idea if Mrs. Higginbotham heard the shot, but he suspected she did. He saw a silhouette race through the den. Moments passed, then the patio door opened ever so slightly as she looked at the shocking scene near the Porsche.

Decisions, decisions. What does one do in these situations? To call for help would be to initiate a scandal that would dra-matically alter her world, and certainly not for the better. The police would bombard her with questions, but she would have no answers. Her husband would probably beat her and then hire every lawyer in town to make sure she was left in the streets, penniless.

What was a girl to do? She had no idea and she wasn't thinking clearly.

Her lover was obviously dead. Or was he breathing? She made the fateful decision to sprint out, take a look at him, and then try to think of the next move. But there would not be one. She opened the door, took one step, and the sniper fired. A millisecond later the bullet hit her in the teeth and rocked her head back so violently that she fell into the brick wall beside the door. She was wearing a short white bathrobe, black string panties, nothing else, and as the sniper scanned her with his scope he thought, Such a waste. She was tanned and toned without an ounce of extra body fat. Her fatal flaw had been a penchant for illicit sex, though she never dreamed she would die for it.

The sniper quickly unsnapped the scope, unscrewed the barrel, and with a few precision moves had the rifle back in its case. He strapped it to his back and began his descent from the white oak. There was no hurry. It would be hours before the bodies were discovered. He and his partner had big plans for a steak dinner in a few hours at Harvey's Rib Shack in downtown Dayton. Over champagne and fine wines they would replay the perfect kills and drink to a two-million-dollar fee. They would check the newspapers in the morning for the shocking story, perhaps see a quote or two from poor Higgs out in Vegas as he reacted with shock to such cold-blooded killings, then they would separate for a few months until their next job.

But a rotted limb changed everything. For an ex–Special

Ops known for his sure-footedness, back in the day anyway, such a mistake was unbelievable, though he would not remember it and never have time to analyze it. Head down, he fell fast and hard with nothing to grab onto and no time to brace for an ugly landing. He hit the hard ground with his forehead, and his neck snapped with such force that he knew he was dead. He blacked out and had no idea what time it was when he opened his eyes again. It was dark. He wanted to check his wristwatch but he couldn't lift his hands. Nothing was moving. The pain in his neck was so excruciating that he wanted to scream. Instead, he stifled a groan, then another. He was on his back and twisted at the waist in an awkward shape that he wanted to adjust, but nothing, not a damned thing was moving. Except for his lungs, and they were labored. He couldn't see the case with his rifle. His cell phone was in a rear pocket but nothing was within reach.

When he wore a real uniform and stalked enemies around the world, he had always kept a cyanide pill in a pocket to end things quickly if the situation called for it. He closed his eyes and dreamed of a pill now. This was not the way he wanted to die.

Even if she found him, his spinal cord was crushed. Trying to move him would just make matters worse.

4.

She heard the groans before she stumbled upon him. She fell to her knees and looked into his eyes. "What happened?" she hissed.

"I fell," he grunted. "My neck."

"Did you get them?"

"Yes, both. Then I fell."

"What the hell."

"I'm sorry."

"I heard sirens down there. We have to move."

"I can't. I'm paralyzed. I can't move anything."

"Bullshit, Rick. I'm getting you out of here."

He closed his eyes and groaned even louder. She stood and walked around the tree, straining for a glimpse of the house, but she could see nothing. With a small laser flashlight, she found the case with the rifle and debated what to do with it. If she took it, and if she got caught with it, she would be toast.

And what to do with him? The fool broke his own neck. Trying to carry him downhill through thick terrain for at least a mile would cause even more neurological damage. She knew that basic truth from her training.

Through his own stupidity he was about to get caught. But not her. And the two-million-dollar fee would not be divided. In the distance she heard a siren.

She walked to a spot beside him and looked down. He opened his eyes and saw her remove a small automatic from her pocket. "No, Karen, no."

She aimed at his forehead.

"No, please."

And she fired twice.

5.

To say Rick Patterson was half dead when they found him would be to seriously overstate his condition. With a crushed spinal cord, two gunshot wounds to the head, half his blood drained to the ground, a pulse of 28 and a diastolic blood pressure of 40, he was well beyond half dead. A crew of first responders and paramedics worked on him for an hour under the tree until he was stable enough to be airlifted to a Cincinnati hospital where he underwent eleven hours of surgery. Forty-eight hours later, he was still listed as critical.

And he was not yet Rick Patterson. There was nothing on his body that revealed identity, address, phone number, nothing. A detective with the Ohio State Police obtained a search warrant and took a partial set of fingerprints while the suspect fought for his life on a ventilator. The prints were finally matched to a U.S. Army veteran, one Rick Patterson of Tacoma, Washington. A brother said he worked in private security. Ballistics tests quickly matched his sniper rifle to the carnage on Higgs's patio, but his two head wounds were caused by smaller bullets from a handgun. Back at the scene, the landscape was scoured with little to show for the effort—a few ineffectual boot markings and some tire tracks.

For days the great mystery baffled the police. The killings of Mrs. Higginbotham and her lover, Jason Jordan, were solved, but who shot Patterson and got away? And why? And who paid him for the contract killings? Mr. Higgs was already being investigated and had hired lawyers.

For days Patterson refused to die. He clung to life with the help of machines and wonder drugs and a tenaciousness the doctors rarely saw.

And on the ninth day, he began to talk.

6.

Bob Cobb had just finished a long walk on the beach, and was pouring a cold beer into a frosty mug for a rest by his pool, when the phone rang. It was Agent Van Cleve from the FBI office in Jacksonville. Bob had met him a month earlier when he began snooping around the island.

Van Cleve asked if Bob could stop by the office tomorrow. Since the office was in downtown Jacksonville and at least an hour away, Bob was hesitant. He was writing these days and, as always, behind, and really didn't want to kill a day with the FBI.

"It's rather important," Van Cleve said. "And we need to discuss it here."

Bob knew that if he pressed he would get nowhere, so he reluctantly agreed to rearrange his entire day and appease the FBI.

He arrived promptly at 10:00 a.m. and followed Van Cleve to a small room with large screens on three walls. Van Cleve was antsy and eager and obviously on to something. As he dimmed the lights he said, "Got a couple of videos for you."

The first one, in color, was from a tiny camera inside the sniper's rifle scope. Van Cleve was saying, "This happened two weeks ago near Dayton, Ohio. The guy getting out of the Porsche is the boyfriend, not the husband, and he's sneaking into the house for a quickie with the wife. Hubbie is in Vegas with the boys but he left the contract behind. Lover boy goes inside, they tango for forty-seven minutes, and then the fun starts. Here he comes, out the door, walks to his car. Bam. Half his head is blown away by the sniper, who's almost four hundred yards away. Twenty-six seconds pass and the missus decides to check on him, and, bam, she loses half of her face."

"This is pretty awesome," Bob said.

"I thought you'd like it."

"May I ask how you got this?"

"The sniper was/is a dumbass who, for some unknown reason, thought it would be cute to film a couple of his greatest hits. Doubt if he planned to post this on Facebook, but more than likely he wanted to present it to the husband. Who knows? A dumb move. Big story in western Ohio. You see it by chance?"

"No, missed that one."

The front page of the *Dayton Daily News* appeared on another screen with the bold headline: **Wife and Lover Dead in Contract Killing.** Below it were large photos of the two victims, then a smaller photo of Higgs the husband.

Van Cleve continued, "The sniper was in a tree, and after the killings he somehow fell and snapped his spinal cord. He couldn't move, so his partner shot him twice in the head, sort of like finishing off a dying animal. The law of the jungle. The police there, along with the FBI, made the smart decision to keep quiet about the sniper, who appears to be a professional. Damned good shot, just not much of a climber. Anyway, not a word in the press about him, so far."

Van Cleve clicked a button and another video ran through its warm-up. "Here's where things get good. The sniper is still alive and four days ago he started talking." The image was of Rick Patterson in a hospital bed, on a ventilator, his head wrapped in heavy white gauze, tubes and wires everywhere, and five stern-faced men in dark suits staring at him. Van Cleve paused the video to say, "That's him, along with his lawyer, a U.S. attorney, a federal magistrate, and two FBI agents." On the other side of the bed were two doctors in scrubs. The wide camera angle was from the foot of the bed and it conveyed a scene that was truly hard to grasp.

Van Cleve said, "Patterson is not expected to survive. He has two small but steady brain hemorrhages that the doctors can't seem to stop, and even if he did hang on his life is pretty much over. He knows it. And so he's talking, or, rather, communicating. Obviously, with all the tubes and crap in his mouth he can't talk, but he has regained some movement in his hands. He can scrawl out messages and grunt his approval. Along with all the other wires and tubes there is one that runs to an audio unit. It's all being recorded in the U.S. Attorney's office across town. Obviously, he's in no condition to answer questions but he insisted. He's very motivated. His doctors objected at first, but hell, they've given him a death sentence so how much does it really matter?"

The judge could be heard explaining some basic legal principles to the patient, who held a black marker and moved it awkwardly across a whiteboard propped on his stomach.

The U.S. Attorney leaned in a bit lower and said, "Now, Mr. Patterson, I'm going to ask you some questions, all of which have been approved by your lawyer. Please take your time. We are in no hurry."

No hurry, Bob thought to himself. Two leaky brain hemorrhages and a broken neck and the man is dying by the minute.

"Were you involved in the planning and murders of Linda Higginbotham and Jason Jordan?"

He wrote the word *yes*, and the U.S. Attorney repeated it for the record.

"Did you in fact kill both of them?"

Yes.

"And you were paid for these killings?"

Yes.

"How much?"

Two.

"Two million dollars?"

Yes.

"Who paid for the killings?"

A long pause as Patterson slowly scrawled the words: Don't know. His lawyer said, "He says he doesn't know."

"All right, more about that later. And did you act alone?"

No.

"How many accomplices did you have?"

One.

"And his name?"

Without hesitating, Patterson wrote the name: Karen Sharbonnet.

"And where was this person during the killings?"

No response.

Van Cleve said, "Guy goes still for about five minutes here and they thought he had croaked. He rallied later and admitted that his partner was close by and found him on the ground. Instead of trying to help, she tried to finish him off. Two pops to the head. Anyway, enough of that. Here's the next video, the one that might interest you. This is inside a high-end gym in Laguna Beach. Obviously, we have it under surveillance."

Eight women in two rows of four were gyrating and sweating to the beat of loud music and the screeching commands of their leader. All were young, toned, California tanned, and attractive. The camera zoomed in on one with short red hair.

Bob smiled and said, "Oh boy. I'd recognize that body any-where."

Van Cleve said, "I think you knew her as Ingrid. Real name is Karen Sharbonnet, former Army Ranger, former contract killer, former partner of Rick Patterson."

"Former?"

"Yes, we grabbed her. After Patterson ratted on her we tracked her down and followed her for three days. She got sus-picious and tried to make a run for it. Picked her up at LAX as she was boarding a flight to Tokyo. On a German passport, one of at least six she used."

Van Cleve clicked again and there was the mug shot.

Bob said, "The short red hair is a nice touch, and effective, but the eyes never lie. That's her all right. Has she said any-thing?"

"Not a word. And we have yet to tell her about Rick. She thinks she left him dead in the woods, doesn't know we found him, and damned sure doesn't know he's communicating."

"How much do you know about her?" Bob asked.

"Well, as I said, it's slow going because Patterson is hanging on by his fingernails. He says that they have been working as a team for about five years, high-end contract killings. They got two million for the Higginbotham job. We tracked her bank accounts, she has about a dozen in at least four countries, and, sure enough, the money arrived on St. Kitts two days ago. Two million bucks."

"Anything about Nelson Kerr?"

"Not yet. As of yesterday, Patterson was still talking."

"Make him talk faster."

"Sorry, but I think he's fading."

7.

Leaving Jacksonville, Bob impulsively turned off Interstate 95 and drove to the international airport where he bought a ticket. He flew to Newark and connected to Boston where he boarded a small commuter for Martha's Vineyard. Seven hours after taking off, he was on the ground and called Bruce's cell phone. Bruce was surprised to hear from him and asked, "What brings you to the Vineyard?"

"You invited me, remember? What time is dinner?"

Bruce most certainly did not remember inviting Bob but immediately realized something was up. He said, "Meet me in the bar at the Sydney Hotel in Edgartown in an hour."

Bruce was waiting, alone, an hour later when Bob strolled in grinning from ear to ear. They huddled in a corner and ordered drinks. Bob began with "You will not believe who the FBI has in custody."

"Tell me."

"Ingrid. Real name is Karen Sharbonnet, lives in Laguna Beach, California."

Bruce was almost too stunned to respond. He gazed away and began shaking his head. Their drinks arrived, and after a long pull on his wine Bruce said, "Okay, let's hear it."

"It's beautiful. You won't believe it."

8.

They watched him closely as he parked his massive SUV in one of the parking lots around the perimeter of the park. He popped the lid and withdrew a large duffel filled with all man-

ner of youth baseball gear. His son, Ford, an eleven-year-old
all-star, was with him, dressed for the game, with his own per-
sonalized batting bag holding more equipment than any professional owned forty years earlier.

Slowly, they trudged along the walkway between two fields,
one of a thousand father-and-son teams ready for action on this
perfect Saturday for baseball.

Sid was not the coach, but rather the equipment manager,
for the Raiders. They found their dugout, greeted other team-
mates and coaches, and relaxed as a grounds crew raked the
infield and laid down chalk. The game was an hour away, and
the boys tossed balls in the outfield as their coaches and fathers
argued over last night's Astros loss to the Cardinals.

Four FBI agents, all dressed casually as baseball dads,
moved in closer.

Eventually, Sid left the dugout and headed toward the concession stand for a soft drink. He bought one and took it to
another field where a game was underway, and as he stood at the
chain-link fence and scouted a future opponent, a man holding
a business card stepped close and said softly enough for no one
else to hear, "Sid, Ross Mayfield, FBI."

Sid took the card, seemed to examine it carefully, and looking at the field asked, "A pleasure. What can I do for you?"

"We need to talk, and the sooner the better."

"About what?"

"About Grattin, Flaxacill, Medicare fraud, maybe even Nelson Kerr. Lot of territory to cover, Sid. There's a huge net out
there, Sid, and it's closing rapidly. We have the goods. You could
be facing forty or more in the slammer."

He actually closed his eyes as if punched in the gut but tried not to show it. His shoulders sagged slightly, but, as the agents debriefed later, he handled that awful moment remarkably well.

"Do I need a lawyer?"

"Oh yes, maybe two or three. Get 'em on the phone and let's arrange a meeting within forty-eight hours."

"And if I choose not to?"

"Don't be stupid, Sid. We'll get a warrant and come kick down your doors at three in the morning. Might be a bit traumatic for your wife and five kids, and the neighbors would see it all. And, Sid, we're listening to everything. One word to Ken Reed or any of the others and a golden opportunity vanishes immediately. Understand? It's time to look after your own neck. Reed's history, and I doubt the company will survive."

Sid clenched his jaw and nodded slightly.

"Twenty-four hours," Mayfield said. "I want to hear from you or your lawyers within twenty-four hours, okay? And we'll meet in forty-eight."

Sid kept nodding.

Early Sunday morning, after a sleepless night, Sid Shennault drove to his lawyer's office in Bellaire, an affluent community in Houston's sprawl. The lawyer, F. Max Darden, was a well-known specialist in white-collar crime and had never heard of either Ken Reed or his company. For two hours, Sid Shennault spilled his guts and told him everything he knew about Grattin, Reed, the management, and the use of vitamin E3, or Flaxacill. He claimed to know nothing about Nelson Kerr.

At eleven, on cue, Agent Ross Mayfield and three of his colleagues, now dressed in the standard black suits, arrived, and

F. Max directed everyone to the conference room of his splendid
office suite. A secretary served coffee and doughnuts as the men
jawed aimlessly in a vain effort to break the tension.

After the secretary was gone, F. Max took control of the
meeting with "I assume you are here to offer my client some
type of deal."

Mayfield said, "That's correct. We are working with the U.S.
Attorney here in Houston and our plans are to indict most of
the top management of Grattin, including Mr. Shennault. We
are certain that your client has been involved in an enormous
Medicare and Medicaid fraud for many years, and he will certainly be indicted for it, along with many others who work for
the company."

"And how would you describe this fraud?" F. Max asked,
probing, though he already knew the basics.

"It involves a drug called Flaxacill, better known throughout the company as vitamin E3. It's registered but unapproved
because it's a bad drug. It was discovered by accident in a Chinese lab about twenty years ago, and at first it was thought to
have enormous potential because it could possibly extend life
by keeping a heart beating. Turned out, though, that it only
works for patients who have lost all other brain functions, plus
it causes blindness that is almost instantaneous. Somehow, the
good folks at Grattin found out about the drug and cut a deal
with the Chinese lab. For the past twenty years Grattin has been
using its miracle vitamin to keep tens of thousands of dementia
patients breathing for a few more months."

"So the drug actually extends life?" F. Max asked, as if in
disbelief.

"For critically injured or advanced dementia patients.

There's also the blindness issue. I'm not sure you want to ask a jury to believe it's really a good drug."

"I know what to do with a jury, Mr. Mayfield."

"I'm sure you do and we just might give you the chance. We're not here to bicker and negotiate. I'm sure you're a real hero in the courtroom, Mr. Darden, but, to put it bluntly, you ain't got no case."

Sid cooled things with "So what's the deal?"

Mayfield took a sip of coffee and continued to stare down Darden. Finally, he put down his cup and addressed Sid. "First, you inform. You have about two weeks to deliver the documents. We need payment routing for the drug. How much and where does the money go? And for how long? Who's involved in getting the money to the Chinese lab? That's accounting and that's your expertise. We also need names of other execs or senior management people who approved of or knew about the drug. Second, we'll get the indictments and make the arrests. These will be carefully coordinated because Ken Reed is an obvious flight risk. So far, we've identified three corporate jets and three homes outside the U.S. You'll be arrested first, and we'll do it quietly, discreetly, no one will know. The next day we'll send in the SWAT team for the big drama. Third, you'll turn state's evidence, give us all the affidavits we need, and prepare to testify if necessary. We'll enter into a plea agreement and ask the judge for leniency."

"How much leniency?" Sid asked.

"No fines, six months max in jail, home arrest."

Sid accepted this with an air of resignation. His glory days were over and he'd had a good run. There was plenty of money in the bank and enough time left to rebuild a future. His wife and kids would stick by him, weather the embarrassment and move on. It was, after all, Texas, a land where pasts were easily forgotten if one picked up the pieces and made more money. There was also a certain admiration for outlaws. And, frankly, he had no loyalty to Ken Reed and his inner circle. Most of the men were on their third wives and pursued lifestyles repugnant to Sid's beliefs. It would be a pleasant day when he walked out of Grattin and never looked back.

F. Max said, "Why can't we go with immunity? I'd feel much better if my client were immune from prosecution. He can still cooperate fully and you'll get what you want."

"There will be no immunity in this case. And that's from Washington."

9.

At the insistence of the FBI, and with its offer to foot the bill, Bob Cobb flew from Boston to L.A. where two agents met him outside customs and drove him to their offices on Wilshire Boulevard. He was led to an unmarked suite on the third floor and introduced to an Agent Baskin, who was all smiles. A victory was at hand and everyone seemed to feel it. Baskin walked him across the hall to a small conference room where a technician was waiting. On a large digital screen, the same image of poor old Rick Patterson trying to die came into clear view.

Baskin said, "I understand you've already seen some of this."

Cobb said, "Yes, in Jacksonville."

"Well, there's more. This was two days ago." Around the bed, all jackets had been removed and the five white men appeared to be weary of their interrogations. The U.S. Attorney held a legal pad and spoke down to the witness/patient. "Now, Mr. Patterson, on August the fifth of last year, a writer by the name of Nelson Kerr was murdered on Camino Island, Florida. Were you involved in any way?"

A painful pause, then a weak and scratchy "Yes."

"Did you kill Nelson Kerr?"

"No."

"Did your partner, Karen Sharbonnet?"

"Yes."

"And this was in the middle of a major hurricane, right?"

"Yes."

"Mr. Kerr died from multiple blunt-force wounds to the head, is that right?"

"Yes."

"Do you know what weapon was used?"

"Yes." A long pause, then his lawyer leaned down to within inches of the man's mouth. Patterson groaned and mumbled something. The lawyer whispered to the U.S. Attorney, who then asked, "The murder weapon was a golf club?"

"Yes."

Bob Cobb couldn't help but chuckle. "That son of a bitch," he said.

"Beg your pardon," Baskin said.

"That kid figured it out the day after the murder. A long story. I'll explain later, or not. Doesn't matter."

Back to the interrogation. The U.S. Attorney asked the witness, "How much were you and Karen Sharbonnet paid to murder Nelson Kerr?"

Another painful pause, then a soft "Four."

"Four million?"

"Yes."

"And you split the money equally?"

"Yes."

"Who paid the money?"

A pause. His lawyer leaned down again and strained to listen. Patterson grunted and the lawyer stood and whispered to the U.S. Attorney, who then asked, "You were paid by a broker?"

"Yes."

"And who is this broker?"

The lawyer whispered again, and the U.S. Attorney asked, "Is the name of the broker a Mr. Matthew Dunn?"

"Yes."

At that point the witness shut down and his interrogators backed off. A doctor stepped forward and whispered to him, then waved them all away. The screen went blank.

Agent Baskin said, "That was it for the day. He's good for about twenty minutes. We found Matthew Dunn and have him under surveillance. A real character. Background in arms trafficking, drugs, even worked as a mercenary in Syria. A bad dude, but we'll catch him soon enough. You want to see your girl?"

"I do."

"A caution. She has no idea that Patterson is even alive. We assume she thinks she finished him off in the woods and she's playing a real tough-girl game right now."

"Let's go."

They walked down one flight to the second floor and stopped at a door that two agents were guarding. Baskin opened the door and motioned for Bob to step inside. Have a go.

Karen Sharbonnet was seated in a metal chair on one side of a wire mesh partition that did not rise to the ceiling. Her left hand was cuffed to a chain bound to the chair. Bob sat across from her and gave her a smile, one she did not return.

He said, "So, how you doing, babe? Looks like they finally caught you."

She shrugged as if she could not have cared less.

"We had some fun, didn't we. One long weekend. Or do you remember?"

"I don't remember."

"What a crusher. We spent the weekend in bed, at my place, had a ball, and you don't remember?"

"I don't remember."

"I guess you're such a whore you can't remember all your boys, right?"

She shrugged again, smiled, nothing would faze her.

"The last time I saw you, you were running away, running down the sidewalk in a Category 4 hurricane, barely able to stand up, like a crazy woman. I yelled and yelled and finally said to hell with you. Woman must be crazy. I didn't know you were headed to Nelson's. You know he called me, said you were at his place, said you were acting crazy, and I said no surprise there. Bitch is crazy."

"I don't know what you're talking about."

"That's because you're a professional with ice in your veins. And you know, even in bed there was something distant about you. No complaints, mind you, but something was never right. You know they found your fingerprints in Nelson's condo?"

"Nelson who?"

The wall behind Bob was plain white drywall, or so it seemed. A section of it was a hidden screen, and behind the screen were three cameras aimed at Karen Sharbonnet's face. Every twitch

and blink was being analyzed by their experts. Every movement
of her eyes and the muscles across her forehead and around her
mouth. She was ice. Her hands were frozen. Her breathing calm.
Her expression never changed. At the thoroughly unexpected
sight of Bob, she had registered nothing.

Until.

"You whacked him with a seven iron?" Bob asked, incredu-
lously.

A slight parting of the lips, as if she needed a bit of air. A
slight hardening of the eyes, as if shocked. Then she narrowed
her eyes and two wrinkles appeared at the top of her nose. Then
she shook it all off with a smile and said, "You must be the crazy
one."

"I've never argued that, but I'm not crazy enough to kill and
not stupid enough to get caught. Look, babe, I'll see you soon.
They'll extradite you back to Florida, the scene of the crime,
and put your cute little redheaded ass on trial. And I'll be there,
in the courtroom, watching, eager to testify against you. I can't
wait. My buddy Nelson deserves a little justice and I'm more
than happy to help."

"I don't know what you're talking about."

Bob stood, walked to the door, and left the room.

10.

Matthew Dunn lived in a rented one-bedroom condo in a
glass tower near the Vegas Strip. Forty-eight hours of surveillance revealed a rather laid-back approach that included a long
walk each afternoon to the Belaggio where he played blackjack at
ten dollars a hand while sipping cheap scotch. His background

was far more interesting. He'd been booted from the Marines for insubordination, then hired by a private U.S. mercenary gang to do dirty work in Iraq. He'd survived two years in a Syrian jail for smuggling guns. He'd been indicted in New Orleans for importing cocaine, but somehow walked. He'd spent three years in a federal prison for an insurance scam, and a week after being paroled landed a five-million-dollar defense contract to supply orange juice to U.S. troops. Somewhere along the way he took up killing for profit and became a go-to guy for high-end contracts. A raid with warrants on his bank accounts revealed little—less than $20,000. The FBI assumed he preferred cash and foreign banks. Monitoring his laptop and listening to his cell phone, the FBI became concerned when he booked a flight to Mexico City. He was arrested without incident at McCarran International and put in isolation at the Clark County Detention Center.

11.

Eighteen days after breaking his neck, Rick Patterson finally died in the ICU at a Cincinnati hospital. He was forty-four, single, had never married, and had little family to speak of. A brother had him cremated and his remains sent by FedEx to a mausoleum in Seattle for "future purposes." There were gaps in his background, but the best guess was that he and Karen Sharbonnet met twenty-one years earlier while on duty in East Africa. Their paths crossed several times and both spent years in Afghanistan and Iraq. They certainly never married and there was no evidence of any serious relationship, other than the business one that led to his death. Attempts to find money

were futile. Like others in his shadowy world, he apparently preferred cash and offshore accounts.

Karen was not informed of his death, and the FBI assumed
she still believed he died in the woods where she left him. She
was in protective custody with no access to newspapers or the
Internet. When she was informed that she was being held for
the capital murders of Linda Higginbotham, Jason Jordan, Nelson Kerr, and a plastic surgeon in Wisconsin, she calmly asked
for a lawyer.

12.

After signing the preliminary plea agreement hammered
out by F. Max Darden, Sid Shennault went to work prowling
through the financial records of Grattin Health. Since he had
implemented the systems and upgraded them over the years, it
was easy work. Within forty-eight hours he was sending F. Max
encrypted emails with financial info so rich and detailed, Agent
Ross Mayfield and his task force were soon drooling. Flaxacill
was indeed a cheap drug. Grattin spent, on average, eighty million a year for it, paid through a web of offshore companies and
accounts to the same trade broker in Singapore, who, of course,
eventually forwarded the loot to the lab in Fujian Province.

The treasure trove of documents soon became an avalanche
as Sid sold his company's soul to impress his new handlers and,
hopefully, squeeze them for an even better deal. After the first
leak he became a traitor, and once a traitor there was no turning
back. After seventy-two hours, he had buried the FBI with more
raw data than they could process, all of it wonderfully admis-
sible in a court of law.

Then, the squeeze. F. Max called Agent Ross Mayfield and requested a one-on-one meeting. They met in a fancy bar near Darden's office late in the afternoon. F. Max ordered red wine; Mayfield, on duty, stayed with coffee. As soon as the drinks arrived, F. Max got to the point. "We want immunity, complete and unrestricted immunity. No indictment, no arrest, nothing. Sid walks away free and clear."

Mayfield shook his head. "We've had this conversation."

"We have. But there's more to the story. What if Sid can deliver the goods on all of Ken Reed's offshore accounts and properties? He has over half a billion stashed in banks from here to New Zealand and Sid can provide the details. He can also deliver the toys—the homes, yachts, airplanes."

"I'm listening."

"Think of the litigation when this goes down. Tens of thousands of lawsuits against the company. Reed will pull a Trump, file for bankruptcy and hide behind the courts for protection. But what if the plaintiffs and their hungry lawyers have access to his hidden fortune? Sounds like justice to me. Reed ends up broke, bankrupt, in jail for the rest of his life. Sid can deliver, but only with immunity."

"I don't know."

"Come on, Ross. Look at the trainload of delicious gossip Sid's already delivered. You guys can't process it fast enough, right? He knows what he's doing and he wants to do more, but at a price. What's the benefit of indicting him and ruining his name?"

Mayfield smiled and nodded and glanced around. He liked it—that much was obvious. "What about the Nelson Kerr matter?"

"Nothing. Not a dime. Sid is convinced Reed did a one-off and paid for the job through some other account, or maybe cash. He kept it far away from the company. He's not that stupid."

Mayfield glanced at his watch and said, "It's five after five. Quitting time. Order me a beer while I take a leak."

The beer arrived before Mayfield returned. He took a gulp and said, "I'm in. I'll call Washington tonight and get it done." He offered a hand and F. Max squeezed it.

13.

On a rainy Tuesday afternoon in mid-May, Bruce was at home on the veranda enjoying the sounds of water splashing on his tin roof and dripping into his pool, and he was reading, off and on, when he wasn't napping. He should have been at the store but there was even less traffic with rain than on normal days. More and more he found the place, and the business, depressing. Noelle had fled the island and was shopping for antiques in New Orleans.

He heard the distant noise from his cheap phone, a rare sound. Once he realized what it was he scrambled into the kitchen and grabbed it.

Dane said, "Hello, Bruce. Got a minute?"

"Of course. Why else would I answer this phone?"

"Something's happening. I'm at home in Houston and I'm safe. Ken's planning to leave in the morning, taking a long trip, to Rio I believe. I've checked my sources and verified as much as I can. Listen carefully."

"Do I need a pen?"

"No. Just listen. He plans to leave Houston Hobby at nine in the morning on his Falcon 900, land in Tyler, Texas, just long enough to fetch his girlfriend, who'll drive from Dallas. Then they're off. Not sure but it looks and smells like the big getaway. Can you notify the FBI?"

"Of course. And you're sure you'll be safe?"

"He's not worried about me right now. He feels the noose and he's acting strange. Please notify the Feds."

Bruce called Bob Cobb and demanded that they meet immediately at a beach dive, one that did not exist before Leo. Bob called Agent Van Cleve in Jacksonville and relayed the message.

14.

At 8:00 the following morning, Ken Reed rode in his chauffeured SUV to the general aviation terminal at Hobby International and boarded his Falcon 900. He was the only passenger bound for Tyler, Texas. The jet took off at 9:01 for the thirty-minute flight. Once Reed was in the air, a small army of FBI agents and technicians entered the lobby of a nondescript twenty-story office building in south central Houston. They cordoned off the top four floors and hustled all employees into three different conference rooms. They confiscated all cell phones and laptops and threatened arrests if anyone breathed too loud. The employees were terrified and some of the women wept.

In Tyler, Ken's girlfriend was hustled to the Falcon by an assistant, who disappeared, leaving the two alone on the jet. The pilots waited for clearance to taxi and take off. Ken attempted to call his secretary but there was no answer. He called assistants and lieutenants—no one answered.

He made the mistake of calling his wife, and when Dane answered he said he was being called away by urgent business.

"Where you headed, Ken?" she asked coolly.

"Washington, then New York. Could be gone a few days."

"That so? Traveling alone?"

"Afraid so."

"Look, Ken. Not sure how to break this to you but the party's over. You're not gonna make it to Rio, and that little cookie you've got with you is going back home to her mommy. You're not taking off and you've had your last ride in that cute little Falcon. The Feds are about to confiscate all your toys, girls included. See you in court."

She ended the call with a laugh.

Ken cursed and looked out a window just as three black SUVs pulled alongside his airplane, each with those pesky blue lights flashing on their dashboards.

CHAPTER TEN
THE STORM

1.

The first week of June brought the first serious heat to the island, and with the longer days summer finally arrived. Ten months after Leo, the cleanup was over and the days were filled with the comforting sounds of electric saws, automatic hammers, diesel engines, and the yells and shouts of busy workers. Crews worked long hours, even double shifts, to repair and renovate cottages, restaurants, shopping centers, churches, and many inland homes. Most of the small beachside hotels and motels were open for business, but the larger ones with hundreds of rooms and far more damage were still months from reopening. The beaches had been picked clean and the eroded inlets had been rebuilt by tons of relocated sand. Most of the private boardwalks had been rebuilt and two new city-owned piers jutted deep into the water and attracted the usual assortment of lonely fishermen.

June also brought back Nick Sutton, fresh from his studies at Wake Forest and with a shiny new degree in English lit but

no prospects of permanent employment. Not that he was trying. His plan, if it could be called that, was to spend the summer the same way he'd spent the prior three, housesitting for
his grandparents while selling a few books, reading even more,
and all the while hanging out at the beach and working on his
tan. When pressed, especially by Bruce, who liked the kid but
was worried about his initiative, Nick had vague ideas about an
MFA degree where he could get a grant and write for two years
while continuing to enjoy the college life. He had even more
vague ideas about writing his first novel.

And he was quick to remind Bruce that he, of all people,
had no business giving career advice. Bruce had been twenty-
three years old and still classified as a junior at Auburn when he
finally walked away.

Nick spent hours each day consumed with the details of the
ever-evolving plots and dramas that began with the death of
his old friend Nelson Kerr. He read everything online and kept
all the stories in neat and indexed research files. He kept every
video of every news report. He scoured the Internet for any snip-
pet of news, recorded everything, and had become in the past six
months a veritable encyclopedia of knowledge about the case.

Each morning at Bay Books, around ten, when he was supposed to punch the clock and get busy at the front counter,
he barged into Bruce's office with the latest news. After a full
report, he usually said something like "And you made it all happen, Bruce. This is all you, man."

Bruce demurred and argued that he had nothing to do with
Danielle Noddin, the informant, coming forward. He had nothing to do with the capture of Karen Sharbonnet, the details of
which had yet to be made public.

Nick would argue: "Okay, what about tracking down the miracle drug and busting Grattin? If you hadn't had the balls to hire that firm at Dulles, we would've never known. Grattin would still be pumping the old folks with E3 and ripping off the taxpayers."

They bantered and argued every morning, and Bruce didn't mind at all. Getting the daily update from Nick saved him the time and trouble. And, before long, Nick let it slip that he was probably going to write a book about the entire episode. However, as of now the story had no ending.

By mid-June, eleven senior executives of Grattin had been indicted, arrested, and dragged to court for their initial appearances. Four were still in jail under exorbitant bonds. Several dozen executives and managers of related companies were under investigation. The case so far had proved to be a bonanza for the Houston legal profession.

Ken Reed was locked away in protective custody, deemed an extreme flight risk, and denied bond. Three of his airplanes had been grounded. His handsome yacht was docked at a Coast Guard lot. His fleet of fancy cars had been hauled in. Dane was living in their Houston home, which had been left alone, for the moment, but three other houses were chained and padlocked. At least six offshore bank accounts had been frozen.

In what appeared to be overkill, the FBI arrested some five dozen Grattin nurses, pharmacists, managers, and even orderlies for dispensing vitamin E3. Most were expected to point fingers at their bosses and escape with fines. Cable news legal experts speculated that the government was grandstanding a bit, flexing its muscle to draw attention to the enormity of the fraud.

Grattin itself was forced into involuntary bankruptcy, and an emergency receiver was appointed to protect its forty thousand patients. The company was far from bankrupt, as the receiver, a Houston law firm now on the clock at $100,000 a month, soon learned. Grattin was flush with cash and had almost no debt. To stay in the game, the receiver convinced the bankruptcy court that it was needed to run the company, which appeared to be a fair argument, according to cable news legal experts. All the bosses were either in jail or out on bond.

Vitamin E3 was immediately removed from circulation. Regulators in fifteen states, suddenly awakened, watched intently, along with a gaggle of journalists, the FBI, the FDA, and who knew how many other government agencies, as the number of deaths among the severely demented spiked in Grattin facilities. Clear proof, agreed the cable news legal experts, that the drug worked. If not for its horrible side effects, what was the problem?

Undaunted by the bankruptcy, and in a frenzy at the smell of fresh blood, the tort lawyers attacked with a vengeance and were soon bellowing from billboards and early morning TV. Class actions sprang up overnight in a dozen states. Cable news legal experts, throwing darts, estimated as many as two hundred thousand potential plaintiffs.

David Higginbotham, Karen Sharbonnet, and Matthew Dunn were indicted in federal court in Ohio for the capital murders of Linda Higginbotham and Jason Jordan. David was in custody there, while Sharbonnet and Dunn fought extradition. The family of Jason Jordan filed a $25 million wrongful death case against all three defendants. According to the *Dayton Daily News,* Higgs's hard-earned net worth was about $15 million. His lawyer, who was expected to get most of the money in fees over the next ten years, vowed to fight all charges until the end of time.

On his deathbed, Rick Patterson had confessed to the murder of Dr. Rami Hayaz, a prominent plastic surgeon in Milwaukee who was at war with some ex-partners over the patent for a medical device. Dr. Hayaz had been murdered outside a shopping center in an apparent carjacking. He'd been robbed, shot in the head, and left for dead. His Maserati was found two days later in a chop shop in a bad part of town. For four years, the police had found no viable clues and the substantial reward money had proved useless. Rick admitted to the killing, the first with his new partner, Karen. The Milwaukee prosecutor called a press conference and announced a full investigation, vowing justice for Dr. Hayaz.

As Karen Sharbonnet's rather substantial legal troubles mounted, she remained in isolation at an unidentified jail in the L.A. area. She spoke to no one, not even the guards. She hired a tough defense lawyer, an aberration in his field in that he ignored the media and hated press conferences. But the flood of attention could not be stanched. Her story was simply too sensational to ignore, and her attractive mug shot, indeed the only known photo of her, was plastered on every tabloid magazine.

Nick collected them all. He missed nothing.

One morning he reported that Danielle Noddin had filed for divorce in Houston. She had hired a fancy New York litigator known for her ability to unravel lopsided prenuptial agreements. There had been several reports of the money Ken Reed had hidden offshore, before and during their fourteen-year marriage, and it now appeared to be fair game. Dane's lawyer had plans to get a chunk of it.

On the literary front, the sensational story of Nelson's murder and its alleged connection to *Pulse* spun the book's presale orders into another orbit. Simon & Schuster announced an earlier release date of October 15, just in time for the holiday season. It also announced an increase in the first printing from 100,000 to 500,000, with plans to perhaps go even higher.

2.

The decision was made in Washington, at the Department of Justice. The question was: Of the three murders on the table, which was their strongest case? For obvious reasons, each of the three U.S. Attorneys wanted the first crack at Karen Sharbonnet. The Attorney General gave each half an hour to plead his case.

Western Ohio went first, followed by Southern Wisconsin.

The U.S. Attorney for the Northern District of Florida made the most persuasive argument. Not only did he have proof that she was in the deceased's condo—a single fingerprint—but he also had an eyewitness who saw her stagger away into the night, into the storm in the direction of the condo. Then the phone call to the witness from the deceased verifying her presence at about the time of his death.

All three cases had the deathbed confessions of Rick Patterson, which would pose enormous evidentiary problems at trial, but at least in Florida Sharbonnet had committed the actual murder. In Ohio and Wisconsin she had been the accomplice.

Another factor was Florida's history with the death penalty. Its U.S. Attorney proudly rattled off the statistics that proved without a doubt that jurors in his state were far more likely to impose death than Ohio. And Wisconsin had abolished the death penalty in 1853.

At the end of the two-hour meeting, the Attorney General, with far more important matters at hand, ordered that Florida would go first.

The following day, Karen Sharbonnet was flown on a commercial flight nonstop from L.A. to Jacksonville. The details of her clandestine trip were somehow leaked and reporters were crawling all around the Jacksonville airport. The U.S. Marshals went to plan B and ducked through a side door, but one camera caught her. For about five seconds she was seen, under a baseball cap and behind thick sunglasses and with hands bound, getting hustled by heavy men in suits as they pushed her into a van.

Bruce watched it in his office, with Nick of course. The cable news legal experts were of the opinion that her trial would be at least a year away. Her codefendants, Ken Reed, a man she'd never met, and Matthew Dunn, one she knew well, would be dealt with later. Of all the charges Reed faced, federal capital was by far the most serious. One expert predicted that Dunn, the middleman, would cut a deal to save his neck and squeal on both Reed and Sharbonnet.

"It's a storm, Bruce, and you're in the eye," Nick said.

"Get back to work."

3.

Two whole days passed with nothing new. Nick seemed lost without any breaking news, then sprang to life one afternoon when he found a story out of rural Kentucky. The police in the small town of Flora had closed their investigation into the death of Brittany Bolton and declared the cause to be just another opioid overdose. They had found no viable witnesses to her disappearance, no sign of foul play. Her family was too distraught to comment.

4.

About once a month, Bruce chatted by phone with Polly McCann in California. She had been following the unpredictable events of the past few months, and while encouraged by the news that her brother's killers might actually be found and brought to justice, she was not looking forward to drawn-out criminal proceedings on the East Coast.

She had recently been approached by a well-established Florida trial lawyer who had proposed the filing of a huge wrongful death claim against Ken Reed and the others. This lawyer had done impressive homework, and even flew to California to meet with her, her husband, and their personal attorney. He was of the opinion that Reed certainly had pockets deep enough to pay a sizable award, and that the wrongful death claim would take priority over all other civil matters. He suggested the sum of $50 million as an opener, with 20 percent for him if the case settled and 30 percent if it went to trial. The lawsuit would not be initiated until after the criminal trial, and, assuming Reed was found guilty, their case would not be difficult to prove.

He knew his turf. His résumé was impressive if a bit too self-congratulatory, but Polly and her husband had been mildly impressed. She asked Bruce's advice on what to do.

He demurred and said that, in spite of the current chaos in his life, he knew very little about the law and really didn't want to learn much. However, if *his* brother had been the target of a contract killing funded by a billionaire crook, then, hell yes, he'd want as much blood as he could squeeze. He agreed to quietly check out the Florida lawyer and gauge his reputation.

Polly left him with the news that she and her husband were planning to spend a week on the island to celebrate July Fourth. She needed to meet with the probate lawyer and so on. Bruce was delighted to offer them a guest room upstairs.

5.

On a calm Friday morning in late June, Agent Van Cleve from Jacksonville called Bruce and asked for a meeting. He was willing to drive up late in the afternoon and perhaps have a beer after hours. He wanted Bob Cobb present, if possible. Bruce was surprised to be included in any discussion, since he had heard little in the previous months. He suggested they meet at Curly's Oyster Bar for happy hour.

Bob was rarely not in the mood for a late afternoon drink, or even an earlier one. Nick got wind of the meeting and would not take no for an answer. The three got a table on Curly's deck near the edge of a marsh and began with a pitcher of beer. It was Friday, the island was tired of another long week of rebuilding, the air was warm but not sticky, and the crowd was in the mood to blow off some steam.

Bruce had met Van Cleve briefly, but Bob had spent more time with him. The agent arrived in shorts and deck shoes and almost blended in with the crowd. It was 5:30 and he had punched the clock for the week.

Bob introduced Nick as a local friend but laid off any insults about unemployment. They poured Van Cleve a beer as he surveyed the crowd. Bruce noticed he did not have a wedding band. A waiter ventured by and they ordered a bucket of boiled shrimp and another pitcher.

Van Cleve got serious and said, "Okay, here's the update. As you know, Karen had a partner, guy named Patterson, and she thought she'd killed him. But he hung on a few and even managed to talk. He gave us the goods on three contract killings, including Nelson Kerr's. A fourth we're still investigating. Over a ten-day period we managed to pull some facts out of him as he was literally dying. Broken neck, gunshot wounds, a mess. Anyway, they were paid four million by Ken Reed, facilitated by the broker Matthew Dunn, to rub out Kerr. They came here together, rented a condo near the Hilton, monitored Nelson, and made plans to strike. The hurricane was just their good luck. Suddenly they had a chance to pull the trigger while absolutely no one was looking. Karen got inside Nelson's condo, whacked him, carried him outside in the storm, and you know the rest."

Nick interrupted with "Excuse me, but what was the murder weapon?"

"One of his golf clubs, probably an iron."

Nick grinned and raised his arms as if to accept their thunderous applause.

"What's this all about?" asked Van Cleve.

Bob was shaking his head. Bruce said, "The day after the murder, while we were babysitting the dead body, the three of us were discussing the meaning of life. Nick here, who reads far too many crime novels, said that the woman was not a guest at the Hilton, was probably staying in a rental close by with a team, that she had met Nelson, thus knew him and talked her way into his condo. She did not take a blunt instrument with her but rather used something of Nelson's."

"The seven iron to be exact," Nick said. "Read it in a Scott Turow novel."

Van Cleve was impressed. "Well, well, are you looking for a job?"

"He damned sure is," Bob said.

"Please hire him," Bruce said. "He's fresh out of college."

Nick said, "And I work cheap. Just ask Bruce."

They enjoyed a good laugh and refilled their mugs. The shrimp arrived and the waiter dumped half the bucket on the checkered tablecloth, sort of a lesser tradition.

Bruce asked, "So, how did they get off the island?"

Van Cleve said, "We'll probably never know. The poor guy shut down after a while."

"And he's good and dead?" Bob asked.

"Yes, may he rest in peace. No more contract killings for him."

"Or for Ingrid!" Bob said, raising his mug. "Cheers."

They laughed some more, drank some more, listened as a country band got tuned up on a stage across the way, and watched the girls come and go.

Nick looked at Van Cleve and said, "So, when do you think they'll put her on trial?"

He shook his head in frustration. "Who knows? Lawyers and judges. Could be a couple of years. She might even cut a deal and avoid a trial."

Nick said, "Oh, I so want a trial. I want to see Big Bob here on the witness stand telling the jury about his wonderful weekend with a cuddly contract killer right before she rubbed out his close friend. Talk about rich."

Bob smiled and said, "I'll have the jury eating out of my hands. And her lawyers won't touch me."

Bruce said, "You can't testify, Bob, you're a convicted felon."

"Says who?"

Bruce looked at Van Cleve, the only one with a law degree. He said, "Well, generally speaking, they prefer not to put on felons because of credibility issues. But that's not always the case."

Bob protested, "I got more credibility than that crazy woman. I want to face her in court."

Nick said, "And they flew you all the way to L.A. to see her in jail? You gotta tell us that story, Bob."

"All right, but order another pitcher." Bruce waved at the waiter as Bob launched into his windy tale. His language deteriorated as his humor gained traction, and soon they were all laughing again. It was almost dark when the shrimp was gone but the party was far from over. They found menus and were discussing the catch of the day when a young blonde in tight shorts and T-shirt approached the table. Heads turned and the music seemed to pause as she stopped by Van Cleve, took his hand, and pecked him on the cheek.

He said, "Hello dear," as he quickly stood. "Sorry, boys, but I gotta go. This is my friend Felicia." She flashed a perfect glowing smile at Bruce, Bob, and Nick, all of whom were too startled to say anything. They returned the smile, and Bruce was about to ask her to join them when Van Cleve said, "It's been real. Thanks for the drinks. I'll catch the next tab." They sauntered away, with every eye on the tight denim shorts.

When Bob finally exhaled he said, "Since when do Fibbies get the girls?"

"Well, Bob, he is about twenty years younger than you."

Nick, still gazing, said, "Wow, that's impressive. Maybe I will hire on at the Bureau."

Bruce said, "Down, boys. Who's hungry? I'm paying, obviously Van Cleve is not. Who wants fish tacos?"

The music cranked up again and the crowd grew thicker. When the waiter brought a platter of fish tacos they ordered another pitcher of beer. As they ate they recalled, with more humor than they had any right to expect, the awful hours after the storm and the scene on Nelson's deck. They laughed at the vision of old Hoppy Durden, Santa Rosa's only homicide detective who doubled as its bank robbery specialist, as he stared at Nelson and scratched his head. And then he strung up enough yellow crime scene tape to stop a riot. They laughed at themselves as the three looters making off with Nelson's thawing meats and pizzas and the best of his booze, in his fine BMW roadster. They laughed at Captain Butler of the state police, strutting around the crime scene in his pointed-toe boots as if on the verge of making an arrest while not discovering anything useful. They wondered if the FBI had informed him that the killer was in Jacksonville, in jail. They laughed and ordered more beer.

Bob and Nick did not answer to women. Noelle was out of town, so the three amigos could let it rip. They needed a blow-out, an all-nighter, because it had been a long time and they were tired of carrying burdens.

Because he was twenty-two, Nick had the standard habit of checking his phone every ten minutes. At 11:15, it vibrated and he yanked it out of a pocket. He began shaking his head and laughing. "Oh boy."

"What is it?" Bob asked.

"It's hurricane season, Bob. Started two weeks ago. And they've already named one: Buford."

"Buford?" Bob said. "What a terrible name for a hurricane."

"Didn't you say the same thing about Leo?" Bruce asked.

Nick held up his cell phone to show them a red mass somewhere in the far eastern Atlantic.

"No projected path?" Bruce asked.

"It's too early," Nick replied.

"Where is he?" asked Bob.

"Two hundred miles west of Cape Verde."

Bruce froze for a second and cocked his head. "Isn't that where Leo came from?"

"Yep."

They ordered another pitcher of beer.